Women's Bodies

Discipline and Transgression

Edited by

Jane Arthurs and Jean Grimshaw

CASSELL
London and New York

Cassell
Wellington House   370 Lexington Avenue
125 Strand   New York
London WC2R 0BB   NY 10017–6550

First published 1999

British Library Cataloguing-in-Publication Data
A catalogue record for this book is available from the British Library.

Library of Congress Cataloging-in-Publication Data
Women's bodies : discipline and transgression / edited by Jane
    Arthurs and Jean Grimshaw.
         p.   cm.
      Includes bibliographical references and index.
      ISBN 0–304–33962–8 (hc). — ISBN 0–304–33963–6 (pb)
        1. Body image.   2. Feminine beauty (Aesthetics)   3. Women—
Psychology.   I. Arthurs, Jane.   II. Grimshaw, Jean.
HQ1219.W65   1997
306.4—dc21   97–34289
                                                  CIP

ISBN   0–304–33962–8 (hardback)
            0–304–33963–6 (paperback)

Typeset by BookEns Ltd, Royston, Herts
Printed and bound in Great Britain by
Biddles Ltd, Guildford and King's Lynn

Contents

Acknowledgements   vi
Contributors   vii

1. Introduction
   Jane Arthurs and Jean Grimshaw   1

2. Don't Touch Me (I'm Electric): On Gender and
   Sensation in Modernity
   Michelle Henning   17

3. Temporality, Materiality: Towards a Body in Time
   Tamsin Wilton   48

4. Racializing Femininity
   Lola Young   67

5. Working out with Merleau-Ponty
   Jean Grimshaw   91

6. 'Doing Looks': Women, Appearance and
   Mental Health
   Liz Frost   117

7. Revolting Women: The Body in Comic Performance
   Jane Arthurs   137

8. Talking Dirty in *For Women* Magazine
   Clarissa Smith   165

9. The Bearded Lesbian
   Mandy Kidd   195

10. The Girls Can't Hack It: The Changing Status
    of the Female Body in Representations of
    New Technology
    Julia Moszkowicz   208

Index   232

Acknowledgements

The initial impetus for this book came from study and research undertaken by staff and students in a range of courses taught at the University of the West of England, particularly in cultural and media studies and women's studies. The editors would like to thank all of those colleagues and students without whose interest and energy the project would not have been undertaken.

The stills in Chapter 7 from *Absolutely Fabulous* are reproduced with the kind permission of Joanna Lumley and Julia Sawahla, the stills from *Through the Cakehole* with the kind permission of Jo Brand and Channel 4.

The photographs in Chapter 8 are reproduced with the kind permission of *For Women* magazine.

Contributors

Jane Arthurs teaches Cultural and Media Studies in the School of Cultural Studies at the University of the West of England, Bristol. Her previous publications have been oriented towards feminist studies of film and television, including '*Thelma and Louise*: On the Road to Feminism', in P. Florence and D. Reynolds (eds), *Feminist Subjects, Multi-media* (Manchester University Press, 1995) and 'Making a difference: women in the television industry', in S. Hood (ed.), *Behind the Screens: Broadcasting in the Nineties* (Lawrence and Wishart, 1994).

Liz Frost is a Senior Lecturer in the Faculty of Health and Social Care at the University of the West of England. A background in mental health practice and extensive involvement with women service users in this field has led her to pursue academic research in both mental health and women's studies. She is currently working on a book dealing with women's appearance in relation to mental health. She is also completing externally funded research into the evaluation of joint health and social services crisis provision.

Jean Grimshaw taught philosophy and women's studies in the School of Cultural Studies at the University of the West of England until 1998. She is the author of *Feminist Philosophers* (Wheatsheaf, 1986) and of numerous articles on feminism and philosophy. She is a member of the editorial collective of *Radical Philosophy*.

Michelle Henning lectures in media practice and cultural theory in the School of Cultural Studies at the University of the West of England. She also works as a visual artist. Her other publications include 'Digital encounters: mythical pasts and electronic presence', in M. Lister (ed.), *The Photographic Image in Digital Culture* (Routledge, 1995) and an interactive artwork, *Externally Yours*, which parodies cosmetic and perfume ads. It was produced in collaboration with Maria Parkes, for a CD-ROM, *From Silver to Silicon* (Artec, 1996).

Mandy Kidd has lectured in women's studies at the University of the West of England, and is currently teaching sociology and psychology at Soundwell College in Bristol. This is her first publication.

Julia Moszcowicz is a part-time lecturer in complementary studies and visual culture in the School of Art at Bath Spa University College. She also teaches at the School of Cultural Studies, University of the West of England. She has recently completed an MA dissertation on gender and new technology. This is her first publication.

Clarissa Smith is a lecturer in journalism studies at the Falmouth College of Art. She is currently undertaking doctoral research into women's uses of and pleasures in sexually explicit material, following the completion of an MA in women's studies. This is her first publication.

Tamsin Wilton is senior lecturer in health studies at the University of the West of England, where she teaches women's studies and lesbian studies. She is the author of several books including *Finger-Licking Good: The Ins and Outs of Lesbian Sex* (Cassell, 1996), *En/gendering AIDS: Deconstructing Sex, Texts, Epidemic* (Sage, 1997) and *Lesbian Studies: Setting an Agenda* (Routledge, 1995). She is currently writing a textbook on sexuality for health and social care professionals; her handbook on lesbian health, *Good for You*, was published by Cassell in 1997.

Lola Young has reviewed films and commented on contemporary culture on both radio and television. She has written widely on the construction of racialized and gendered identities and contemporary culture; her most recent publication is *Fear of the Dark: 'Race', Gender and Sexuality in the Cinema* (Routledge, 1996). She is currently Professor of Cultural Studies at Middlesex University, and is working on a collection of essays on cultural criticism.

1

Introduction

Jane Arthurs and Jean Grimshaw

In recent years, there has been a veritable explosion of academic interest in the body. Books and collections of essays have proliferated; a new journal, *Body and Society*, devoted wholly to issues concerning the body, commenced publication in 1995; the body is commonly a particular focus of interest at academic conferences.

In many ways, interest in the body has been a constant theme in and subtext to a great deal of nineteenth- and twentieth-century theory and discourse. A history of theorizations of the body would need to include, for instance, nineteenth-century Darwin-inspired theories of the physiology or physiognomy of criminality; Charcot's displays of the body of the hysteric at the Salpetrière; Freud's account of the body of the hysteric; and Wilhelm Reich's view of the constitutive role of the 'armouring' of the body in neurosis. Much contemporary discussion, however, owes a debt to two things in particular.

The first is the work of Michel Foucault. Contemporary theorizations of the body owe a great deal to Foucault's discussion, in *Discipline and Punish* (1979), of the formation of the body of the soldier through the minutiae of bodily disciplines, and of the increasing interest taken by the modern state in the bodies of its citizens. A debt is also owed to the view of the discursive production of régimes of sexuality in Volume 1 of Foucault's *The History of Sexuality* (1981), and to the later accounts in Volumes 2 and 3 (1987, 1988) of technologies of the self in classical times which deployed detailed procedures of bodily regulation.

The bodies of the citizen and the soldier in Foucault's analysis were, however, paradigmatically male ones. A second important source of much recent work on the body has been feminist writing. Some of the central themes and issues were formulated by Simone de Beauvoir. In *The Second Sex* (1983) she analysed the ways in which the female body was disciplined and constrained. At times she even seemed to conclude that, unlike the male body, which she saw as unproblematic, the female body constituted an intrinsic handicap for women in the attempt to achieve 'transcendence'.

Since the emergence of 'second-wave' feminism in the late 1960s, the disciplining of the female body has been a constant theme in a great deal of feminist writing. In the 1970s, books such as *Little Girls* (1976) by Elena Belotti gave vivid accounts of the ways in which girls, unlike boys, were required to behave in 'ladylike' ways which discouraged them from physical activity and initiative. There was also a great deal of discussion and analysis of the ways in which the female body was constrained not only by conventions of feminine movement and behaviour, but by the apparatuses of fashion, beauty and the media.

Since then, the range and scope of feminist analyses of women's bodies has broadened considerably. A particular concern has been the issue of the normalizing power of ideals of body shape, size and youthfulness, and the relation of these ideals to ethnicity. They have subtly shifted since the 1960s and 1970s. The 'ideal' female body is no longer *simply* thin, but firm and toned and lightly muscled. What is the significance of this shift? Why is the practice of dieting carried to such extremes, and why are anorexia and bulimia on the increase? Why do so many women undertake expensive, invasive and frequently dangerous forms of cosmetic surgery? In addressing these issues, feminist writers have at times deployed the work of Foucault; but it is a mistake to see feminist writing on the body simply as Foucault-inspired and important to note its independent roots in feminist concern about the diverse forms of bodily constraint and discipline to which women have been subjected.

Feminist film studies have also provided an important arena for new developments in theorizing women's bodies, following the publication in 1975 of Laura Mulvey's analysis of the Hollywood narrative film and its construction of women's bodies as passive objects of spectacle, denied the full subjectivity of the active, desiring hero. The power relations of patriarchy were theorized as being reproduced through the regimes of looking institutionalized by Hollywood, which were, in turn, a re-staging of the Oedipal processes of gender formation analysed by Freud. This psychoanalytic model of film, combined with the semiotic analysis of the visual codes of masculinity and femininity – found, for example, in advertising, women's magazines and pornography – dominated feminist analyses of 'images of women' in the late 1970s and early 1980s. The assumption that men and women, both as spectators and readers, were 'subject' to these ideologically powerful representations, unable to resist the binary logic of their pre-ordained place in the hierarchy of gender, led to a sustained campaign to produce counter-images to these dominant forms or, in the case of pornography, to censor those images which, it was argued, served to present women's bodies as the passive object of male sadistic and fetishistic fantasies.

It became clear that these analyses of women's place in the regimes of visual representation left out any consideration of women as active, desiring subjects; popular culture also provided pleasurable fantasies for women. Attention shifted to the ways in which women's desire could be expressed in mainstream media forms, including utopian fantasies of power, with the emergence of the more ambivalently gendered 'active female hero' of Hollywood films such as *Aliens* and *Thelma and Louise*. At the same time, many feminists argued against the censorship of pornography, rejecting the assumption made by anti-pornographic feminists that representations of sex were a primary cause of men's violence towards women and arguing the importance of constructing a space for explicit representations of sex which were addressed to women's desires.

The new emphasis on pleasure and fantasy and the active appropriation of the proliferating range of images on offer has been accompanied by a changed understanding of the relationship between bodily appearance and gender identity. Following Butler (1990), the idea of gender as a performance which has no prior reality was compatible with other postmodern theories of signification where the gendering of bodies is constructed as a series of masquerades. The notion of an ideal feminine appearance which was in some way an outward expression of an inner identity has been partly displaced by a self-conscious manipulation of possibilities, a manipulation in which excess, stylization and irony are brought to the fore. The ways in which this game is played both by producers and by consumers of media images mean that it is difficult to make any straightforward assumptions about the influence of the body imagery in circulation on women's conceptions of self.

Interest in the body, then, has been a recurring theme of feminist theory since the early 1970s. But why the more recent dramatic increase in writing about the body? The first thing to point to is the increasing 'visibility' of the body in contemporary culture. One aspect of this is the proliferation of discourse concerning sexuality in the media. The thresholds of acceptability of explicit representations and images of sexuality and sexed bodies have changed dramatically in the wake of the post-1960s liberalization of régimes of representation. Although censorship is still a publicly debated and contentious issue, we have become accustomed to a vast array of explicit images and representations of sexuality that would have been unthinkable in the 1950s or early 1960s.

The body has become visible in other contexts as well. Contemporary discourses of health, fitness and beauty intersect in powerful new ways. During the 1960s and 1970s, pursuits such as frequenting a gym were largely seen as the preserve of school-children, or of those who participated in 'sport' in specialized ways. Discourses of 'beauty', such as proposed dietary regimes or the use of cosmetics, bore little relation to notions of 'health'; the objective of diets was simply to get thinner, and the use of cosmetics was simply an exercise in concealing 'natural' blemishes or emphasizing facial features in ways regarded as 'attractive'. The 'make-over' was no more than skin deep. Fashion and sportswear barely intersected. The body in Aertex shirt and shorts on the playing field or in the gym bore little relation to the body in fashion advertisement or display. It was not, on the whole, coded as 'sexual'.

During the last fifteen years or so, the 'fitness' industry has exploded. 'Health' clubs, gyms, exercise classes and the availability of personalized exercise training are now routine features of popular culture. Publications have proliferated, and a cursory glance along the magazine racks in newsagents or supermarkets reveals an increasing range of magazines devoted exclusively to exercise and fitness, with photographs of 'ideal' male and female bodies on their covers. But in addition, discourses of health, fitness and beauty have become scarcely separable from each other. The body which is most commonly coded for sexual attractiveness *is* the 'fit' body – toned, lightly muscled and gleaming. Sportswear intersects with fashion; shoes and leotards may have designer labels, and fashion on the catwalk might at times equally be seen in the gym. Being slim and toned is 'healthy'; diets are recommended in the name of 'health' rather than simply thinness. Skin care is no longer a matter of the superficial application of creams and cosmetics. Régimes should start from the 'inside' and the beautiful skin is the healthy skin (in the healthy body), whose 'health' is supposedly aided by the bewildering array of 'scientific' skin care preparations which are advertised as operating 'deep down'.

In the 1980s, this increasingly powerful intersection of the discourses of health, fitness and beauty operated within a culture characterized paradoxically both by the theme of 'enterprise' and by an increasing level of pessimism about the future of the planet. The world might be yours for the taking. In addition, you could have the body you wanted; it is not something to which you are simply subject, but it is something that you can work on, care for and fine tune, and in the last resort alter by means of surgery. It is *itself* part of the story of your success. Success is something you can dress for, and the workout becomes a symbol of the way in which your life as a whole might work out.

At the same time, however, the world of the future began increasingly to appear as one in which no one might much want to live. There was a nagging suspicion that perhaps your body is the *only* thing you can hope to control (even if this control will always elude you in the end). Your job might be subject to the vagaries of the market and of recession. Your health is insistently under attack from pollution of all forms; you no longer have any idea what goes into the food that you eat. But you can perhaps preserve yourself by a rigorous programme of 'healthy' eating, exercise and skin care. Much as the anxieties of the Victorian ruling class about the seething and potentially unruly 'masses' in the new industrial towns were frequently displaced onto fears of and attempts to control working-class sexuality, perhaps late twentieth-century anxieties about the vagaries of global economic systems, the potential nightmares of environmental catastrophe and the dystopias created by the technological manipulation of nature are accompanied by a retreat from a belief in the efficacy of politics, and displaced onto new forms of cultural fetishization of the body. The trajectory of the life of Jane Fonda, one of the most important cultural icons of the fitness industry and the new kinds of concern with the body, might stand as a parable for these cultural shifts. Fonda became a film star and sex symbol in the 1960s and early 1970s. Her subsequent involvement with politics in the 1970s transmuted itself in the 1980s into a new kind of concern with the body as 'fit' and healthy rather than simply as sexually desirable. In this huge success story Fonda's body was itself the project and example, and political energy (including feminist energy) at times seems to have been displaced or replaced by the energy of the aerobically fit body. But Fonda's 'aerobic' body drew nevertheless on the earlier construction of Fonda as sex symbol and was a potent sign of the increasing intersection between the discourses of fitness and those of sexuality.

The cultural emphasis on the body can also be seen as related to current crises and uncertainties in gender relations. An additional feature of popular discourse about the body since the 1980s is the way in which it has increasingly involved men. Care for the body is no longer primarily a female preserve, or that of the relatively few men who participate in specialized sporting activities. Fashion and cosmetic aids for men proliferate and, alongside this proliferation, the gender coding of bodies has in some respects become less absolute and more difficult to fathom. Male bodies are routinely shown in erotic and seductive poses which would formerly have been coded as female, and female eroticism itself (as in the case of Madonna) is often coded as assertive or even aggressive in a way that might formerly have been seen as masculine. But this new 'androgyny', unlike that of the 1960s and 1970s, is chameleon-like and premised on artifice. The body can be 'written on' in any way that one chooses. The denial in much academic writing of the 'naturalness' of the body and the stress on its discursive construction is played out in some of the more transgressive forms of sexual politics, notably in 'queer' theory and activism, which have aimed to deconstruct gender binarism and subvert gendered norms of dress and bodily presentation or representation.

Tamsin Wilton (Chapter 3) notes the veritable epidemic of body-transformative actions that characterize contemporary culture. Transsexuals submit to surgical sexual re-assignment. Body-builders transform their bodies into monstrous displays of striated muscles. In addition, 'Bodies are exercised, starved, depilated, shaved, pierced, tattooed, cut, stapled and stitched. Skin is bleached with chemicals or darkened with radiation, fat is vacuumed out of breasts, thighs, stomachs and buttocks, bones are cracked, hair is shaved or removed, breasts are stuffed with gobs of plastic.' Most of these body-transformative actions, Wilton suggests, are undertaken in total conformity with heteropolar conceptions of gender. Others, however, resist heteropolarity in transgressive ways. But whether conformist or transgressive, projects of body-transformation have come to seem more viable than projects of changing or rewriting current gender scripts. Changing one's body may seem the only achievable route whereby the profound anxieties, generated by the feeling that one's own gender identity and performance have 'failed', can be addressed.

The essays in this book are orientated around four main themes:

The materiality of the body

Much feminist theory from the 1970s onwards has been anchored in the distinction between 'sex' and 'gender'. Sex was seen as 'biological', something that was given in nature, while gender, on the other hand, was seen as cultural. This distinction was of crucial importance in allowing a wedge to be driven into theories of 'woman's nature', which were biologically determinist. More recently, however, it has been seen as problematic, for two main reasons. First, it has been argued that 'sex' is itself gendered; the assumption that there are only two sexes, and the insistent quest for 'sexual difference' premised on a sharp sexual binarism, is itself a product of a gendered and heterosexist ideology. Second, it has been argued that the body itself cannot be seen as given, as brute nature, a *tabula rasa* on which culture, conceived of primarily as a kind of ideology, writes. Rather, the body is itself the subject of constant social inscription; it is discursively constructed and 'written' on by innumerable forms of social discipline: there is no possibility of a sharp distinction between 'nature' and 'culture'.

The distinction between nature and culture not only fails adequately to think the 'body-as-flesh'; it fails also to recognize how modes of human experience of the world, which might be thought of as universal, are in fact historically constructed in highly specific ways. Michelle Henning's chapter explores the ways in which concepts of 'sensation' in modernity are both historically specific and gendered. She discusses, for example, how sensation came to be conceptualized in metaphors derived from the newly harnessed phenomenon of electricity, and how women were often seen as more vulnerable than men to the 'shocks' of modernity. For some writers, such as Simmel, the sensory stimulation of mental life required a 'shield' of consciousness; Freud also suggested that consciousness functions as a shield which protects against the excessive stimulation of the external world. Henning discusses the ways in which theories and ideas about sensation and its importance in modernity were negotiated in relation to the categories of masculinity and femininity. She appropriates aspects of Walter Benjamin's and Siegfried Kracauer's writings of the 1930s – about the ways in which capitalism both opened up and closed down sensation – to offer a critique of the opposition between active intervention and passive absorption which characterized so many late nineteenth- and early twentieth-century theorizations of sensation.

But do theories which stress the discursive or historical construction of the body allow for the recognition of its materiality, of the corporeality that is involved in sexed and gendered identities? In Chapter 3 Tamsin Wilton notes that while the body can never be posited as prior to signification, there is a problem with theories which have seemed to try to displace it altogether. There is indeed a need to resist theories of the body which are biologically determinist. But theories which suggest, for instance, that there are no differences between queer and non-queer bodies, or which see gender as purely 'social' – if by that is meant that it can be understood wholly as a matter of display, performance, narrative or career which need involve no reference to the materiality of the body – fail to recognize the problems with ideas of the infinite plasticity of the body. Given that the oppression of women, queers and people of colour involves the discursive constitution of bodies, it is understandable that talk of bodies is sometimes greeted with suspicion. But social construc-tionism cannot make sense of oppositional body practices, nor of such things as the strong need felt in the case of gender changes for the physical alteration of bodies. Wilton argues that the interventions of feminism and queer studies which have sought to counter the hegemony of heteropolarity need grounding in an oppositional theory of the body. Such a theory, she suggests, should conceive of the body not so much as an object located in space, which is easily amenable to control or manipulation, but rather as an event situated in time. Being male or female is an embodied, time-situated social process, which involves a lifetime of interactions at the interface of the body and the social. Bodily events and worries about the body are immensely significant for gender identity and sexual identity. Bodies are chronically changeable and subject to time and to processes that are frequently beyond our control. Gender is a process rather than a property of bodies, in which the 'conversation' between the body and the social is continually recreated.

Disciplining women's bodies

It is important to recognize and at times to resist the normative pressures to which women's bodies are subjected through the discourses and practices of such things as fashion, fitness and beauty, and to bring to prominence the ways in which these are used to maintain hierarchies of power. Ideals of beauty, for instance, have been based on racial hierarchies, although, as Lola Young points out in Chapter 4, this racialization has not always been explicit or acknowledged. Nineteenth-century philosophic and medical discourses constructed beauty as an aspect of a person's ontological value, which then became an indicator of moral worth. These modes of classification were then applied to entire 'races': a link was developed between outward physical attributes and 'fitness' to reproduce. The eugenics movement, which advocated selective breeding in order to avoid the degeneration of the human species, rested on the construction of a hierarchy of beauty which placed white women at the top and black African women at the bottom. The fact that black women were considered 'ugly' and 'degenerate' then constituted them as a sexual threat. If white men were enticed into sexual relations with black women they would contaminate the purity and 'health' of the white races. Black women came to represent the forbidden 'other' for white men, a position which has produced a history of fetishistic fascination in which desire and revulsion are intermingled. White men's sexual fantasies about black women emerge in grotesque representations where they occupy an ambivalent position on the borders between the animal and the human. This ambivalence is also there in the attractions of androgyny, where the black woman is constructed as the antithesis to the delicate and fragile ideal of white femininity. Young argues that these historical discourses are still influencing contemporary representations of black women, such as the widespread practice of assuming a white normative ideal in women's magazines or in the construction of 'exotic' imagery of black women as objects of white men's desire.

In a great deal of feminist writing the female body has appeared primarily as the disciplined body. Sometimes the 'disciplined' female body has implicitly been contrasted with a 'natural' female body. In the wake of Foucault, however, and of other theorizations on the social/discursive construction of the body, most writers now take pains to stress that their critiques of the kinds of discipline to which female bodies are subject are not premised on the idea of a 'natural' body.

But attempts to analyse the relationship of women themselves to these practices raise complex questions concerning female agency, motivation and pleasure. Some accounts of the disciplinary nature of the body practices that women adopt have tended to construe women simply as victims of a pernicious patriarchal system or ideology which deploys body practices and the fetishization of certain types of body in ways that constrain all women. But if women are victims, they seem very frequently to be willing victims. If at times they experience the dictates of fashion, beauty and norms of bodily appearance as constraining, they also frequently gain pleasure from articulating their own self-presentation in relation to these things. How are female pleasure and desire to be understood? How is one to respect and acknowledge pleasure and desire while also recognizing that women's responses to body norms and practices may involve constraint and oppression? How can female agency and choice be understood in ways that neither see women merely as 'dupes' of a patriarchal order nor, in postmodern vein, see choice or pleasure merely as the free play of unconstrained desire?

Some of these issues are addressed in the chapters by Jean Grimshaw and Liz Frost. Jean Grimshaw discusses a range of feminist critiques of exercise and fitness practices, in particular those of aerobics and going to the gym. She argues that no woman can be perceived as 'autonomous' in the sense that she could be wholly immune from the more malign kinds of pressures and ideology which frequently surround these practices. Nevertheless, the kinds of motivation often assumed in feminist critiques – such a heteronormative ideal of being 'attractive' to men, for instance, or a desire to preserve an appearance of youthfulness – cannot in fact give an adequate or exhaustive account of these practices. She suggests that aspects of Merleau-Ponty's work can provide an account of the 'body-in-the-world' on which we can draw in rethinking the phenomenology of bodily activity in relation to one's other projects in the world. In addition, she suggests that some accounts of the constraints to which female bodies are subjected may implicitly contrast a 'repressed' female body with an 'unrepressed' male body in ways that fail to recognize adequately the constraints to which men's bodies, too, are subject.

In Chapter 6, Liz Frost discusses the question of women's appearance, of 'doing looks', in the context of women's mental health. Women's concern with their appearance has frequently been ascribed a set of negative meanings, from Christian views which condemn it as sin or vanity to some strands of contemporary feminist thinking which see it as proof of a colonized consciousness. However, it has also been used as a measure of 'mental health'. Frost notes that in psychiatric hospitals it has been quite common for psychiatrists or psychiatric nurses to judge a woman's progress to 'health' by the extent to which she is concerned with properly 'feminine' dress and make-up (provided that this is not construed as 'excessive' or achieved in ways that transgress norms of 'proper' feminine behaviour). Many women, including some who have been hospitalized themselves, have seen this concern by hospital authorities and medical staff as a further reinforcement of the sorts of injustice and oppressive social norms which were themselves largely responsible for hospitalization in the first place.

Frost argues, however, that it will not do to see *all* concern with looks or appearance in this light. For one thing, all human beings are embodied; they cannot wholly disconnect themselves from the question of how they look, and the inability to see how one looks, as in the case of blindness, might lead to forms of disorientation for which compensation would have to be found. To suppose that looks might be wholly unimportant and have nothing to do with a woman's (or anyone's) sense of self is to suppose the possibility of a curious mind/body split, whereby the 'real' self is identified with a mind or spirit which has nothing to do with bodily appearance. Frost argues that therapeutic programmes in mental hospitals which offer 'beauty' programmes, fashion groups or other forms of therapy (such as performance arts teaching and the use of costume and make-up) should not always or necessarily be seen as reinforcing oppressive patriarchal norms. Mental distress may lead to a sense of fragmentation of the self, and constructing a new relationship with one's appearance and bodily demeanour, in which agency, decision and choices are involved, may be one aspect of a therapeutic strategy aimed at integrating a 'public' and 'private' self in more viable ways. 'Doing looks' does not necessarily have oppressive or patriarchal meanings. There is a need to recognize the empowerment and sense of skill and competence which women may gain from a renewed involvement with their appearance. The kinds of choices which may be available do not necessarily have to conform to stereotypical or studio-constructed fantasies of womanhood.

Representing female sexuality and desire

A considerable amount of feminist writing has argued that there is little space within contemporary representations of female sexuality and desire for representing an autonomous or actively desiring female sexuality, nor a female desire that is outside the bounds of heteronormativity. It has been held by Andrea Dworkin (1981), for instance, that in pornography woman is constructed simply as the passive object of male lust, power and aggression. Catherine Mackinnon (1987) has argued that 'sex', as constructed by heteronormative patriarchal domination, simply *is* the eroticization of female subordination.

Representations of sexuality have always involved not only gender but also class and race. In the nineteenth century, for instance, as Jane Arthurs notes in Chapter 7, any active expression of female desire tended to be associated with prostitutes and lower-class women, and the kinds of concealment and euphemistic language which veiled all references to sex or bodily functions were associated with gentility and good breeding. By the end of the nineteenth century, the 'civilizing' process of attaching shame and disgust to bodily indecorum was well in place, and bodily indecorum or unrestrained indulgence was associated with the lower classes. The kinds of desires which infringed decorum were deeply repressed in the bourgeois unconscious, in a potent mixture of disgust and desire.

Clarissa Smith (Chapter 8) questions whether the representation of female sexuality is always as monolithic as the analyses, such as those of Dworkin and Mackinnon, would seem to suggest. She discusses *For Women*, a popular magazine which aims to offer women a range of explicit comment and discussion about sex, as well as representations of the male body that might be seen as 'pornographic'. The magazine remains within a heteronormative framework. It does not, however, in any way suggest that female sexuality and female desire should be wholly orientated towards pleasing men. At times it takes an ironic, detached and humorous view of sexual practices, and it invites readers into a 'conversation' with other female readers from which men are excluded. In addition, while it presents detailed and explicit discussion of sexual techniques and possibilities, it constantly stresses the importance of women refusing to be constrained or browbeaten into engaging in any sexual practice which is not congenial to them. According to *For Women*, women should be autonomous sexual subjects within the parameters of safety, which is also a constant preoccupation of the magazine. Smith discusses the ways in which the magazine encounters, while never explicitly engaging with, feminist debates about male violence and the sexual subjugation of women. *For Women* might indeed be seen by some as 'vulgar' in that it transgresses canons of 'good taste' or 'decorum' in its constant refusal to 'prettify' sex, and its explicit references to the messiness and 'bodiliness' of sexual practices.

Transgressive bodies

The final two chapters explore aspects of the contemporary interest in transgressive gender practices, and in representations which aim in some way to subvert or denaturalize gender binarisms. Jane Arthurs discusses the ways in which female comedians challenge prevailing standards of female decorum and the cultural construction of the female body as an object of reverence and revulsion. She argues that there is a kind of 'licensed transgression', institutionalized by comedy, which provides a space within popular culture for the expression of female anger and for the 'unruly' woman who inverts the power relations of gender by breaking the codes of bodily decorum and unsettling dominant categories such as masculine and feminine, upper class and lower class, respectable and not respectable. She focuses on the character of Patsy Stone in *Absolutely Fabulous*, and on the performance of the 'stand-up' female comedian, Jo Brand.

Patsy, she argues, can be read as a drag performance, which both parodies femininity and dissociates it entirely from any maternal or nurturing element. It also embodies elements of masculinization and an anti-bourgeois attitude to bodily decorum. Jo Brand's comic persona is dependent on her body, mainly its size, and the challenge in her comic performance is to translate cultural disgust at large women into laughter, without positioning herself as the powerless 'victim' of the joke. Brand refuses the social norms of femininity, claims the right to be as 'uncivilized' as men, and uses the kind of 'deadpan' which both apes the lack of expressiveness demanded of powerful bourgeois men and is used by male comedians to establish their authority. She also breaks the strong cultural taboos surrounding women and food both by her size and by her celebration of food as an alternative to sex.

Mandy Kidd discusses the bodily transformations undergone by Della Grace, most notably the growing of a beard. Within queer theory, the acquisition by a woman of 'masculine' characteristics such as a beard may be presented as a powerful strategy in deconstructing gender binarisms and subverting norms of 'feminine' appearance. Kidd argues, however, that in the end the acquisition of 'masculine' characteristics in this kind of way is in danger of being recuperated by the very kind of binarism it apparently aims to subvert. She suggests that the kinds of 'playing' with gender and the appropriation of aspects of gay male culture which have characterized queer theory and activism have tended to reinstate the masculine as the norm, failed to recognize the power differentials underlying gender oppression, and rendered the lesbian still marginal and invisible.

In Chapter 10, Julia Moszkowicz focuses on representations of female identity and subjectivity in relation to computers and the new information technology. Women have often been perceived, and have perceived themselves, as being at the margins of technological development; the image of the computer hacker, for instance, is a masculine one. Moszkowicz argues, however, that representations of women and new technology are not monolithic. Female protagonists are at the centre of narrative production in some recent films concerned with aspects of the digital age. Moszkowicz suggests that it is female rather than male bodies that have become the central signifiers for a particular aspect of the digital age – the fluidity of the subject and the possibility of traversing gendered positions. She focuses on the character of Angela Bennett in the film *The Net*, a topical technophobic movie which depicts the nightmare of the obliteration of Bennett's identity through the obliteration of computer records. Bennett is herself a 'hacker', as competent within the world of computing as her enemy Jack Devlin. Moszkowicz argues that the claims to represent 'universal' problems about technology are articulated and played by Bennett, as she struggles with Devlin. Bennett is not a 'cyborg' and retains her female form throughout the movie. Nevertheless Moszkowicz suggests that it opens up a space for her to traverse conventionally coded gender positions.

Conclusion

The essays in this book recognize the power of the normative processes and ideals to which women are subjected and the representations which they confront. These include norms of sexual orientation and desire, of sexual behaviour and the bounds of decorum, of body shape and size. They do not, however, see women's bodies as entirely disciplined or constrained by the relations of power operating in society. On the other hand, neither do they see women as able to transcend their bodies in the way suggested by de Beauvoir, or by more recent theorizations of the social construction of gender, which seem to displace the body and its materiality. Instead they pay attention to the complex and dialectical relations between our embodied selves and the cultural processes in which we are engaged as active desiring subjects.

References

Belotti, E. (1976) *Little Girls*. London: Writers and Readers.

Butler, J. (1990) *Gender Trouble*. London: Routledge.

de Beauvoir, S. (1983) *The Second Sex*. Harmondsworth: Penguin.

Dworkin, A. (1981) *Pornography: Men Possessing Women*. London: Women's Press.

Foucault, M. (1979) *Discipline and Punish*. Harmondsworth: Penguin.

Foucault, M. (1981) *The History of Sexuality,* Vol 1. Harmondsworth: Pelican.

Foucault, M. (1987) *The Use of Pleasure*. Harmondsworth: Penguin.

Mackinnon, C. (1987) *Feminism Unmodified*. London: Harvard University Press.

Mulvey, L. (1975) Visual pleasure and narrative cinema. *Screen*, **16**: 6–18.

2

Don't Touch Me (I'm Electric):
On Gender and Sensation in Modernity

Michelle Henning

Apparently I am at risk. The stresses of a busy urban lifestyle, pollution and holes in the ozone layer are undermining the protective role of that important bodily organ – my skin. Unprotected, I start to display the symptoms of an illness called ageing. Happily, though, there are skin creams which can restore the protective power of my skin. Scientific research has produced a new 'skin technology' which can save me. It will isolate me in a laboratory world as bland as my newly smoothed skin. It will keep me in a kind of suspended animation. Which, considering I am thirty next birthday, is just in time.

Current advertisements for anti-ageing skin creams seem to be simultaneously futuristic and old-fashioned. Many of them present a modernist narrative of technological and scientific progress, yet also address their audience's awareness of the negative aspects of technological modernity. They play on women's fears about ageing, but they tend to represent ageing as something done to us. The female body is represented as vulnerable – under attack – and its protector is Science (with its traditionally 'masculine' associations).

Ideas of women as vulnerable and in need of protection have a long history. In contemporary advertising, skin 'problems' are linked to stress, which in turn is linked to a working lifestyle (in one ad a woman is shown using a mobile phone), as well as to pollution. In the nineteenth century, women – especially young women – were thought to be particularly vulnerable to new technologies and new lifestyles. It seemed to some observers

17

Are you wearing your
anti-oxidants today?

Estée Lauder invents
DayWear
Super Anti-Oxidant Complex

Starting today you can give your skin a dose of
anti-oxidant protection. Good things like
green tea, grape seed extract, vitamins E and C
DayWear from Estée Lauder. This super
anti-oxidant moisturiser actually neutralises
environmentally-triggered oxidants, before
they can visibly age your skin. DayWear helps
supplement skin's own defences, too.
In the exclusive oil-free formula:
• 8 super anti-oxidants.
• Plus all-day moisture.
• And an SPF 15 sunscreen.
DayWear. Only from Estée Lauder.

ESTĒE LAUDER

Figure 2.1 Advertisement from *Marie Claire*, April 1997. The image of
a cityscape is unusual in skincare ads, but the concerns it evokes – about
pollution and ageing, and the need for 'protection' – are not.

(mostly, but not all, male) that women were ill-suited to modern
life, and that middle-class women in particular were ill-suited to
the education and work to which they had fought to gain access.
(As I'll show, women's 'vulnerability' is figured differently
according to class.)

In this essay I look at the ways in which ideas about bodily
sensation have been articulated in terms of feminine vulnerability. I
want to show how attempts to understand the effects of modern life
on people's bodies have linked 'femininity' with passivity and
'masculinity' with agency. At stake in the struggle over these
categories was what constituted agency and who counted as
political actors. By coupling femininity with passive responsiveness
and political conservatism, many writers in the nineteenth century
and the early part of the twentieth century managed to dismiss
women as social agents at a time when they constituted a significant
political threat. In the late twentieth century many commentators
on the media still tend to accept the opposition between critical
distance and absorption, assuming that an openness to and
absorption in sensation is related to passive acceptance.

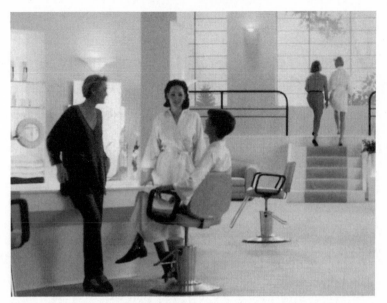

Figure 2.2 The 'Pond's Institute'.

This chapter is divided into five parts. The first looks at the ways in which the physical and psychological effects of modernity were linked to ideas of femininity through association with hysteria. The second part looks at the construction of an ideal masculinity linked to the figure of the armoured warrior. Part three considers the transformation of this idea in the work of Georg Simmel, Walter Benjamin and Sigmund Freud; some of the ways modern life seemed to undermine existing models of masculinity and femininity; and how gender categories were renegotiated. In the fourth part I look at the emergence of the understanding of sensation in terms of nerves and electrical currents. Part five explores representations of women of different classes as 'hypnotized' and 'intoxicated' by an onslaught of sensations. At the end I appropriate aspects of the writings of Walter Benjamin and Siegfried Kracauer to dismantle the opposition between critical distance and sensory absorption.

The feminizing of the symptoms of modernity

In the late nineteenth century and first part of the twentieth new forms of machinery seemed to be taking their toll on people's bodies and minds. In the British popular press, concerns about the damaging effects of technology came to the fore in the years preceding the First World War. In 1914 *Pearson's Weekly* listed the 'ailments' produced by technological progress, ' "wireless anaemia", paralysis from vibration of a car, aeroplane deafness and "picture palace headache" ' (Broks, 1997: 111–18). The dangers of factory labour were documented early in the nineteenth century: not only were industrial accidents very common but the everyday repetitive jolts of industrial machinery were taking their toll on the body of the labourer. But arguably less attention was paid to this than to the dangers of railway travel, which was the nearest many middle-class people came to experiencing industrial machinery. An 1857 study documented the effects of the vibrations of the trains, which had no suspension, on the bodies of railway engineers. Middle-class train passengers experienced these vibrations to a lesser extent, cushioned by the upholstery of the seats in the first- and second-class carriages. As well as this physical shaking, they were subjected to the deafening sounds of the train, and the rapid shifts in the field of vision produced by travelling at speed (Schivelbusch, 1986: 117).

Commentators noted that these attacks on the body did not necessarily produce straightforward physical symptoms. The effect could be indirect: physical symptoms could be the 'expression' of the psychological traumas provoked by sudden or extreme stimuli. In industry, workers were exhibiting psychological as well as physical strain, and seemed traumatized by industrial accidents. People suffering shock after railway accidents, despite having no visible injuries, were initially thought to be suffering from 'railway spine', 'a supposed microscopic deterioration of the spine'. Only in the 1880s was this understood in psychological terms as 'railway brain' (Schivelbusch, 1986: 134–49). The linking of neuroses with the physical 'jolts' and sudden shocks of industrial modernity became commonplace. For example, Jean-Martin Charcot, well-known for his studies of neuroses such as hysteria, suggested that certain forms of hysteria could be brought on by an accident.

The phenomenon of shell-shock in the First World War posed new problems for understanding neuroses. Significantly, the term 'shell-shock' was coined because soldiers' neuroses were initially seen as specifically caused by the new explosive shells – the sound they produced, the suddenness with which they exploded, and the horrific way in which they could reduce a human body to fragments. A more convincing argument is that war neuroses were a response to the combination of these new technical developments in modern warfare with changes in the organization of troops and strategies of warfare (such as the use of trenches), changes which have been described as a kind of 'mechanization' of warfare.

Nevertheless, the feature of modernity thought to produce neuroses was its capacity to surprise, jolt or shock. One of the effects of these 'shocks' was to close down sense perception. Symptoms common amongst hysterics, shell-shocked soldiers and industrial labourers included loss of feeling in parts of the body and loss of sight or hearing. Although both men and women suffered from neuroses, it was the classification of women suffering from these symptoms as hysterical which enabled the symptoms to be 'feminized'. Hysteria had traditionally been thought to be an effect of female biology, socially produced only insofar as it occurred in women who did not fulfil their 'natural' function of childbirth. Charcot, who popularized the theory that hysteria could be brought on by trauma, still rooted it in female biology, believing that although men could also suffer from hysteria, young women were more likely to be hysterics, because they were more 'impressionable', 'weaker' and subject to 'nervous attacks'. It was thought that women and overly 'feminine' men could temporarily lose sensation as a result of trauma. Nevertheless Charcot linked hysteria with modernity. As modern life became faster and more technological, hysteria was thought to be on the increase.

In Britain and America the medical profession attempted to draw a distinction between symptoms related to hysteria and those related to 'neurasthenia' (also termed 'nervous exhaustion'). These boundaries are tenuously drawn, with the neurasthenic woman often sharing the same symptoms as the 'hysteric', yet treated with more sympathy because of her apparent 'refinement' and 'ladylike' qualities (Showalter, 1987: 134–5). In other words, neurasthenia and hysteria were distinguished according to the class and 'breeding' of the sufferers. In addition, neurasthenia was more explicitly linked to the social and technological transformations that characterized modern everyday life for the bourgeoisie. In the 1860s George Miller Beard had defined it as an 'American nervousness', stating that:

A deficiency in nervous energy was the price exacted by
industrialised urban societies, competitive business and social
environments, and the luxuries, vices and excesses of modern life.
Five characteristic features of nineteenth-century progress – the
periodical press, steam power, the telegraph, the sciences, and
especially the increased mental activity of women – could be held
to blame for the sapping of American nervous strength.
(Showalter, 1987: 135)

Apparently, in the United States neurasthenia was not seen as a
feminine condition; instead it was linked to the stresses of
business and money and even seen as 'an impressive illness for
men' (Showalter, 1987: 136). For women and for men, neurasthenia was thought to be caused by excessive stimulation and the
'incapacity' of the individual to react to this stimulation (Buck-
Morss, 1992). Nevertheless, the majority of American neurasthenics were educated, middle-class women, and their symptoms
were thought to be brought on by overstretching their minds.
Even this could be understood in physical terms. Psychologists
and physicians conducted experiments exploring the relationship
between 'mental fatigue' and physical sensation and sensitivity,
which suggested that mental fatigue could be measured by
measuring changes in the sensitivity of an individual's skin,
although opinions varied as to whether mental fatigue increased
or decreased skin sensitivity and awareness of pain (Rabinbach,
1992: 149; 343, note 26).

Usually, hysteria was associated with hypersensitivity. Perhaps
the most interesting instance of this is dermographism, in which a
condition of the skin makes it so sensitive that touching or
scratching produces welts which may last for up to forty-eight
hours. Women in general, and hysterical women in particular,
were thought to be most prone to this condition, and male
sufferers were found to have 'feminine qualities', being 'emotional' and 'impressionable' (Beizer, 1994: 20–9). To demonstrate
the condition doctors would write on the anaesthetized skin of the
patient and then photograph it. As Janet Beizer points out, this
hypersensitive skin and the practice of writing on it reinforced the
idea of the hysteric's body as 'expressive' (an idea later taken up
by the surrealists Louis Aragon and André Breton) yet what it
'expresses' are merely the whims of the doctor (they drew abstract
patterns and lines or wrote the diagnosis, the patient's name, their
own name, or, more unsettling still, the sign of the devil). Beizer

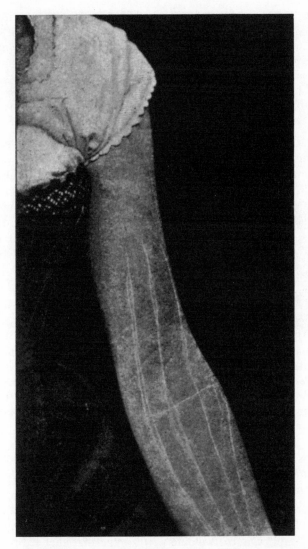

Figure 2.3 Etchings on young woman's arm. Women – especially hysterics – were said to be more impressionable than men; consequently they were thought to be more often subject to dermographism, the immune reaction that doctors appropriated as skin-writing or skin-drawing, and sometimes referred to as autography or lithography. (Published in T. Barthélémy, *Etude sur le dermographisme ou dermoneurose toxivasomotrice*, 1893; photo Bibliothèque Interuniversitaire de Médecine, Université René Descartes, Paris.)

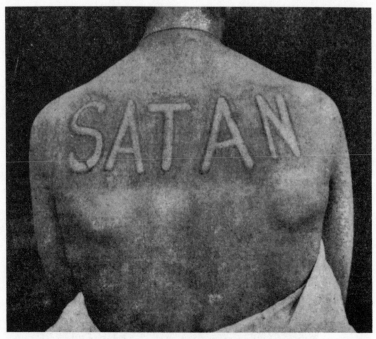

Figure 2.4 Doctors fascinated by dermographism often used the sign of the devil in their writing experiments. The clarity of this photograph suggests that it may have been retouched. (Published in T. Barthélémy, *Etude sur le dermographisme ou dermoneurose toxivasomotrice*, 1893; photo Bibliothèque Interuniversitaire de Médecine, Université René Descartes, Paris.)

shows that dermographism reinforced the perception of the woman as 'impressionable', by making her become a 'medium of communication between men' (Beizer, 1994: 291).

Overall, women were thought to be more vulnerable to the over-stimulation of modernity – whether mental stimulation (ideas, competition in business) or direct physical stimulation.

Armoured masculinity

Some writers have suggested that the occurrence of hysterical symptoms in male soldiers in the First World War urged a rejection of the image of the weak, impressionable and feminine sufferer. Yet, as Beard's work on neurasthenia would suggest, symptoms would be read completely differently according to the class and sex of the sufferer. Joanna Bourke has shown that, in Britain, the wartime appearance of hysterical symptoms in men did not straightforwardly 'masculinize' hysteria as shell-shock (Bourke, 1996). Hysterical and anorexic women had often been seen as 'malingerers' by Victorian doctors and represented as deserving of 'punitive cures' in Victorian literature (Showalter, 1987: 138–9). Similarly, in the early years of the war it was thought that men who seemed to be suffering from neurasthenia were malingerers, faking the symptoms in the hope of gaining discharge from the army. Although malingering in the army was punishable by death, medical practitioners believed 'that all that separated the neurotic from the malingerer was intention' (Bourke, 1996: 110). In other words, while the malingerer simulates symptoms in order to deceive, the hysteric simulates symptoms without knowing he is doing so – a kind of unconscious malingerer.

By 1917 military hospitals viewed most cases of neurasthenia as genuine. The numbers and type of soldier suffering from neurasthenia made it difficult for the War Office not to recognize it, since the alternative would have been to execute large numbers of experienced and committed soldiers. Most significantly, as Bourke shows, the official attitude to shell-shock shifted because of the social class of the sufferers. Although only one in thirty British Army men at the Front was an officer, they counted for one in every six hospitalized neurasthenics. Rather than accuse officers of malingering (and, therefore, of cowardice), distinctions were made between different kinds of war neuroses:

> most sympathy was reserved to those suffering anxiety neuroses (the form predominantly experienced by officers) as opposed to hysteria (the form predominantly reserved for privates). (Bourke, 1996: 112)

The distinction between these two different kinds of neurosis in working-class soldiers and officers hung on the notion that the privates were more susceptible to sensations of fear, sensations to which an officer's public school education and training had taught him to pay no attention. The 'hysterical' soldier was feminized, 'seen as simple, emotional, unthinking, passive, suggestible, dependent and weak – very much the same constellation of traits associated with the hysterical woman' (Showalter, 1987: 174–5). By contrast, the officer, even when neurasthenic, fitted an ideal notion of masculinity, nobly repressing his fear for the sake of the other soldiers.

This notion of a masculinity founded on the closing-down of the senses emerged in the modern period. For instance, in Kant's 'aesthetic judgement' the man most worthy of respect is the warrior who refuses to follow his senses which tell him he is in danger, and who seeks to control reality rather than allow it to control him by being armoured against or resisting sensory responses:

> Kant's transcendental subject purges himself of the senses which endanger autonomy not only because they unavoidably entangle him in the world, but specifically, because they make him passive ('languid') instead of active ('vigorous'), susceptible, like 'oriental voluptuaries', to sympathy and tears. (Buck-Morss, 1992: 9)

When Kant wrote about 'aesthetics' he distanced himself from the eighteenth-century cult of sensibility. This, for Kant, is associated with femininity and effeminacy. Indeed, Goethe praised Kant for having 'brought us all back from the effeminacy in which we were wallowing' (quoted in Buck-Morss, 1992: 10). Masculinity, then, becomes associated with being sense-dead and self-contained while an openness and responsiveness to sensation is associated with femininity and lack of control. Femininity also had historical associations with fluidity – the female body 'spills over' while the (idealized) male body has defined boundaries. This association is there in Goethe's formulation, in the idea of 'wallowing' in effeminacy. The epitome of the bounded male body is in the armoured figure of the warrior. The ideally masculine soldier refuses sensation in order to subject himself to its extremes. Yet in the First World War the soldier became the antithesis of this: the hysterical, feminized body which, because it is caught up in sensation ('hyper-sensitive'), consequently suffers from a deadening of the senses (the loss of sight, hearing and feeling which count amongst the symptoms of hysteria).

Klaus Theweleit argues that this modern construction of bounded masculinity has its roots in the expansion of trade in the medieval period, which opened up new sensations to the merchant classes:

> Every new trade route disclosed a novel pleasure; every new object from some foreign land held the possibility of a new feeling. Pepper took its place alongside the salt of the earth. Paprika and silk: those were once words for new sensations. (Theweleit, 1987: 303)

As available experience and sensation expand, instead of becoming open to sensation the European man becomes increasingly 'self-confined': he becomes a 'tough armored ship that can be sent out to seize and "order" the world according to the European perspective' (Theweleit, 1987: 302). The process of colonization constructs an ideal masculine self based in the distancing of sensation and on individualism. This ideology of armoured manhood can be seen at its most extreme and explicit in the writings, analysed by Theweleit, of German Freikorps officers. These soldiers identify with armoured masculinity and oppose it to the fluid, feeling and therefore relatively unbounded bodies of women. They associate their fear of and disgust towards women with the threat of Communism, perceiving Communism in terms of the 'mass' which threatens to engulf the individual and women as similarly engulfing (the most fear and hatred is saved, therefore, for the 'Red woman'). In this way women are metaphorically linked to the collective experience of the mass, or the crowd, and mass experience becomes feminized (Theweleit, 1987).

The consciousness shield: Simmel, Freud, Benjamin

Theweleit argues that it is consciousness that armours the masculine self. This armoured consciousness is both the ideological product of, and the justification for, men's roles in war and colonization. Yet for the sociologist Georg Simmel, writing at the turn of the century, the sensory stimulation and 'rhythm of life' of the modern city itself necessitated a kind of mental armour:

> The metropolitan type of man – which of course exists in a thousand individual variants – develops an organ protecting him against the threatening currents and discrepancies which would uproot him. ... The reaction to metropolitan phenomenon is shifted to that organ which is least sensitive and quite remote from the depth of the personality. Intellectuality is thus seen to preserve subjective life against the overwhelming power of metropolitan life. (Simmel, 1964: 410–1)

Although Simmel refers to metropolitan 'man' he does not directly associate this armouring with masculinity, and it is possible that for Simmel it applied to women too. The protective 'organ' to which Simmel refers is the conscious mind, the seat of the intellect and (cold) reason. It protects 'the more unconscious layers of the psyche', where emotion, deep feeling and habit reside. In this Simmel seems almost to prefigure the argument Freud was to make twenty years later in *Beyond the Pleasure Principle*. In that essay Freud was addressing questions raised by war neuroses in men, drawing upon previous work on the similar neuroses related to industrial labour, and hysteria in young middle-class women. He develops a new version of the body 'armoured' against sensation.

Freud tentatively suggests that consciousness functions as a kind of shield, protecting against the 'excessive energies' of the external world. Consciousness protects us against the 'shocks' that these stimuli provide by preparing us, producing the necessary anxiety. If we are prepared for these shocks, i.e. if consciousness succeeds in cushioning us against them, then we reconcile them with our experience. If, however, we are totally unprepared, if consciousness fails in its job as a shield, they produce a sensation of fright and we become traumatized. In the event of trauma, we can attempt to 'master the stimulus retroactively' – either through dreams in which we reproduce the anxiety we would have had, had we known what was about to happen, or through recollection (Freud, 1984).

In Freud's and Simmel's essays the conscious mind is conceived as a protective shell. Far from simply taking on board sensory information it actually guards against it. If modern experience is characterized by an increase in stimuli and in technologically produced abrupt shocks, consciousness must continually be on the defence, the individual increasingly cushioned against experience. Thus the armoured body shifts from a general philosophical ideal (Kant's transcendental subject) to an explanation of a peculiarly modern form of consciousness resulting from the barrage of stimuli characteristic of industrial society and modern warfare. Yet it remains tied to masculinity. It is not that women cannot form this shield, indeed they must in order to survive, but it took an 'epidemic' of hysteria in men to arrive at this conclusion. In other words, Freud arrives at an apparently ungendered set of speculations about the modern subject and undoes the association of the armoured body with masculinity, yet he only does this as a result of the crisis in gendered distinctions brought about by shell-shock. Furthermore, we can speculate that since more women than men suffered hysterical symptoms, this shield is supposed to be less effective in women. As Harvie Ferguson puts it,

> The pliant female body, unprotected by a hard reflective shell of intellect, was continually falling into a state of helpless torpor in which it was receptive to a multiplicity of uncontrolled and disordered impressions.' (Ferguson, 1996: 45)

The theory Freud develops in *Beyond the Pleasure Principle* is a sophisticated stimulus-response theory. He explains trauma using neurological terms (suggesting that consciousness corresponds to the outer cortex of the brain). Freud, who had moved away from thinking about neuroses in terms of the 'nerves', moves back to it in *Beyond the Pleasure Principle*. Previously he had refused to see hysteria in women as resulting directly from the barrage of stimuli that constitutes modern life. He produced instead the 'seduction theory' of hysteria, positing hysterical women as 'victims of the breakdown of idealised bourgeois family relations' (Ferguson, 1996: 49). Recent feminist studies have criticized this theory for its unacknowledged assumptions about female sexuality, and instead have explained hysteria in terms of a 'bodily protest' against femininity and powerlessness. However, they do seem to agree at least with his rejection of immediate physical cause, in favour of understanding it in relation to the broader social structures of modernity (Bernheimer and Kahane, 1985). But in *Beyond the Pleasure Principle*, Freud was returning to an interest in traumas that seemed to be brought about more directly, by actual events, and to what he himself had referred to as 'the old, naive theory of shock' (Schivelbusch, 1986: 148). The explanations of hysteria which seemed appropriate to young women could not, it seems, explain similar symptoms in male soldiers and officers.

While Freud's return to neurology was motivated in part by assumptions to do with sexual difference, neurology also serves to give the essay the authority of science (this has been used as one explanation for Freud's about-turn). And it is old-fashioned. Some of the biological theories Freud uses were discredited by the time he wrote this. For example, he quotes Hering and uses terminology close to that of Hering such as the idea of a 'memory trace'. Hering was one of the main early theorists of 'organic memory'. He argued that memory occurred when sensory stimulation physically altered body tissue and left what he termed 'living traces' which could be inherited across generations. Organic memory theory is linked to the belief that moral life, experience and tendencies are biologically inheritable and accumulative. Not surprisingly, it was used to naturalize and justify racial and social classifications (Otis, 1994).

In fact, these theories about the ability to inherit acquired traits and memories could be seen to contradict the view that 'nervous maladies' are the result of the 'shocks' of modernity, and are linked to the older belief that they were inherited. In France, many nineteenth-century experts on neurasthenia accepted the view that certain supposedly 'inferior' races had hereditary tendencies towards it but that others suffered from it due to the conditions of modern life (Rabinbach, 1992: 148).

Another criticism of Freud's essay could be that, like all stimulus-response theories, it reduces experience to stimuli, and the person to a receptor of stimuli, even if Freud does qualify the idea of straightforward reception through the idea of the 'shield'. Stimulus-response models tend to consider only the ways the world acts on the human subject, instead of also considering humans as acting on the world. In this sense they construct a passive model of the human subject: a body simply receiving, or defending itself against, stimuli.[1] Insofar as it is a stimulus-response theory, Freud's theory could be said to produce a passive, not an active, subject. Armoured masculinity had previously been conceived in highly active terms, as enabling the control and conquest of nature. Yet Freud's essay envisages this armour in entirely defensive (and physiological) terms.

Beyond the Pleasure Principle has been peculiarly influential. Walter Benjamin used it in his 1939 essay on the poetry of Charles Baudelaire, poetry which for Benjamin exemplifies the nineteenth-century urban experience of 'shock'. He elaborates Freud's theory: modern urban experience is characterized by an increase in stimuli and in technologically produced abrupt shocks, so consciousness must continually be on the defence. Freud had stated that if consciousness succeeds in cushioning us against shock experiences then we reconcile them with our experience. In other words, as Benjamin explains, consciousness gives the incident the character of having been lived, and it does so by assigning it a temporal status – it remains 'in the sphere of a certain hour of one's life', it becomes a memory, but, as Benjamin states, 'at the cost of the integrity of its contents' (Benjamin, 1989: 117).

As a result of this process, according to Benjamin, there is a price to be paid for the armoured self, which is loss of 'aura' – that is the replacement of the experience of historical continuity and collective experience with the fragmented experience characteristic of modernity. In this essay, Benjamin is ambivalent towards the loss of 'aura'. On the one hand it is indicative of the alienation and isolation of the modern individual, but on the other hand it might also open the possibility of new forms of collectivity and consciousness. For Benjamin and other writers Freud's essay points to the ways in which the sensations of modernity are reconciled through the construction of a continuous, coherent self. Just as Baudelaire's poetry 'exposes the passing moment in all its nakedness', Freud's essay exposes the continuous ego as a fiction, a mere defensive strategy.

In an earlier essay, 'The Work of Art in the Age of Mechanical Reproduction', Benjamin seems to suggest that the destruction of aura in modernity might have two possible consequences. One is exemplified by the Italian Futurist manifesto, written prior to Italy's entry into the First World War, which extols armoured masculinity and glorifies the sensations and destructiveness of war – representing war in terms of aesthetic pleasure (some of the Futurists, like some of the Freikorps officers, went on to become Fascists). This is, for Benjamin (1992: 235), the most extreme form of alienation. The alternative possibility, the potential of which Benjamin sometimes saw in Communism, was the making of everyday sensory ('aesthetic') experience the basis of political, revolutionary action.[2] In this sense Benjamin's argument goes back to Marx and *The Communist Manifesto* in which the proletarian revolution is envisaged as 'man' stripped of illusions, standing on the precipice of history and facing the real conditions of existence. Curiously, although revolution is almost always described in terms of masculine heroism, this image of revolution evokes a nakedness and a vulnerability – that openness to the sensory world usually associated with femininity.

The 'feminizing' implications of changed ways of conceptualizing the subject were not lost on turn-of-the-century writers and artists. Individualism and the privatization of experience emerge in the modern period, but urban modernity also threatened the boundaries of the individual who, despite attempts to remain bounded, became inextricably caught up in sensation, especially

31

when jostled in the city crowd. Some celebrated this disintegration. For example, the *fin-de-siècle* decadents revelled in the search for sensation. In doing so they contested the existing polarity of femininity as absorbed in sensation and masculinity armoured against it. In some ways this appropriation of the qualities assigned to femininity did provide a space for a negotiation of masculinity in relation to homosexuality, but it was to have very little effect on the existing perception of women. Similarly, in the twentieth century the surrealists looked to everyday sensory experience to disrupt bourgeois ideology. Yet here too the re-evaluating of sensation did not attach value to femininity but marked the appropriation of those qualities of sensory openness, absorption and lack of bodily control previously associated with femininity. For them, as for the Italian Futurists, femininity itself still represents all that is conservative, traditional and backward looking.[3]

Responses to the disruption of existing gender categories could be crudely characterized according to two poles: one that attempts to shore up and re-armour the individual, seeing masculinity as under siege and modernity as dangerously feminizing; another that attempts to rescue those attributes consigned to femininity – particularly an openness (or 'vulnerability') to sensation – and make them available to men, without in the process disputing women's inferiority.

The electrical body and gender

One new way of comprehending perception, sensation and sensitivity was through the idea of electricity and the nerves as electrical. This produced particular and contradictory gendered meanings. Christoph Asendorf shows that a central idea of Viennese modernism was the new conception of the body as a bundle of nerves and reality as simply a set of stimuli. This derived from the work of Hermann Bahr and from Ernst Mach's *The Analysis of Sensation* (1885) in which the ego was seen as simply a fiction; the idea of the individual as made up of currents of sensation replaces the idea of the unified subject. Bahr wrote in 1891 of the 'new people' as being

> nerves; the rest is extinct, withered and barren. They live now only through the experience of nerves; they only react on the basis of nerves ... (quoted in Asendorf, 1993: 171)

Benjamin's writing on Baudelaire also draws attention to the way in which the electrical impulses of the nervous system transgress the separation of the body from the world:

> Moving through this traffic involves the individual in a series of shocks or collisions. At dangerous crossings, nervous impulses flow through him in rapid succession, like the energy from a battery. Baudelaire speaks of a man who plunges into the crowd as into a reservoir of electric energy. (Benjamin, 1989: 132)

This passage makes explicit the link between the concept of modernity as shock and the late nineteenth-century fascination with electricity. Although nerves had been long understood in terms of electricity, it wasn't until the last decades of the nineteenth century that electricity began to have a visible presence in people's everyday lives. It was only in the 1870s and 1880s that the first central electricity stations were put into operation and some European cities began to install electric (arc) lighting in place of gas lamps to light the major shopping streets (Schivelbusch, 1995: 58, 65, 115). The length of time it took for Europe to become fully electrified suggests why electricity was one of the primary signifiers of modernity as late as the 1930s. That electricity unequivocally stood for progress is exemplified in Lenin's formula 'electrification + Soviet power = communism'.[4]

Since the eighteenth century, electricity was thought of as a kind of life force, even bringing to life dead bodies, like Frankenstein's monster. Even the electric chair was seen in these terms – the electricity seemed to be trying to reanimate the person, even after it had killed them (Asendorf, 1993: 163). Medical practitioners could finally put to use their fascination with electricity when patented devices using electricity as cure became available in the 1880s. George Beard himself was an advocate of the use of electricity in treating neurasthenia. (His *Medical and Surgical Uses of Electricity* was published in 1874.) The many uses of electricity alongside the neurological understanding of electrical charges in the body combine to reinforce the idea of electricity as a life force. In addition, analogies were drawn between electro-magnetism and sexual attraction.

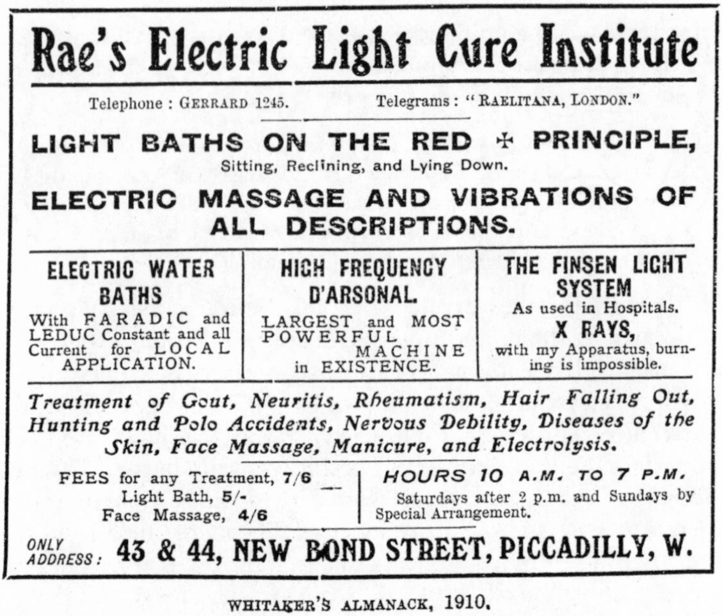

Figure 2.5 Advertisement in Whitaker's Almanack, 1910. Note the inclusion of 'nervous debility' amongst the list of conditions which can be treated.

Electricity thus becomes feminized, linked to women's roles as the bearers of new life and as erotic spectacles. Turn-of-the-century images of electricity and electrification depicted women emanating electricity from their fingers, holding together the wires of the newly electrified city. In literature and art, women's hair (already an erotic object) represented the flow of electricity. Rimbaud's poem 'Les Chercheuses de Poux' makes use of the idea of electricity flowing from women and the static electricity in hair but links this more with death and somnambulism as it describes a young boy being de-loused by his sisters:

> He hears their lashes beat the still, sweet air;
> Their soft electric fingers never tire –
> Through his grey swoon, a crackling in his hair –
> Beneath their royal nails the little lice expire.[5]

Rimbaud's poem may be exceptional in bringing together this idea of women as electrical with an emphasis on the banal, organic and (usually) non-erotic lice infestation. But it does point

Figure 2.6 Advertisement listing hysteria amongst the conditions that an 'electric corset' might alleviate. By permission of Adam Hilger Ltd.

Figure 2.7 Turn-of-the-century illustration symbolizing electricity and the electrification of the city through the image of a woman. Reproduced in C. Asendorf (1993), *Batteries of Life: On the History of Things and Their Perception in Modernity*, Berkeley: University of California Press. Reproduced here by permission of Anabas-Verlag.

to the association of women as electrical with the image of the deadly seductress or vamp. This association is there in the 1927 film *Metropolis*, in which an electro-chemical process transforms the robot into the false Maria – the Vamp, and in Symbolist images of women's flowing hair which link the idea of electricity 'as the flowing current of life' to the image of Medusa (Huyssen, 1986: 80; Asendorf, 1993: 164–5). In these examples the ambiguous gift of electricity, that murderous life force, is brought together with the fear/enticement that the woman as Vamp suggested.

In these representations electricity is personified as women and women are understood in terms of electricity. In some ways this is a continuation of the idea of women as more open to sensation and more vulnerable to the shocks of modernity. Yet women were also seen as lacking in energy, more prone to fatigue. Theories of the conservation of energy linked the argument that women were overusing their minds with the idea that women were particularly vulnerable to 'the excessive energies at work in the external world'. Against the demands being put by feminists and suffragists, some doctors argued that women needed to conserve the limited nervous energy they had, since their nerve centres were more unstable than men's (Showalter, 1987: 125).

Though electricity was often associated with women's bodies and the erotic charge they seemed to hold, it was also used as a violent means of restoring 'proper' masculinity. The treatment of hysterical soldiers from the First World War with electricity makes explicit the relationship between punishment and cure, and the stakes of gender. The soldier must be disciplined, made masculine again, jolted (literally) out of his feminine passivity. This is shown at its most extreme in the work of Dr Lewis Yealland, discussed by Showalter. As part of the effort to get soldiers back to the front, Yealland 'treated' a twenty-four-year-old private suffering from loss of speech or 'mutism', a symptom associated with hysteria. The patient was subjected to a variety of treatments, with little success, until Yealland finally tied him to a chair and forcibly applied strong electric shocks to his pharynx for four hours. Even though the patient cried out, Yealland would not stop until he spoke without a stutter. This doctor may have dealt so violently with the man's mutism precisely because it smacked of feminine passivity.[6]

Mutism was common amongst shell-shocked soldiers and, like hysteria in women, has been linked to frustrated anger at subjugation:

> To be reduced to a feminine state of powerlessness, frustration and dependency led to a deprivation of speech as well ... Ernst Simmel argued that mutism was a symptom of the soldier's repressed aggression towards his superior officers, a censorship of anger and hostility by turning it in upon the self. Thus shell-shock may actually have served the same kind of functional purpose in military life – defusing mutiny – that female hysteria served in civilian society. (Showalter, 1987: 175)

The medical use of electricity also shored up the doctor's masculine control by drawing a clear distinction between him and the patient. Unlike hypnosis, the other common method of treatment, it did not allow patients to fake symptoms and it put the doctor in control of the spectacle (treatments were sometimes carried out in front of an audience, as in Charcot's Salpetrière). Armed with such a technology, he was firmly positioned as 'scientist' rather than 'mesmerist' (McCarren, 1995: 761, 767). Electric shocks were used to restore sensitivity to numb or paralysed parts of the body but also to stop convulsions and in the process stop sensation too.

Electricity is a central theme in new representations of modern sensory experience in this period. It is used to naturalize sexual difference as biological differences in the 'energy' and 'nerve centres' of men and women, and as a violent technical means of enforcing a supposedly masculine denial of sensation and emotion.

Sleepwalking and intoxication

Another way in which women's susceptibility is figured is through the linked ideas of the hypnotic trance and intoxication. It was thought that an overdose of sensation, or faulty/fragile nerves, could lead to loss of self-control and an intoxicated, sleepwalking state.

The most extreme manifestation of this was hysterical 'dissociation', also known as 'multiple' or 'split' personality (and often treated with electric shock). This was most common in women and undermined the idea of the unified self. In the late nineteenth century, more and more cases of multiple personality were recorded. One expert, Binet, compared it to sleepwalking. Just as the person who sleepwalks at night has no memory or knowledge of what they did, so each persona of the hysteric has no knowledge of the other. In effect, she has two distinct personalities or 'double consciousness' (Ferguson, 1996: 41–2).

Some commentators thought that large numbers of women were beginning to experience minor versions of dissociation as a calculated effect of capitalism in the department stores which were designed to intoxicate the female shopper with sensations. The most famous representation of this is Emile Zola's *Au Bonheur des Dames* which suggests the 'systematically disoriented sensorial experience of the women shoppers' (Ross, 1988: 101–2). Poor, vulnerable women, so open to sensation they fall under the spell of the commodity. Thus bewitched, they become like sleepwalkers, experiencing shopping as a dream detached from everyday reality. Yet if this is, as Kristin Ross expresses it, the 'ordered disorganisation promoted by capitalist culture', it has an outcome that hardly benefits that culture: shoplifting.

Middle-class women's shoplifting was diagnosed as a form of hysterical dissociation – termed 'kleptomania'. While working-class women stole from necessity (and were therefore seen as common criminals) 'respectable' bourgeois women seemed to be stealing for the hell of it. It was suggested that these women were like magpies, helplessly attracted to the shiny baubles on display in department stores (Schwartz, 1989: 415). Kleptomaniacs were distinguished from other shoplifters by apparently being in a trance-like state. The kleptomaniac caught stealing would vigorously deny the crime, then express shame and surprise when the stolen articles were found, claiming to have been in a daze, or to have no recollection of taking them, and through her confession, shifting the blame onto someone else, another self who had momentarily taken over (Schwartz, 1989: 415–19). But as with war neurasthenia later, kleptomania tended to be treated seriously only amongst middle-class women – who didn't really need what they stole. Impoverished women who stole and then claimed they were in a daze were usually assumed to be faking.

Although shoplifting could be seen as working against capitalism, and the kleptomaniac's apparent trance-like state a means of releasing her from the restrictive bonds of bourgeois femininity, commentators instead viewed middle-class female shoppers as the passive victims of modernity. This was not helped by the fact that the hypnotic trance was associated with feminine helplessness and suggestibility and was used in the treatment of hysteria. In one view hypnosis was thought to be effective only for hysterics or potential hysterics because of weaknesses in their nervous system; in another, hypnosis itself produced a 'feminine' suggestibility.[7] So, although some medical practitioners used hypnosis on shell-shocked soldiers in the First World War, arguing that it worked by enabling both the recovery of the repressed traumatic event and the 'liberation of pent-up emotion', for others the association of hypnosis with suggestibility, weakness and theatrics made it inappropriate for the treatment of male soldiers – hypnosis was thought to exploit and encourage an 'effeminate' passivity in conflict with the soldier's 'masculine' qualities of self-discipline and autonomy.[8]

So the hypnotic trance is already understood as feminine and feminizing. But the trance induced by the phantasmagoria of the department store was also understood as a kind of drunkenness or drugging of the senses. Department stores were noted for the ways they played on all the senses, but the sense most associated with 'drugging' is the sense of smell. In the traditional hierarchy of the senses, smell is inferior, associated with women, so-called primitive peoples and animals (Classen, 1993; Classen *et al.*, 1994). Scent is represented as a means by which women intoxicate (seduce) men but it is also seen as something women are attracted to and easily intoxicated by. One critical perspective on modernity emphasizes the ways in which intoxicating substances and spectacles were increasingly deployed in the interests of capitalism. Thus, Susan Buck-Morss (1992: 24) points out that 'perfumeries burgeoned in the nineteenth century'. However, equally notable are the ways in which bourgeois society aired its concerns about the dangers of intoxication for women in general and for the working classes in particular. Again, using the example of perfume, Alain Corbin has shown how the use of scents by bourgeois women was carefully policed. Only a small range of perfumes were permitted, with floral odours encouraged and animal perfumes (such as musk) discouraged. Nineteenth-century descriptions of the negative effects of perfumes on women are quite revealing in the constellation of fears they muster. Corbin (1994: 184) quotes Dr Roster, writing in 1826:

> Misuse of perfume gives birth to all the neuroses ... hysteria, hypochondria and melancholia are its most usual effects.

Corbin summarizes that,

> the charm of perfumes, the search for 'base sensations', symptoms of a 'soft, lax' education, increased nervous irritability, led to 'feminism' and encouraged debauchery.

It's clear that here the intoxication by perfume of bourgeois women was seen as a threat to social order. In fact, intoxication can be a sign of rebelliousness and even an important part of revolution. Benjamin's social history of Paris makes this clear: he describes how opposition to the wine tax was one issue that united the French proletariat and the peasantry. To find cheap wine, whole families would leave the confines of the city and, according to police reports of the time, would return home making open and defiant display of their drunkenness (Benjamin, 1989).

But working-class drunkenness was also used to naturalize and justify class differentiations. Kristin Ross has written about how the bourgeoisie characterized the 'bad' worker as either drunk or idle and used the assumption of drunkenness to attack 'the masses' during the Paris Commune of 1871. The terms used by monarchist journals to refer to the crowd – *la crapule* and *la canaille* – are both associated with being drunk.[9] And drunkenness in working-class women was read as a sign of loose moral character and sexual availability – Parisian laundresses gained their place in the pornographic fantasy world of the bourgeois man partly because of the amounts of wine they consumed to counter the heat and hard labour of the laundry (Lipton, 1980).

Working-class women were considered particularly susceptible not only to alcohol but to the intoxicating effect of capitalist spectacle via the new technology of the cinema. The cinema was one of the few places women were able to congregate *en masse*. Until 1908 German law prohibited women from assembling in public or taking part in politics, and Patrice Petro (1989: 69–70) suggests that even later the appearance of women at public gatherings was considered 'scandalous' or 'immoral'. But the film industry actively encouraged the female audience. In an early study (1914) linking gender and cinema attendance in Germany, the sociologist Emilie Altenloh represented her own sex as 'particularly prone to cinematic representation' precisely because of women's reputed unmediated, emotional response to sense impressions. She distances herself from other women, by contrasting this attentive absorbed form of reception to that of 'intellectual people' (quoted in Hake, 1987: 160). In fact the majority of commentators on women filmgoers identified them with a closeness and absorption in the film that was the very opposite of the 'distance' necessary for critical consciousness.

The word used in German cinema criticism to describe this absorbed form of attention (and the films themselves) was *Zerstreuung*, which has been translated as 'distraction' or 'diversion'. It usually had negative connotations, signifying passive, uncritical consumption of mere entertainment.[10] Two German writers, Walter Benjamin and Siegfried Kracauer, critiqued the class assumptions which shaped the cultural critics' attitude, in which the bourgeois self-perception as individual spectator capable of critical distance is set against their perception of the working classes as collective subject, producing 'the same ancient lament that the masses seek distraction whereas art demands concentration from the spectator' and 'self-pitying complaints about this turn towards mass taste' (Benjamin, 1992: 232; Kracauer, 1987: 93).

Nevertheless Kracauer recognized that the extravagant new picture palaces of the 1920s were designed to produce a sensory intoxication and effectively prevent contemplative attention, 'The stimulations of the senses succeed each other with such rapidity that there is no room left for even the slightest contemplation to squeeze in' (Kracauer, 1987: 94). Thus the picture palaces use spectacle and sensory 'intoxication' to produce distraction for the mass audience. Distraction is not passive since (as Benjamin argues) knowledge and new perceptions are not formed by contemplation alone; we can also learn through habit and use. Benjamin sees film as a medium particularly conducive to distraction because it privileges this kind of apperception.[11] In addition, both Kracauer and Benjamin contextualize distraction as a mode of attention in terms of the cinema as leisure, and the formal qualities of the medium of film as compensating for and reflecting the superficiality, fragmentation and unfulfilling nature of modernized labour. For Benjamin, film as a medium is linked to factory labour through its similarity to the conveyor belt, and to the shock experience of modernity through the rapid shifts in perspective that editing produces. For both writers this lends a realism to the medium:

> Here, in pure externality, the audience encounters itself; its own reality is revealed in the fragmented sequence of splendid sense-impressions. Were this reality to remain hidden from the audience, they could neither attack nor change it. (Kracauer, 1987: 94)

Yet the cinema audience included large numbers of young women who did not work in factories. According to Patrice Petro, women in the Germany of the 1920s were employed in a wide range of low-paid jobs with much less economic and social stability than men. For many women, modernity meant simply an increase in the difficulty, monotony and stress of their traditional domestic roles. Nevertheless, Petro (1989: 76) still views cinema as compensatory for these women, providing a 'heightened sensory experience' as compensation for the 'sensory deprivation' of everyday life.

When Kracauer discusses the female audience, he refers to them disparagingly as 'little shopgirls'. In his essay 'The Little Shopgirls go to the Movies' he seems to share with the journalists their contempt for women cinema-goers – femininity once more represents a conservative passivity and complete vulnerability to ideology. He represents the female audience as unable to distinguish between real life and the romantic film, and he comments scathingly on the way the 'little shopgirls' respond physically to the film by weeping. This essay is discussed by both

Patrice Petro and Sabine Hake, who suggest that a combination of fear and fascination shaped the male critics' attitude to the female audience and that this is linked to women's increased political visibility (Hake, 1987: 14). As Petro points out, Kracauer's essay tells us more about bourgeois masculinity than it does about working-class women. It was the male critics' own investment in individualism and their own fear of 'loss of self' that enabled women's absorption to be constructed as vulnerability (1989: 71). Yet this comes from the same writer who, like Benjamin, is also capable of seeing in this sort of attention the potential for social change.

The contradictory nature of Kracauer's and Benjamin's writings on 'distraction' is perhaps produced out of the tension between this bourgeois masculinity and their commitment to the (historically 'feminized') 'mass'. They support the potential of the working-class 'mass' to enact social, revolutionary change. However, they also recognize the ways in which distraction might mobilize people to different and opposite political ends. Writing in 1926, Kracauer sees how the new cinema attempts to contain and seduce its audience but sees its potential to feed into a tension which he senses on the streets of Berlin – the feeling that things will suddenly 'burst apart'. A decade later Benjamin recognizes that Nazism has harnessed the collective power of the 'distracted masses', yet he still sees everyday bodily, sensory experience as the source of political change.

To summarize: when the mass is not only 'feminized' but predominantly female, its absorption in sensation is read as passive vulnerability. In the period and the texts I have discussed, femininity is considered virtually incompatible with the ability to act on and transform the social world. Yet there also emerges a recognition that a precondition for social change is a collective consciousness and bodily involvement in the world – that lack of distance and immersion in sensation historically associated with women and defined as 'femininity'. The feminine turns out not to be so passive after all.

Acknowledgements

Thanks to Ben Highmore and Martin Lister for their ideas and comments on earlier drafts of this essay, Mike and Chrys Henning for finding illustrations, John Parish for finding the title, and

Rebecca Goddard and Sue Beale for providing distraction. The title of this essay is taken from the song *Don't Touch Me (I'm Electric)* by Bill Nelson's Red Noise (1979).

Notes

1. One critic of stimulus-response theories of consciousness was the Soviet psychologist Vygotsky (1896–1934). David Bakhurst has argued that Vygotsky's work shows that we do not simply respond to stimuli but 'engage in the specific practice, social in origin, of the production and interpretation of narrative forms' (see Bakhurst, 1990: 212).

2. My reading of this owes much to Susan Buck-Morss's 'Aesthetics and Anaesthetics' essay and to Terry Eagleton's book *The Ideology of the Aesthetic* (1990). Buck-Morss (1992: 5) applies Eagleton's explanation of aesthetics as sensory cognition to Benjamin's 'Work of Art' essay.

3. The surrealists' celebration of the hysteric and of women murderers may have been to do with their transgression of gender boundaries but they have nothing to say about the actual suffering of the hysteric. The futurist Marinetti's glorification of war and Fascism, and denigration of femininity is well known yet he also expressed support for the women's suffrage movement.

4. Lenin quoted in Asendorf (1993: 169). It was Asja Lacis, the Latvian revolutionary, who had explained what was happening in Moscow to Walter Benjamin: 'She spoke of how she had not understood Russia in the least at the outset. ... Gradually she had realised what was in fact taking place here: the conversion of revolutionary effort into technological effort. Now it is made clear to every communist that at this hour revolutionary work does not signify conflict or civil war, but rather electrification, canal construction, creation of factories' (Benjamin, 1986; written 1926–7).

5. Quoted in Ross (1988: 106).

6. The association of loss of speech with passivity is so strong that in December 1996 I heard a radio debate in which a doctor (advocating the use of electroconvulsive therapy) uses the 'mutism' of patients as justification for conducting ECT without their permission.

7. Charcot argued that hypnosis was effective because of a weakness in the nervous system of the subject: only hysterics or potential hysterics could be hypnotized. Against this, Hyppolite Bernheim saw suggestibility as the underlying factor: hypnosis *produced* hysteria and created suggestibility. For Bernheim, the hypnosis which 'induced' or 'cured' hysteria in Charcot's patients was 'a phenomenon of suggestion and suggestion was increasingly a

feature of public life. More and more people were being urged to walk about in a 'waking dream' (Ferguson, 1996: 41–2). Freud had abandoned hypnosis as a cure for hysteria in the 1890s.

8. The quote in favour of hypnosis is from Brown, cited in Leys (1994: 625). According to Leys, in response to these criticisms, hypnosis is made masculine, retheorized as consensual and participatory in the period following World War I.

9. *Crapule* is derived directly from the Latin *crapula* (drunkenness). *Canaille*, from the Latin *canis* (dog), carries with it associations of debauchery and specifically drunkenness (Ross, 1988: 16, 148).

10. Hake (1987: 147) The term implies not a lack of attentiveness but a particular kind of absorbed attention: 'Distraction and concentration form polar opposites which may be described as follows: A man who concentrates before a work of art is absorbed by it. ... In contrast the distracted mass absorbs the work of art' (Benjamin, 1992: 232).

11. He explains this through a parallel with another art form – architecture. Benjamin's point is that we experience buildings both 'by use and by perception – or rather by touch and sight'. Whilst the visual contemplation of a building is emphasized in the treatment of it as a work of art or a tourist site, the tactile experience of it is the experience of everyday life. We don't contemplate a building through the sense of touch, rather we get to know it. This isn't simply a distinction between these two senses – though we can contemplate a building through vision, most of the time we simply notice it, in order to find our way round it (Benjamin, 1992: 233).

References

Asendorf, C. (1993) *Batteries of Life: On the History of Things and Their Perception in Modernity*. Berkeley: University of California Press.

Bakhurst, D. (1990) Social memory in Soviet thought. In D. Middleton and D. Edwards (eds), *Collective Remembering*. London: Sage.

Beizer, J. (1994) *Ventriloquized Bodies: Narratives of Hysteria in Nineteenth-Century France*. Ithaca, NY: Cornell University Press.

Benjamin, W. (1986) *Moscow Diary*. Cambridge, MA: Harvard University Press.

Benjamin, W. (1989) *Charles Baudelaire: A Lyric Poet in the Era of High Capitalism*. London: Verso.

Benjamin, W. (1992) The work of art in the age of mechanical reproduction. In *Illuminations*. London: Fontana.

Bernheimer, C. and Kahane, C. (1985) *In Dora's Case: Freud, Hysteria, Feminism*. London: Virago.

Bourke, J. (1996) *Dismembering the Male: Men's Bodies, Britain and the Great War*. London: Reaktion Books.

Broks, P. (1996) *Media Science Before the Great War*. London: Macmillan.

Buck-Morss, S. (1992.) Aesthetics and anaesthetics: Walter Benjamin's artwork essay reconsidered. *October*, 62, 3–31.

Classen, C. (1993) *Worlds of Sense: Exploring the Senses in History and Across Cultures*. London: Routledge.

Classen, C., Howes, D. and Synott, A. (1994) *Aroma: The Cultural History of Smell*. London: Routledge.

Corbin, A. (1994, orig. 1986) *The Foul and The Fragrant: Odour and the Social Imagination*. London: Picador.

Eagleton, T. (1990) *The Ideology of the Aesthetic*. London: Blackwell.

Ferguson, H. (1996) *The Lure of Dreams: Sigmund Freud and the Construction of Modernity*. London: Routledge.

Freud, S. (1984) Beyond the pleasure principle. In *Pelican Freud Library, Vol. 11, On Metapsychology: The Theory of Psychoanalysis*. Harmondsworth: Penguin (first published 1920).

Hake, S. (1987) Girls and crisis: the other side of diversion. *New German Critique*, 14(40), 147–64.

Huyssen, A. (1986) *After the Great Divide: Modernism, Mass Culture and Postmodernism*. London: Macmillan.

Kracauer, S. (1987) Cult of distraction: on Berlin's picture palaces. *New German Critique*, 14(40), 91–6.

Kracauer, S. (1987) The little shopgirls go to the movies. *New German Critique*, 14(40).

Leys, R. (1994) Traumatic cures: shell shock, Janet and the question of memory. *Critical Enquiry*, 20, 623–62.

Lipton, E. (1980) The laundress in nineteenth-century French culture: imagery, ideology and Edgar Degas. *Art History*, 3(3).

McCarren, F. (1995) The symptomatic act circa 1900: hysteria, hypnosis, electricity, dance. *Critical Inquiry*, 21.

Otis, L. (1994) *Organic Memory: History and the Body in the Late Nineteenth and Early Twentieth Centuries*. Lincoln: University of Nebraska Press.

Petro, P. (1989) *Joyless Streets: Women and Melodramatic Representation in Weimar Germany*. Princeton, NJ: Princeton University Press.

Rabinbach, A. (1992) *The Human Motor: Energy, Fatigue and the Origins of Modernity*. Los Angeles: University of California Press.

Ross, K. (1988) *The Emergence of Social Space: Rimbaud and the Paris Commune*. Minneapolis: University of Minnesota Press.

Schivelbusch, W. (1986) *The Railway Journey: The Industrialisation of Time and Space in the Nineteenth Century*. Los Angeles: University of California Press (first published 1977).

Schivelbusch, W. (1995) *Disenchanted Night: The Industrialisation of Light in the Nineteenth Century*. London: University of California Press (first published 1983).

Schwartz, H. (1989) The three-body problem and the end of the world. In Michel Feher *et al.* (eds), *Fragments for a History of the Human Body*, Part 1. Cambridge, MA: Zone/MIT Press.

Seremetakis, C. N. (1994) *The Senses Still: Perception and Memory as Material Culture in Modernity*. Oxford: Westview Press.

Simmel, G. (1964) The metropolis and mental life. In Kurt H. Wolff (ed., trans.), *The Sociology of Georg Simmel*. New York: The Free Press. (first published 1902–3).

Showalter, E. (1987) *The Female Malady: Women, Madness and English Culture, 1830–1980*. London: Virago.

Starobinski, J. (1989) The natural and literary history of bodily sensation. In Michel Feher *et al.* (eds), *Fragments for a History of the Human Body*, Part 2. Cambridge, MA: Zone/MIT Press.

Synott, A. (1993) *The Body Social: Symbolism, Self and Society*. London: Routledge.

Theweleit, K. (1987) *Male Fantasies. volume 1*. Minneapolis: University of Minnesota Press.

3

Temporality, Materiality: Towards a Body in Time

Tamsin Wilton

The idea of the body and the discourses and apparatuses of power which construct and act upon bodies are of particular interest to queers and women, perhaps especially the practices and knowledges of medicine which have commandeered the intellectual and cultural territory of the body, re-presenting sexual 'difference' and sexual object-choice deviance as properties of bodies. Medicine is not unique in this. It is simply the most overt (and most powerful) exemplar of a wider social project to subject queers and women to disciplinary control (Foucault, 1976; Wilton, 1997). Since queers and women are both arguably gendered 'feminine' within and by the operations of discourses of embodiment (see below), the disciplinary control in question is itself expressive of male power. I look to the social, academic and political interventions of sociology, feminism and Queer[1] to resist and oppose this assertive male hegemony which organizes its truth-claims around corporeality.

Yet sociology, feminism and Queer have so far failed to engage in any direct way with this encarnation of hegemony. Moreover, although the new activism of Queer Nation and the proliferating gender-performances of the queer milieu do, to some extent, succeed in problematizing gender by means of bodily/embodied signifying practices, no radical theory of the body has yet coalesced out of such counter-hegemonic interventions. Indeed, the recent theoretical tendency has been to downplay the significance of carnality in favour of a constructionist model which purposefully detaches 'sex', in all its manifold meanings, from the flesh (Frank, 1991; Butler, 1993; Plummer, 1995), leading some to urge that the time has come to bring back the body. As Judith Butler indicates, it is 'difficult to know what to retrieve under the sign of the body' (Butler, 1993: 28). 'What to retrieve under the sign of the body' is precisely what concerns me here, since practices of hegemony which depend upon embodiment demand that we develop an adequate oppositional theory of the body, rather than simply vacating the space it has been constrained to occupy. I am also concerned to move away from the current position of mutual hostility that exists between feminists (e.g. Harne and Miller (eds), 1996; Jeffreys, 1990) and queers (as discussed in Merck, 1993, and Wilton, 1996), since the co-constitutive relations among genders and sexualities demand a theoretical and political alliance between us.

The difficulty in making sense of bodies lies in disaggregating the body both from the dubious legacy of biological determinism which haunts it and, as Butler (1993: 30) suggests, from its ironic position as the discursively constituted pre-discursive ground:

> The body posited as prior to the sign is always *posited* or *signified* as *prior*. This signification produces as an *effect* of its own procedure the very body that it nevertheless and simultaneously claims to discover as that which *precedes* its own action. [emphasis in original]

Not only constructed as a *tabula rasa*, the privileged signifier of extra-discursivity (authenticity?), the body has also been constructed by some as extra- or pre-social. Any counter-hegemonic theory of the body has to engage with these difficult questions. Ken Plummer (1995: 156) calls for 'a way of telling stories about the body that enables us to see it not simply as a bounded, "there", "in us" but something which resonates socially'.

I want, therefore, to interrogate the ideation of the body in order to identify corporeality as the site of a power struggle between discourses which have largely spoken 'past' each other, and to respond to Plummer's call for a new way of telling stories about the body. I am also motivated by Butler's suggestion (1993: 32) that 'feminists ought to be interested, not in taking materiality as an irreducible, but in conducting a critical genealogy of its formation'. Whereas Butler tends to take 'materiality' to be coterminous with physicality, in the longer term I believe we need to reconstruct a less literal version of materiality, one which is more strategically and theoretically useful to feminists and to queers. In order to do this, it is first necessary to clarify the 'nature' of the body itself. Moreover there is always a sense in which the body is a text. As such, traces of the operations of power and resistance are inscribed upon the body both by the disciplinary practices of the state (Foucault, 1976) and by the transgressive and (putatively) disobedient practices of marginalized and disreputable people (Polhemus and Randall, 1994). It becomes important to decide whether the body is a text, a palimpsest or a conversation, and I am especially interested in asking this question in the context of body-transformative practices, such as weight-training and 'gender-reassignment' surgery, which take gender and sexuality as their matter.

Identify and control

For both feminists and queers, the social construction of bodily difference is perceived – I think rightly – as constituting the very core of oppression. Contrary to Foucauldian accounts, modern scientific medicine did not originate this socio-political project of bodily difference (Foucault, 1976). Rather, its roots lie in much older attempts to read sex into/from the human body, which can be traced with some confidence back to Plato and Aristotle.

Here we run instantly into the problem of semantics. 'Sex' stands for a truly chaotic cacophony of meaning-making across the biological, the social, the psychological, the cultural and the political, all of which have their own tangled histories. Any reasonably sophisticated theory of sex must recognize this. West and Zimmerman (1991), for example, propose 'sex, sex category and gender' as three distinct though intersecting strands. The notion of 'sex category', here interposed between sex and gender, allows for phenomena such as transsexualism or gender transience by recognizing that 'it is possible to claim membership in a sex category even when the sex criteria are lacking'. They define gender as 'the activity of managing situated conduct in the light of normative attitudes and activities appropriate for one's sex category' (West and Zimmerman, 1991: 14). In this paradigm, however, sex is restricted to questions of male and female and properties or activities of masculinity and femininity. The erotic – sexuality – is excluded.

But it is, I suggest, important to recognize the privileged role of the erotic in constituting and maintaining dominant ideologies of gender. By 'sex', I mean here both the attribution of maleness or femaleness and the different but inextricably related question of desire, arousal, activity and pleasure which may loosely be termed 'the erotic'. Both are contributive to and derivative from the social construction of 'gender' (Kaplan and Rogers, 1991; West and Zimmerman, 1991; Grosz, 1990), and both are sets of meanings which lay claim to being 'read from' the flesh and its nature.

'Biological' sex and 'social' gender are all too often mistakenly seen as natural fact and cultural artefact, with an (authentic?) biological reality preceding and giving rise to a culturally contingent (artificial?) social construct. A focus on the erotic enables us to recognize that they are, rather, co-dependent and mutually reinforcing. In dominant discourse the erotic generally takes an unreflexively gendered position; masculinity and femininity coalesce around the possession and gender-appropriate use of sexual organs. This conceptual and ideological co-dependency of biological sex, a gendered erotics and the socio-cultural construction of gender is what I term 'heteropolarity', since its rubric is structured around a naturalized model of heterosexual desire as the 'charge' across two sexes seen as polar opposites (Wilton, 1995, 1997). It is also important to note here that this heteropolar paradigm is intrinsically phallocentric, constructing masculinity and femininity relative to the possession or lack of the phallus. The central irony of this, as many feminist writers have pointed out, is that while masculinity is the norm and definitive absolute of power and agency, individual men – whether queer or not – are condemned to experience it as an endlessly aspirational state, since the fleshly penis can never do more than 'stand for' (pun intended) the phallus. For women – whether lesbian or not – the consequences of being assigned the status of referential 'other', lacking both penis and phallus, and of the heteropolar construct of heterosex around penile activity have been widely theorized (de Lauretis, 1994; Grosz, 1995; Wilton, 1996, 1997).

Heteropolarity, although differently nuanced at different times and locations (locations of class, religious affiliation and ethnicity as well as of geopolitical status), is generally constructed as a scientific 'truth' which 'explains' gendered relations of power. The relations of power which it supposedly explains in fact determine its conditions of production and gain reinforcement from its operations. This is not, contrary to received wisdom, a situation which followed on the heels of the Industrial Revolution and the separation of public/private spheres. Indeed, Thomas Aquinas, in the thirteenth century, proposed that heterosex is the natural biological origin for the domestic division of labour then current:

> Male and female are joined together in humans, not only on account of the necessity for generation ... but also for domestic life, in which there are different jobs for the man and the woman, and in which the man is the head of the woman. (quoted in Cadden, 1993: 193)

With the rise of what we think of as the 'scientific' paradigm, which in Europe (partially) superseded the religious/spiritual paradigm during the Enlightenment, increasingly detailed mappings of the body-as-gendered develop. From the beginning of the nineteenth century, as Thomas Laqueur (1990: 5) suggests, 'writers of all sorts were determined to base what they insisted were fundamental differences between ... man and woman, on discoverable biological distinctions'. The imperative to fix sexual difference in the flesh became, with the increasing transparency of the body to the medical gaze, ever more fine-tuned. By 1847 a doctor writing on hysteria could insist that womanliness was located in every aspect of female corporeality:

> All parts of her body express the same differences: all express woman; the brow, the nose, the eyes, the mouth, the ears, the chin, the cheeks. If we shift our view to the inside, and with the help of the scalpel, lay bare the organs, the tissues, the fibres, we encounter everywhere ... the same difference. (Bracket, 1847, quoted in Laqueur, 1990: 5)

Here, sexual difference saturates the very material of bodies. This drive to differentiate became urgent in response to political struggles over women's suffrage. As the medical gaze zoomed in from bodies to organs to cells, the threat to patriarchal ideology outstripped the technology of looking; at the turn of the century Patrick Geddes was suggesting that gender was imprinted at the cellular level. The male body, he proposed, was composed of 'catabolic cells', cells that gave off energy, while female body cells were 'anabolic', cells which stored and conserved energy.[2] Calling on Darwinism to justify male supremacy he proclaimed that

'What was decided among the pre-historic protozoa cannot be annulled by an act of Parliament' (Geddes, 1889, quoted in Laqueur, 1990: 6, 7).

Biological essentialism, the belief in an 'essence' of femaleness and maleness, cannot be seen as underlying in any straightforward way the scholarship of the scientific medical paradigm. As Laqueur (1990: 88) suggests:

> The history of the representation of the anatomical differences between man and woman is ... extraordinarily independent of the actual structure of organs, or of what was known about them. Ideology, not accuracy of observation, determined how they were seen and which differences would matter.

The phrase 'which differences matter' neatly exposes the productive interface between corporeality and the social.

Erotics and hierarchy: sexualizing relations of power

At this point it should be remembered that/the great oppressive political binaries of the modern era – 'race', gender, class – have all been sexualized| The animal sexuality of black women, the excessive potency of black men, the predatory syphilitic Jew, the uncontained sexual licence of the working classes, the passionless middle-class woman, the irrational, unstoppable force of male lust, all are signs marking power struggles whose agenda is bounded by corporeality (McClintock, 1995; Terry and Urla, 1995; Wilton, 1997). I agree with Laqueur that 'the sexed body ... comes to illustrate the major political and cosmic ruptures of a civilisation' (1990: 55) but I would insist that we incorporate the erotic into the idea of 'the sexed body'. This is not to suggest that the erotic and the sexed body have the same history but to refuse the theoretical abandonment of eros as both marker and instrument of gender regulation/regimentation.

It is hardly surprising, given the co-dependency of gender and the erotic in the heteropolar paradigm, that queer sexuality – queer by reason of its disruption of that paradigm – should be re-presented as a pathology of gender. The rigidity of heteropolarity, whereby masculinity is achieved, expressed and defined by fucking women, mandates that the desires, identities and bodies of those men who fuck men and those women who fuck women must be somehow recaptured within its conceptual matrix in order to protect the coherence of the paradigm itself. Thus, as Judith Butler (1993a: 27) suggests, 'the homophobic terror over performing homosexual acts … is often also a terror over losing proper gender'.

Since the medical gaze, whether scientific or pre-scientific, en/ corporates gender, locating it in the body, sexuality too must be so located. And, indeed, medical discourse is clamorous in its attempts to assert queer desires as corporeal, measuring height, weight, strength of grip, ability to whistle and 'solidity' (among other variables) in an attempt to categorically distinguish between queer and non-queer bodies (Ruse, 1988).

As with gender, the increasing subtlety of the medical gaze has relocated the presumptive corporeality of queer desire from the macro – questions of body morphology and genital structure – to the micro. Western scientific medicine now proposes the queering of the body as a function of hormones, brain structure and finally, of 'gay genes'. In this tendency to squirrel after increasingly microscopic final causes, homosexuality-as-pathology is no different from any other pathology. The attempt to locate socially unacceptable desire in the body is of an order with the more widely accepted attempt to locate disease in the body (Armstrong, 1989) and the project to 'cure' homosexuality is not radically different from any other curative project. What is at stake is not only the brittle irrationality of the heteropolar paradigm but also the hegemony of medicine itself, in what is by now a familiar postmodern refutation of the truth-claims of the scientific rational project.

Abandon ship! fleeing the disciplined body

Given that the oppression of women, queers and people of colour is predicated upon a discursive constitution of gendered and sexed *bodies*, it is unsurprising that politically and culturally opposi-tional discursive practices should have strategically displaced the body. Certain feminists have proposed a radical disaggregation of gender – seen as an institution and organizational matrix of power – from biological sex (Firestone, 1979), while assimila-tionist lesbian and gay activists have traditionally insisted that there is *no difference* between queer bodies and non-queer bodies (Cruikshank, 1992).

Radical social/political movements have not been alone in

casting out the body, nor did they originate this trend. Within the academy the body has long been regarded with deep suspicion in certain quarters. Indeed, Turner (1991: 6) suggests that the development of sociology itself can in part be seen 'as a somewhat hostile reaction to Darwinistic evolutionism, eugenics or biologism'. More recently, feminist biologists have destabilized taken-for-granted assumptions that there is such a thing as 'biological sex' at all (Birke, 1991, 1992; Bleier, 1991).

The result is that gender has come to be understood by many as a purely social entity: a role (Fuss, 1989), display (Goffman, 1976, quoted in West and Zimmerman, 1991), performance (Butler, 1991), career (Tully, 1992) or narrative (Plummer, 1995), depending on your paradigm of choice. Located in the social arena rather than in the body, gender has become a behaviour not an attribute, as this passage from West and Zimmerman (1991: 14) suggests:

> Doing gender involves a complex of socially guided perceptual, interactional and micropolitical activities that cast particular pursuits as expressions of masculine and feminine 'natures'.

Because gender and sexuality are co-dependent within the heteropolar paradigm, a social-constructionist model of gender presupposes a social-constructionist model of sexuality. From Mary MacIntosh to Foucault the notion of dynamic nominalism has developed (Hacking, 1992). It is suggested that 'numerous kinds of human beings and human acts come into being hand in hand with our invention of the categories naming them' (Hacking, 1992: 87). In the beginning was the word, and the word was made flesh and dwelt among us!

Bringing the body back in

For many queers and feminists, social constructionism offered a useful way out of biologism, a refutation of oppressions predicated on the doctrine of encarnation. Yet others chose rather to mark or manipulate the body, treating it not so much as the foundation or originary matter of difference but rather as the semiotic/lexicographic ground of a *conversation* about difference. Here, a hermeneutic cycle is established between hegemonic and oppositional readings of a body-as-text, with *oppositional bodies* being constructed as speech acts by queers, gender transients, sex-radicals (largely non-queer), new tribalists and others (Polhemus and Randall, 1996). A 'purely' social constructionist model for the body makes no sense in any sophisticated way of these practices, nor of radically body-transformative practices such as transsexualism, or the gender-disruptive consequences of female body building. It is a moot point whether such behaviours disrupt or reinforce hegemonic regimes of gender (see Mandy Kidd, Chapter 9). It seems particularly important to interrogate here the construction (literal as well as social) of the transsexual body, since it is on the putatively transsexed body that the cultural scripts and anxieties of heteropolarity are most brutally inscribed.

Transsexualism, enthusiastically co-opted as gender-disruptive and *queer* by some queer activists, seems to me to be an alarmingly legitimate child of the marriage between heteropolarity and the late capitalist consumerization of the body. For, as Mike Featherstone (1991: 177–8) suggests, 'the tendency within consumer culture is for ascribed bodily qualities to become regarded as plastic – with effort and "body work" individuals are persuaded that they can achieve a certain desired appearance.'

This vision of the plastic body stretches human be-ing far beyond simple Cartesian dualism, and it is a vision which leads some women body-builders to identify their bodies as gender-transcendent. In an exciting reflexive essay on her body-building, Marcia Ian takes Judith Butler's notion of gender-performance as drag a step further, identifying the body itself as drag. Ian (1995: 75) recounts a meeting with a male body-builder in a gym, who asked her, 'How do you wear your body?' The question was something of an epiphany for Ian:

> As I thought about his question, my body seemed to peel away from my mind like a suit of clothes from my skin, and I experienced a Cartesian separation of my consciousness from my body such as I had not felt since the experience of 'natural' childbirth. In a flash the notion of 'wearing' one's body seemed to cut in two the very unity of mind and flesh which body-builders go to the gym to forge.

Body here becomes costume; 'one may experience oneself as an essence (or self or subject) wearing a body as a kind of drag as one cruises life, cruises the living' (76).

Since bodies and costumes are always already gendered – indeed, since they always already *signify* gender – it seems as possible to 'do drag' by means of a cross-gendered body as by cross-gendered costume. As Ian (1995: 72) comments, 'In a way, but only in a way, all body-builders' bodies, male or female, are masculine, and the activity of body-building is a masculinizing praxis, given the conventional association of physical strength and lean muscularity with maleness.'[3]

Of course a woman with muscles does not, in any inevitable sense, become or appear more 'masculine'. And, eventually, the social visibility of muscular women may catalyse a shift in the social construction of gendered body-shape. If she has muscles, then muscles are feminine. Ian Hacking (1992: 84) reminds us that the social/cultural construction of gender/sexual identity is a dynamic and two-way process with its own dialectic. He writes of:

> the vector of labeling from above, from a community of experts who create a 'reality' that some people make their own. Different from this is the vector of the autonomous behaviour of the person so labeled, which presses from below, creating a reality every expert must face.

In other words, gender and sexual identities are constructed at the nexus of a dynamic interchange of meanings between the 'self' and the 'social'. This model is problematic, in that it implies an extra-social or pre-social self. I would argue that the 'self', always already 'by definition' gendered and sexually oriented, is *itself* constituted at the dynamic interface between the body and the social. Additionally, 'body' and 'social' are mutually co-constitutive. It is currently fashionable for sociologists to identify the 'self' as constituted by and consisting in a 'reflexive narrative project' (Mellor and Shilling, 1993). My own preference is to see 'self' not as a narrative project (which implies an *authoritative* author and a product which is then available to be 'read') but as a *conversation* between the body and the social, in which the 'matter' of the conversation is continually created and recreated in the dynamic, temporally located, interlocution.

In this 'conversation', it is much easier for an individual to control what the body 'says' than what is said by the society in which the self is obliged to function. Thus the current social crisis in gender is marked by a veritable epidemic of body-transformative actions intended to assert control of the gender-speaking of the bodied self. Bodies are exercised, starved, depilated, shaved, pierced, tattooed, cut, stapled and stitched. Skin is bleached with chemicals or darkened with radiation, fat is vacuumed out of breasts, thighs, stomachs and buttocks, bones are cracked, hair is shaved or removed, breasts are stuffed with gobs of plastic. Despite the degree of attention paid to subcultural practices such as scarification, piercing and tattooing, body transformation is overwhelmingly a set of practices undertaken in utter docility to heteropolar scripts of gender. Much is also carried out in the interests of conforming to white racist notions of acceptability, notions which are themselves gendered. For every goth or queer dyke whose shaved labia are (transgressively) bedecked with multiple piercings there are innumerable women whose desperate obedience to the doctrine of femininity is signalled by the scars of plastic surgery.

At the apotheosis of this butchers' conversation about sex and sexuality are the transsexuals. Here, compliance with heteropolar doctrine is so absolute that the social complexities of gender become fixed in the flesh with a tenacious naivety that is startling. Of course, there are radical transsexuals who identify as transsexual rather than as 'normal' members of their post-operative gender. For example, Sandy Stone (1991: 289) is highly critical of male to female transsexuals who 'replicate the stereotypical male account of the constitution of woman: dress, makeup and delicate fainting at the sight of blood'. But such radicals acknowledge that they are in a minority and that what the majority of transsexuals want is to be absorbed, seamlessly, invisibly, into 'normal' gender relations. This is certainly the impression given by clients interviewed at a British clinic by Bryan Tully (1992) who demonstrate a remarkably intransigent account of gender-as-morphology.

> I want people to see that it cannot be expected of me that I will drink beer, be confident, mend things and leer at women. (198)

> A female body is that which is done to ... and the male body is that which does it. (20)

> As a woman I feel domesticated, tidier and happier. (126)

> I have dropped out of the gay scene now I am a normal woman. Really my hairdresser has helped me the most. (192)

> My outlook on life ... not wanting to smoke and drink in pubs, makes sense to me now. It explains why I have a greater appreciation of small, delicate and pretty things like clothes. (217)

It is a powerful indicator of the potency of the heteropolar paradigm and of its utter saturation of industrial Western societies, that these men believe that in order to avoid drinking beer, smoking, being confident, mending things, leering at women and being untidy, in order to appreciate clothes and be sexually passive, they must submit themselves to castration and the life-long indignities and discomforts of what is at best a primitive and partial 'surgical drag'.

Introducing history

From the time of Plato through to the techno-fix of gender reassignment surgery, medical discourse has maintained the hegemony of heteropolarity by its insistent mapping of difference onto bodies. Moreover, heteropolarity expresses and maintains its hegemony through the material appropriation of women's bodies (Guillaumin, 1981). Counter-hegemonic interventions, whether queer or feminist, must therefore be grounded in an oppositional theory of the body. My suggestion is that such an oppositional theory is best organized around an idea of the body, not as an object located in space whose dimensions may be successfully manipulated in order to re-present gender and the erotic, but as an event situated in time and continuously subject to the co-constitutive dialectic of the organic and the social. Those transsexuals whose radicalism obliges them to refuse easy identification with their non-genetic gender-of-choice share an awareness that gender is not a property of bodies but rather a *process* of bodies. Thus Stone (1991: 295) recognizes that 'transsexuals do not possess the same history as genetic "naturals" and do not share common oppression prior to gender reassignment', while one of the pre-operative transsexuals interviewed by Tully (1992: 183) comments: 'I have seen TS call themselves "she" but clearly they are not ... I think I might feel like a disguised male, after all, I have not had the physical experiences of women, pregnancy, menstruation, abortion and so on'.

So, is it the 'physical experiences' which make someone a woman? Must we return to biological essentialism? Clearly not, for there are self-evidently genetic women who have never experienced pregnancy, abortion or even menstruation. Equally, where biological sex is indeterminate, as in the case of hermaphrodites or those born with chromosomal disorders, sexual and gender identity appear to be more significantly shaped by personal biography than by any biological indicators.

> Money and his associates have followed up scores of hermaph-rodites and have concluded that individuals of the same hermaphroditic diagnosis, if reared in completely opposite gender roles, differentiate a gender identity in agreement with their biography, *irrespective* of chromosomal, gonadal and hormonal sex. (Tully, 1992: 12; emphasis in original)

Tully's proposal is that we think of gender as a *career*. Within this paradigm, ' "gender-dysphoric careers" are proposed as fluctuat-ing enterprises in the construction of meanings' (xiii) and 'gender fluctuation and experiment as a gender career process' (8). This model allows us to understand shifts and contradictions in an individual's 'gender identity', and to recognize that some individuals feel compelled to 'fix' a gender identity experienced as uncomfortably fluid by attempting to re-write the meanings of their bodies. That they do so in obedience to the most restricted constructions of heteropolarity indicates the totalitarian nature of the heteropolar regime.

However, the attempt to erase one set of embodied speech acts – those that speak 'man' for example – and to replace them with another set – those that speak 'woman' – is not and cannot be successful. If there were no more to gender or to sexuality than performances, roles or presentation, there would be no felt need to alter physical bodies. Equally, if there were no more to gender or to sexuality than crude bodily structure then surgical reconstruction would succeed in 'turning' men into women or vice versa. That neither of these is the case points to a profound complexity of acts, meanings, interpretations and experiences sited in and on the socially located body.

If a body is an object, changing its shape changes its nature. But be-ing male or female is about more than body shape, as the gender-disruptive problematics of bodybuilding suggest. Be-ing a man is about a lifetime of meaningful and meaning-giving interactions at the interface of the body and the social. It is about wet dreams, the need to protect vulnerable testicles, fears of prostate trouble, the burden of cultural phantasms such as premature ejaculation or impotence, negotiating a comfortable position relative to socio-cultural suppositions about penis size, etc. Likewise, be-ing a woman is about managing the social and cultural pressures which coalesce around the biological ability to become pregnant and give birth, including the significance of the menstrual cycle. It is about a relationship with the state and the medical profession based on one's breeding potential, about fears of cervical and breast cancer, etc. In other words, 'manning' or 'womanning' – 'maling' and 'femaling' as Richard Ekins (1996) has it – is an embodied time-situated social process. Bodily events are immensely significant in terms of gender identity and sexual identity. The stressful and inevitably harmful business of contraception, for example, simply vanishes in a quite delightful way for a woman who re-locates from heterosexuality to lesbianism, and intrudes often unexpectedly in the lives of women making the journey in reverse (Clausen, 1990).

Conceptually, the contingent, time-bound nature of bodies seems hard to theorize. Frank (1991: 49) proposes a model whereby ' "the body" is constituted in the intersection of an equilateral triangle, the points of which are institutions, discourses and corporeality'. While there seems to be no problem in understanding the culturally and historically contingent nature of institutions and discourses, both dominant and oppositional discourses tend to construct corporeality, 'the body', as an object-state.

This is somewhat ironic given the European romantic tradition of bewailing the brevity of life: 'A fragile dew-drop on its perilous way/From a tree's summit', as Keats has it in 'Sleep and Poetry' (ll. 86-7). It is also cruelly ironic in the light of AIDS, which surely, more than anything else, should force down our throats the chronic changeability of bodies, the absolute and inescapable situating of bodies in time, the body as event. As Roberta McGrath (1990: 144–5) points out, the clinical manifestations of AIDS lend themselves to fearful fantasies of bodily disintegration, since AIDS 'creates a body which turns upon itself, killing not through a single disease but through a cumulation of our most feared diseases [which] ... not only mark the body on the outside, but dissolve it from within'. Mellor and Shilling (1993) write of the sequestration of death, the enormous amounts of time, energy and resources spent on a general cultural denial of the inevitability of change, decay and mortality. Perhaps after all it is not so surprising, in this terrifying time of AIDS, that we appear to cling with increasing panic to our illusions that the body is an object, that it is amenable to control and willed transformation. Yet it will not be possible to develop an adequate oppositional theory of gender or of sexuality unless we can grasp the idea that the body is an event in time. Once this premise is accepted, then 'gender' and 'sexuality' become not merely culturally and historically contingent social fictions or narratives, they can be seen as dynamic conversations between a body-event and the social meanings in which that event is embedded, and of which, in turn, the body-as-event is productive. Only by working from such a model of the body, a model which is dynamic and hence amenable to transformation (perhaps even in some sense transubstantiation), can feminism and Queer move towards our social, political and cultural objectives.

Acknowledgements

This is an extended version of a paper 'Sex in Time: Towards a Time-Situated Model of Gender', which I gave at the Sexuality and Medicine conference in July 1995 at the University of Melbourne. I would like to thank Lisa Adkins for helpful comments on the original paper.

Notes

1. By 'Queer' I mean both the cultural and political interventions of activist groups such as Queer Nation and Homocult and the academic enterprise, Queer Theory, which has currently taken the lead in theorizing gender and sexuality. When I use the lower case 'queer', I refer to lesbian, gay and bisexual people. In this case, queer is used in preference to 'homosexual' which, as well as being a quasi-medical term and hence oppressive, is simply inadequate to the task of describing queerness without reinforcing a heterosexist binary paradigm.

2. This idea is interesting in terms of reasserting the 'magical' character of science, since it so closely parallels notions of masculine and feminine as expressed in spiritual and philosophical traditions such as Taoism or Tantric Hinduism. For example, the traditional Chinese exercises known as t'ai chi are based on a doctrine which states that men's 'chi' or life-force comes into the body from the sky, through the top of the head, while women's comes in from the earth, through the feet. There are many other such gendered doctrines of bodily energies, such as the idea of yin and yang. Clearly, the claim

of science to objectivity is somewhat shaken by its demonstrable tendency to privilege the magical status of key cultural beliefs such as these over the evidence of its own practice.

3. In this context I was interested to hear the trainer who ran the introductory weight-training course I joined repeatedly reassuring the 'ladies' that weight-training wouldn't give them muscles. Male and female muscle fibres, he assured us, were fundamentally different, and no matter how hard we pumped iron, we 'ladies' would not compromise our femininity by developing 'male' muscles. He was flummoxed by my (mischievous) complaint that muscles were precisely what I wanted.

References

Acker, Joan (1991) Hierarchies, jobs, bodies: a theory of gendered organizations. In Judith Lorber and Susan A. Farrell (eds), *The Social Construction of Gender*. London: Sage.

Armstrong, David (1989) *An Outline of Sociology as Applied to Medicine*. London: Wright.

Birke, Linda (1991) Transforming biology. In Helen Crowley and Susan Himmelweit (eds), *Knowing Women: Feminism and Knowledge*. Cambridge: Polity/Open University Press.

Birke, Linda (1992) In pursuit of difference: scientific studies of women and men. In Gill Kirkup and Laurie Smith Keller (eds), *Inventing Women: Science, Technology and Gender*. Cambridge: Polity/Open University Press.

Bleier, Ruth (1991) A critique of biology and its theories on women. In Sneja Gunew (ed.), *A Reader in Feminist Knowledge*. London: Routledge.

Butler, Judith (1991) Imitation and gender insubordination. In Diana Fuss (ed.), *Inside/Out: Lesbian Theories, Gay Theories*. London: Routledge.

Butler, Judith (1993) Critically Queer. *GLQ: A Journal of Lesbian and Gay Studies*, 1(1): 17–32.

Cadden, Joan (1993) *Meanings of Sex Difference in the Middle Ages*. Cambridge: Cambridge University Press.

Clausen, Jan (1990) My interesting condition. *Outlook*, 7 (Winter), 11–21.

de Lauretis, Teresa (1994) *The Practice of Love: Lesbian Sexuality and Perverse Desire*. Bloomington: Indiana University Press.

Ekins, Richard (1996) Male femaling: telephone sex and the case of intimacy scripts. In Richard Ekins and Dave King (eds), *Blending Genders: Social Aspects of Cross-dressing and Sex-changing*. London: Routledge.

Featherstone, Mike (1991) The body in consumer culture; and with Mike

Hepworth, The mask of ageing and the postmodern lifecourse, both in M. Featherstone, M. Hepworth and B. S. Turner (eds), *The Body: Social Process and Cultural Theory*. London: Sage.

Firestone, Shulamith (1970) *The Dialectic of Sex: The Case for Feminist Revolution*. London: Women's Press.

Foucault, Michel (1976) *The History of Sexuality: An Introduction*, Vol. 1. Harmondsworth: Penguin (trans. 1979).

Frank, Arthur (1991) For a sociology of the body: an analytical review. In M. Featherstone, M. Hepworth and B. S. Turner (eds), *The Body: Social Process and Cultural Theory*. London: Sage.

Fuss, Diana (1989) *Essentially Speaking: Feminism, Nature and Difference*. London: Routledge.

Grosz, Elizabeth (1990) Conclusion: a note on essentialism and difference. In Sneja Gunew (ed.), *Feminist Knowledge: Critique and Construct*. London: Routledge.

Grosz, Elizabeth (1995) *Space, Time and Perversion: Essays on the Politics of Bodies*. London: Routledge.

Guillaumin, Colette (1981) The practice of power and belief in nature. Part 1: the appropriation of women. *Feminist Issues*, 1(2): 3–28.

Hacking, Ian (1992) Making up people. In Edward Stein (ed.), *Forms of Desire: Sexual Orientation and the Social Constructionist Controversy*. London: Routledge.

Harne, Lynne and Miller, Elaine (eds) (1996) *All the Rage: Reasserting Radical Lesbian Feminism*. London: Women's Press.

Hart, Nicky (1985) *The Sociology of Health and Medicine*. Ormskirk: Causeway.

Ian, Marcia (1995) How do you wear your body?: bodybuilding and the sublimity of drag. In Monica Dorenkamp and Richard Henke (eds), *Negotiating Lesbian and Gay Subjects*. New York: Routledge.

Jagger, Alison (1992) Human biology in feminist theory: sexual equality reconsidered. In Helen Crowley and Susan Himmelweit (eds), *Knowing Women: Feminism and Knowledge*. Cambridge: Polity/Open University Press.

Jeffreys, Sheila (1990) *Anticlimax: A Feminist Perspective on the Second Revolution*. London: Women's Press.

Kaplan, Gisela and Rogers, Lesley (1991) Introduction (Biology and Feminism). In Sneja Gunew (ed.), *A Reader in Feminist Knowledge*. London: Routledge.

Lash, Scott (1991) Genealogy and the body: Foucault/Deleuze/Nietzsche. In M. Featherstone, M. Hepworth and B. S. Turner (eds), *The Body: Social Process and Cultural Theory*. London: Sage.

Laqueur, Thomas (1990) *Making Sex: Body and Gender from the Greeks to Freud*. Cambridge, MA: Harvard University Press.

McClintock, Anne (1995) *Imperial Leather: Race, Gender and Sexuality in the Colonial Contest*. London: Routledge.

McGrath, Roberta (1990) Dangerous liaisons: health, disease an representation. In Tessa Boffin and Sunil Gupta (eds), *Ecstatic Antibodies: Resisting the AIDS Mythology*. London: River Oram.

McIntosh, Mary (1968) The Homosexual Role. *Social Problems* 16(2): 182–92.

Marshall, Stuart (1990) Picturing deviancy. In Tessa Boffin and Sunil Gupta (eds), *Ecstatic Antibodies: Resisting the AIDS Mythology*. London: Rivers Oram.

Mellor, Philip and Shilling, Chris (1993) Modernity, self-identity and the sequestration of death. *Sociology* 27(2): 411–32.

Merck, Mandy (1993) *Perversions: Deviant Readings*. London: Pandora.

Patton, Cindy (1994) *Last Served?: Gendering the HIV Pandemic*. London: Taylor & Francis.

Plummer, Ken (1995) *Telling Sexual Stories: Power, Change and Social Worlds*. London: Routledge.

Polhemus, Ted and Randall, Housk (1994) *Rituals of Love: Sexual Experiments, Erotic Possibilities*. London: Picador.

Ruse, Michael (1988) *Homosexuality: A Philosophical Inquiry*. Oxford: Blackwell.

Stone, Sandy (1991) The empire strikes back: a posttranssexual manifesto. In Julia Epstein and Kristina Straub (eds), *Body Guards: The Cultural Politics of Gender Ambiguity*. London: Routledge.

Terry, Jennifer and Urla, Jacqueline (eds) (1995) *Deviant Bodies: Critical Perspectives on Difference in Science and Popular Culture*. Bloomington: Indiana University Press.

Treichler, Paula (1988) AIDS, homophobia, and biomedical discourse: an epidemic of signification. In Douglas Crimp (ed.), *AIDS: Cultural Analysis, Cultural Activism*. Cambridge, MA: MIT Press.

Tully, Brian (1992) *Accounting for Transsexualism and Transhomosexuality: The Gender Identity Careers of over 200 Men and Women Who Have Petitioned for Surgical Reassignment of Gender Identity*. London: Whiting and Birch.

Turner, Bryan (1991) Recent developments in the theory of the body. In M. Featherstone, M. Hepworth and B. S. Turner (eds), *The Body: Social Process and Cultural Theory*. London: Sage.

Vance, Carole (1992) Social construction theory: problems in the history of sexuality. In Helen Crowley and Susan Himmelweit (eds), *Knowing Women: Feminism and Knowledge*. Cambridge: Polity Press/Open University Press.

West, Candace and Zimmerman, Don (1991) Doing gender. In Judith Lorber and Susan A. Farrell (eds), *The Social Construction of Gender*. London: Sage.

Wilton, Tamsin (1995) What do I have to do to prove I exist? Lesbians and healthcare. Plenary paper presented at the Researching Women, Gender and Health Conference, University of the West of England, Bristol, June.

Wilton, Tamsin (1996) Genital identities: an idiosyncratic foray into the gendering of sexualities. In Lisa Adkins and Vicki Merchant (eds), *Sexualising the Social*. London: Macmillan.

Wilton, Tamsin (1996a) *Finger-Licking Good: The Ins and Outs of Lesbian Sex*. London: Cassell.

Wilton, Tamsin (1997) *EnGendering AIDS: Deconstructing Sex, Texts, Epidemics*. London: Sage.

Witting, Monique (1992) One is not born a woman. In *The Straight Mind and Other Essays*. London: Harvester Wheatsheaf.

4

Racializing Femininity

Lola Young

> Black is the intensity of all colour; therefore to wear it one must be
> prepared to feel interesting and alert, intense in every detail,
> faultlessly groomed, unworried, and glowing in a clean fresh sort
> of way. Black should not be worn simply because it is the only
> clothing without colour, and because it does not show the dirt, but
> because it is arresting. (Verni, 1933: 227)

Although this extract from a 1930s beauty book for women
makes no explicit references to racial identity, it is significant for
a number of interrelated reasons. The 'arresting' nature of the
black garment must be, in part at least, due to its contrast with
white skin, thus emphasizing the whiteness of the wearer.
Noteworthy too is the way in which it is perceived that behaviour
is dictated by the expectations raised by the wearing of this
'colour'. Verni (1933: 227) states that 'any coloured type, except
the sun-burned woman, can buy a black dress'. However, 'white
is for the deeply sunburned and ruddy of any age'. The passage is
also suggestive in its contradictory usage of black in its
description as 'the intensity of all colour' and yet 'without
colour'. Such contrasting qualities are analogous to those ascribed
to black people and their appearance and the historical slippage
between black the 'colour' and black as a racial term has been
noted elsewhere.[1]

Through a critical account of comments concerned with 'race'
and beauty starting with the eighteenth century, I will argue that
historically notions of beauty and femininity have long been
racialized although this racialization has not always been explicit
or acknowledged. This leads to an examination of the ways in

which the constructs of blackness, whiteness and femininity intersect and may be mutually dependent, and I will address this through the use of examples of white male investment in black and white women's physical appearance

Although concerned with images of black women in relation to beauty, this essay does not seek to give an annotated list of the kinds of stereotyped representations of black women which continue to mark our presence in the West. However, I will argue that black women have been historically imagined and represented through their bodies which bear the markers of their deviance from white norms of feminine propriety and attractiveness.

On the racialization of beauty

She had a way of pouting her lips exactly like what we have observed in the orang-utan. ... Her lips were monstrously large ... I have never seen a human head more like an ape than that of this woman. (George Cuvier, scientist, referring to Sarah Bartmann, the 'Hottentot Venus'.)[2]

rosy cheeks and coral lips. ... In what other quarter of the globe shall we find the blush that overspreads the soft features of the beautiful women of Europe, that emblem of modesty, of delicate feelings. (Charles White, surgeon, on the virtues of European womanhood)[3]

There have been three main depictions of black women to which I would like to draw attention. First the stereotype which depicted black women as desexualized mammies, servants and wet-nurses whose large bosoms were available to suckle and to care for the slave-owners' children but not their own. Another key stereotype was that of the 'tragic mulatta' whose skin colouring afforded her the opportunity to 'pass' for white: even though her skin allowed her to exploit her duplicitous nature, there was usually something to give her away, thus averting the degeneration of the white 'race' through inadvertent 'racial-mixing'. The final pervasive image was that of the black woman whose lasciviousness and hypersexuality were inscribed on her body in the form of excessively proportioned genitalia and buttocks. None of these images of black femininity have been conducive to allowing women of African descent to share the position on the pedestal of transcendental beauty with white women on equal terms. Indeed, in 1766, the German writer

Gotthold Lessing found the whole notion of black standards of beauty and attractiveness derisory:

> Everyone knows how filthy the Hottentots are and how many things they consider beautiful and elegant and sacred which with us awaken disgust and aversion. A flattened cartilage of a nose, flabby breasts hanging down to the navel, the whole body smeared with a cosmetic of goat's fat and soot gone rotten in the sun, the hair dripping with grease, arms and legs bound about with fresh entrails – let one think of this as the object of an ardent, reverent, tender love; let one hear this exalted language of gravity and admiration and refrain from laughter. (quoted in Hannaford, 1996: 217)

Even these brief quotations regarding the repulsion caused by black people's physical appearance give a sense of the strength of the investment in assessing the way people look. Nonetheless, in his extensive historical study of beauty, Arthur Marwick (1988: 20) writes:

> All the complicated talk of politics and power struggles and male conspiracy and oppression seem to me to miss the simple heart of the matter: the sheer uncomplicated joy of going to bed with a beautiful woman.

Besides undermining any claim to academic objectivity, Marwick's attempt to direct the reader's attention away from the politics of beauty is ill-conceived and historically incorrect.

In the nineteenth century, craniology – the study of skull shapes – contributed significantly to scientific racism and, by naming Caucasian skulls as the most beautiful, served to legitimize and normalize the racial predicates of beauty. As is indicated in the quotations from Cuvier, White and Gotthold, the observer or measurer of the object's beauty was invariably male and the object of the scientist's discerning eye was, in the context of debates about the beauty of Europeans, almost always a woman. It is at this moment that hierarchies founded on sexual, racial and class differences were systematized and intertwined (Goldberg, 1993: 28).

Goldberg argues that, during this period, the notion of beauty was also racialized through its links to economic wealth. Importantly beauty – and now wealth – was not simply about how a person looked, 'Beauty, for classical aesthetics, was a property possession which determined subjects' ontological value'

(30). Stafford (1991: 286) also points to the assumed 'tight link between normal or abnormal physical appearance and the general moral makeup of a person'. By the end of the eighteenth century, the moral worth of racialized individuals was implicated in definitions of beauty, at the same time as the norm of white skin, straight hair and so on was established by European scientists and philosophers. From being a set of judgements about individuals, the discourse of beauty shifted to being about entire 'races':

> When translated into the discourse of the favoured versus the ill-favoured races, one major aspect of the aesthetics of health and illness surfaces. It is the association of the beautiful with the erotic; the ugly with the unerotic. ... Only the fecund are truly beautiful for they reproduce the race. (Gilman, 1995: 55)

Thus the broader significance of beauty, in racial terms, was as indicative of the health and fitness of the 'race' so that the notion of beauty was implicated in the emerging discourse of eugenics (54).

It is noteworthy that the discussion of beauty and ugliness was not confined to a comparison of the relative merits of black and white. On Jewishness and ascriptions of ugliness, Gilman (1995: 107) quotes the late-seventeenth-century 'orientalist', Johann Jakob Schudt:

> they are either pale and yellow or swarthy; they have in general big heads, big mouths, everted lips, protruding eyes and bristle-like eyelashes, large ears, crooked feet and hands that hang below their knees, and big shapeless warts, or are otherwise asymmetrical and malproportioned in their limbs.

The need to identify and catalogue the signifiers of racial difference was coupled with an imperative to assess the value of the people who exhibit such signs. The object of this judgement is pathologized because their physical features were deemed symptomatic of a general deviance from the 'norm' and indicated their weakness and degeneracy as a 'race'. Another account of 'typical' Viennese Jews in the 1780s makes explicit the association of Jewish and black peoples, 'Excluding the Indian Fakirs, there is no category of supposed human beings which comes closer to the orang-utan than does a Polish Jew ... their necks exposed, the color of a Black' (quoted in Gilman, 1995: 108).

Thus the black and the Jewish 'races' were described in viciously derogatory terms which likened them to animals and categorized them as subhuman. They were termed ugly and not eroticized (although they were sexualized inasmuch as they were deemed to be sexual threats to the purity of white womanhood). With reference to these 'alien races', procreation was viewed as problematic since the ugly would reproduce their ugliness and their depraved character. In this respect, women are particularly important because of their reproductive function since, as Gilman indicates, there is 'a long medical tradition of associating female health and beauty, positive reproductive capacities and the maintenance or improvement of the race' (Gilman, 1995: 58). As will be shown later in this essay, the links between feminine beauty and fitness for reproductive duties are still the object of scientific enquiry.

The valorization of white skin was not without its contradictions as Stafford (1991: 283) observes with regard to the public exhibitions of images of the 'grotesque' and the 'deformed':

> This medical panorama, unfurling the universal garb of rot, instantaneously clarifies the premium placed during the Enlightenment on an aesthetics of immaculateness. Given the prevalence of perceptible illnesses, the perfect eighteenth-century countenance – oval in shape, with regular features, a white flawless complexion, and lightly carmined cheeks – was as rare and mystic as the ideal work of art.

The materials used to achieve that perfectly white look were often comprised of toxic substances which caused visible and lasting damage to the wearers' skin thereby marring the surface they were meant to perfect.

During this same period, when white women were praised for their delicacy and modesty, black female bodies were subjected to extensive scientific examination and placed on public display in fairs and exhibitions as curios and freaks: one of the best known subjects of such an exhibition was Sarah Baartman. Assigned what would have been perceived as the contradictory title of the 'Hottentot Venus' by the likes of Gotthold Lessing, Baartman was seen as representing the absolute difference between African and European classical standards of female beauty. Nonetheless, although Baartman's anatomy was seen as racially anomalous, her 'excessive' genitalia and extended buttocks were taken to be

71

indicative of the sexually anomalous nature of all women, particularly those white women seen as deviant such as prostitutes and lesbians (Gilman, 1985: 77).

It would be mistaken, however, to assume that there was unanimity regarding the inherent ugliness of the African as opposed to the beauty of the European. A number of artists and philosophers participated in debates about what constituted the beautiful, and, as David Dabydeen (1985: 41–7) argues, this debate was inflected with nationalistic overtones. William Hogarth the artist entered into the controversy surrounding judgements about beauty in nineteenth-century England with his monograph, *The Analysis of Beauty*, which was first published in 1753: 'Without doubt the way Judging of objects by comparison, might be conclusive enough could we always be sure of the Value of the standard, by which we take our measures' (1955: 189). Questioning the absolute judgements about beauty and aesthetics, Hogarth (189) argues from a relativist position:

> we must be liable to mistakes in Judgement, through the many Prejudic'd opinions, proceeding from custom, Fashion, persuasion and delusion. Hence it comes to pass, that the subject of Beauty, continues in so vague a state, mankind being confounded with a variety of contradictory opinions, I have at length in some measure given up and discarded beauty as a reality, concluding it can only exist in Fancy and Imagination.

Hogarth (189–90) addresses 'race' and beauty explicitly and asserts that 'the power of custom is strongly seen in the most remarkable instance ... the Negro who finds great beauty in the black Females of his own country, may find as much deformity in the european Beauty as we see in theirs'. In spite of his relativism – or, perhaps as a symptom of it – an ambivalence regarding the relative merits of black and white emerges which is signalled by the following: 'But as white is nearest to light it may be said to be equal if not superior in value [in comparison with black] as to beauty' and also, 'whereas [other colours] lose their beauty by degrees as they approach nearer to black, the representative of darkness' (128). Here again, there is evidence of a slippage between black as colour and black as people, and the equation of black with darkness is a troubling one, an issue which is noted with regard to Edmund Burke's pronouncements on blackness and the sublime.

Burke's *Philosophical Enquiry into the Origin of Our Ideas of the Sublime and the Beautiful* was first published in 1757, and it is said to be one of the most influential philosophical essays on aesthetics of the eighteenth century (Hipple, 1957: 83). Burke's speculations – some of which were in response to Hogarth's arguments – initially seem to offer a generalized, non-prescriptive definition of what constitutes female beauty. 'By beauty I mean, that quality or those qualities in bodies by which they cause love, or some passion similar to it', and he argues that 'good' proportions do not necessarily guarantee beauty (1990: 89). Burke returns to this subject on a number of occasions, clarifying his notion of beauty with each foray into the topic:

> Beauty in distress is much the most affecting beauty. Blushing has little less power; and modesty in general, which is a tacit allowance of imperfection, is itself considered as an amiable quality, and certainly heightens every other that is so. (100)

Burke warms to his theme of women and their physical qualities:

> Observe that part of a beautiful woman where she is perhaps the most beautiful, about the neck and breasts; the smoothness; the softness; the easy and insensible; the variety of the surface, which is never for the smallest space the same; the deceitful maze through which the unsteady eye slides giddily. ... An air of robustness and strength is very prejudicial to beauty. An appearance of *delicacy*, and even of fragility, is essential to it. (105)

Of course, black females, most commonly known as slaves in the Caribbean and the Americas, as anatomical anomalies in Africa, and as domestic labour in Britain, could never fulfil Burke's criteria for the beautiful. For Burke, a black woman is important in another context, that of experiencing the sublime, that is, being in a state of terror of the unknown, or of anticipated danger or pain. Burke asserts that to be surrounded by darkness – darkness defined as an absence, a lack – is to experience the sublime and this again is where differences between objects, physical phenomena and people are elided. Of particular note is the slide between 'the dark', 'blackness', 'black objects' and 'a black woman' in the account Burke (1990: 131) gives of the aftermath of an operation to remove cataracts from the eyes of a boy blind from birth:

Perhaps it may appear on enquiry, that blackness and darkness are in some degree painful by their natural operation, independent of any associations whatsoever. I must observe, that the ideas of darkness and blackness are much the same; and they differ only in this, that blackness is a more confined idea. Mr Cheselden [the surgeon] has given us a very curious story of a boy, who had been born blind, and continued so until he was thirteen or fourteen years old; he was then couched for a cataract, by which operation he received his sight. Among many remarkable particulars that affected his first perceptions, and judgments on visual objects, Cheselden tells us, that the first time the boy saw a black object, it gave him great uneasiness; and that some time after, upon accidentally seeing a Negro woman, he was struck with great horror at the sight. The horror, in this case, can scarcely be supposed to arise from any association.

Burke's desire to naturalize a fear of black people is not surprising given a context where rationalizations for the enslavement and ill-treatment of black people were continually being advanced. It is of interest here that it is a black female who generates the anxiety in the boy. What is the terror engendered by the 'accidental' sight of a black woman? The association with darkness is worthy of more detailed consideration than is possible here. For now, I would suggest that Burke's observations seem to indicate that anxiety arises not just because the white male is confronted with that which is seen as totally other, not connected to the self in either racial or gender terms: it occurs at the moment when he is forced to contemplate the idea of 'darkness'. This absence of light characterizes the space from which people come and the space into which people go, and the inexorable progress from birth to death – in spite of continuing attempts – have still not been brought under full control. The association of darkness and blackness as with the links between blackness and dirt, evil and ugliness are, of course socially constructed connections which have become naturalized in racially stratified societies. Burke concedes that there may be some grounds for thinking that 'the ill effects of darkness or blackness seem rather mental rather than corporeal' but nonetheless holds on to his intriguing belief that 'seeing' too much darkness can cause physical pain (1990: 133).

While Marwick (1988: 15) claims that beauty is 'a physical attribute, distinct from morality, or intelligence, or any other quality: it is autonomous'; and that beauty is an 'autonomous characteristic to be ranked along with social position, wealth education, race, etc.', it is clear that the value judgements embedded in the term militate against any such autonomy.

Having discussed the historical nature of the racialization of beauty, I will now move to an examination of some contemporary texts which refer to female beauty. The objective is to foreground the ways in which whiteness is rendered both invisible, through lack of specific references to it, and highly visible on account of its pervasiveness.

What are angels made of?

accompanying skin must be bleached to the pink of wild rose and the white of snow ... the hands must be bleached, as well as the face and neck. During the process of bleaching, the back of the neck must receive special attention. (Verni, 1933: 225–6)

You've been caught up in this thing because you know, you worked my grandmother, and after that you worked my mother and then finally you got hold of me. ... You thought that you was *more* [original emphasis] because you was a woman, and especially a white woman, you had this kind of angel feeling that you were untouchable. (Fannie Lou Hamer, civil rights activist)[4]

The distance between our super-sophisticated, postmodern, post-feminist society and eighteenth-century thinking sometimes seems to be very little. In terms of its obsessions, its discriminatory practices, and the construction and maintenance of oppressive discursive regimes, the continuities are more striking than the differences. With the development of mass mediated forms of dissemination, there are clearly many more opportunities to influence and shape the ways in which people think about their bodies and their appearance and arguably, there is a greater diversity of images of racial and sexual difference. However, when examining those images, what passes itself off as heterogeneity frequently recalls earlier, long established patterns of conventionalized beliefs.

The glossy women's magazine, *Marie Claire*, prides itself on its serious, high-quality journalism and seeks to distance itself from other, less up-market women's magazines which are dominated by personal testimonies of tragic circumstances and the minutiae of domestic experiences. As Susan Bordo (1993: 264) has pointed out in relation to the black women's magazine *Essence*, there is often a contradiction between the progressive messages of the editorials and articles, and the exhortations of the advertisers in such texts (Bondo, 1993: 264). In the *Marie Claire* article, 'What is Perfect Beauty?', there is little evidence of such contradictions, since it makes only a token concession to the idea that there might be more to a woman than the arrangement of her physical features. We read that the blonde white woman, (pictured by Britt) 'with good skin and hair, and even, pleasant features ... does not conform to conventional "rules of beauty" as set down by ancient philosophers and modern-day beauty experts' (Bailey, 1996: 293). Even though it might be argued that the article is not to be taken too seriously, the constant reference to male scientists and doctors serves to legitimate the need for women to strive to achieve arbitrary standards of physical perfection.

Francette Pacteau's psychoanalytic study of beauty as a symptom of (white) male subjectivity refers to a number of historical instances from literary and visual culture, where the necessity of fragmenting the female body and its facial features in order to construct the perfect feminine image is evident (1994: 57ff.). This process of fragmenting the female body – the violence of the metaphor 'cutting up' is most apt in regard to the 'work' of plastic surgeons – is explicit in the search for feminine physical perfection:

> Psychologist Dr Dave Perrett of the University of St Andrews produced an image of the perfect female beauty, based on the results of a nationwide survey. This superwoman had Audrey Hepburn's eyes, Michelle Pfeiffer's eyebrows, Sharon Stone's cheekbones, Brigitte Bardot's lips and Meg Ryan's jawline. Dr Perrett explained that this combination produced a woman who exuded youth and fragility. (Bailey, 1996: 292)

While the use of the terms, 'superwoman' and 'youth' to describe this beautiful artifact suggest her reproductive capabilities and suitability for continuing the 'race', the fragility might be thought to work against the rigours of childbirth. However, misgivings on this count have been dispelled in a previous passage:

> Certain physical features in women are now believed to indicate greater or lesser levels of fertility. According to anthropologist Dr Douglas Botting ... the main factor in determining female beauty is jaw size. A *delicate* [my emphasis] jaw indicates good levels of

oestrogens, and suggests that a woman is ready to breed. (Bailey, 1996: 292)

Again the recurring invocation of 'delicacy' is noteworthy, especially as in this context what constitutes 'delicacy of jawline' is not stated and its existence is not questioned: indeed, with further recourse again to science and common-sense notions of the idea of beauty, the reader is told that Max Factor constructed a calibrating machine which was designed to measure the features of his female clients and compare them to his calculations of what constituted the ideal face, thus reinforcing the naturalization of this discursive regime (Bailey, 1996: 292).

As noted earlier, the qualities of 'delicacy' and 'fragility' attributed to the idealized white woman are not commonly associated with black women. In this article, *Marie Claire*, in common with other modern formulations of feminine beauty, privileges the young, the slim and the blonde (and, incidentally, the non-British). Its refusal to contemplate the juxtaposition of 'black' and 'beautiful' is achieved by the denial of the racial specificity of the 'ideal face' by omitting any reference to the ideal skin colour. The exclusion of any reference to black women is emphasized by two other factors. First, Britt's face fills virtually two whole pages – we see her 'before' and 'after' the digitized 'improvement' of her looks – and visually dominates the article. Second, the article is preceded by a full page advertisement illustrated by another blonde and immediately following the first image of Britt there is another advertisement illustrated by a dark haired white woman in a white bathing suit. Thus the ideal of whiteness as perfect beauty is being constantly reinforced through the visual and written discourse of the text.

Referring to the complicity of women's gaze with the models' on the covers of women's magazines, Janice Winship (1987: 11) notes:

we see ourselves in the image which a masculine culture has defined. It indicates symbolically, too, the extent to which we relate to each other as women through absent men: it is 'the man' who, in a manner of speaking, occupies the space between model image and woman reader.

Given that I have argued for factoring in the racial with the feminine and the beautiful, what are the vectors of racial identification involved in this 'exchange of looks'? Certainly black women have a heightened consciousness of how the ways in which they have been represented historically affect their social relations on a day-to-day basis. They are also made aware of how this society's preoccupation with white females as exemplars of the beautiful textures their feelings about how they and other black people look and are looked at (Mama, 1995; Marshall, 1996; Blackwood and Adebola, 1997; Weekes, 1997). Significantly, the extent to which black men might occupy that gap between the image and the reader and the ways in which they look at black women seem not to have been explored.

The scientific endorsement of perfect beauty is considered important, no doubt, for *Marie Claire*'s discerning, relatively affluent readership but the linking of beauty and physical attraction to men to genetic inheritance and reproductive capabilities is potentially pernicious if Gilman's arguments regarding the association between reproductive fitness and beauty, and the eugenicist discourse of the healthiness of the 'race' are considered.

The next article which I want briefly to consider is another example of contemporary journalism, written this time by a man and published in a national broadsheet newspaper. Perhaps to contemporary readers, Burke's and White's eighteenth-century homages to women would seem anachronistic and of limited interest in their invocation of the awe-inspiring nature of physically perfect white femininity, but reflect on the following:

> Taped to the wall over my desk is a full-page advertisement from the *New York Times* of Thursday, October 17, 1991. It depicts a young woman, to me terrifyingly beautiful, reclining in mid-air, clad in a black slip and spiked heels. Her head tilts back, exposing the delicate line of her neck and making a Niagara of her thick golden hair. The backs of her hands press coquettishly against her tapered waist. She curls one of her slender legs under her perfectly shaped bottom, the other she kicks up to the top of a page like a dancer in a chorus line. (Lewis, 1994: 14)

The language and mode of dissemination have, of course, changed but there is a clear continuity of thought and similarities of expression between Lewis' tribute to white womanhood and the others cited. This self-indulgent eulogy to 'the Bloomingdale model' – her name is never revealed – chronicles the attractions of 'possessing' a beautiful woman: a woman the author eventually married in spite of the terror he claims she provoked. One of the many male endorsements of his choice of desirable object that Lewis cites is that of O. J. Simpson. Lewis writes, a 'normally temperate friend' rings him to say, 'There is a woman here you should meet in a hurry. As I speak, she is being chased from one end of the room to another by O. J. Simpson.' So the woman – whose golden hair is a guarantee of her whiteness/purity/angelic qualities – must be saved from the unleashed black male and, some weeks later 'the Juice [O.J. Simpson] was pumping my hand and telling me with unnerving enthusiasm how lucky I was.'

The awe which afflicts men when confronted with their ideal is not only evident and permissable in journalistic discourse. As I have already indicated, Marwick's study of beauty can hardly be described as dispassionate. Another example of his writing serving as a cloak for discussing the women to whom he is attracted is that of his description of Twiggy's attractions as transcultural and transhistorical: 'Twiggy was beautiful because her figure was perfectly proportioned and because she had an astoundingly lovely face' and 'Twiggy in any era would have the same devastating impact on living human beings as she had when she first went among them in the 1960s' (1988: 32). The comment regarding the significance of Twiggy's presence in the human race suggests some quasi-religious persona or perhaps an extra-terrestrial being, someone who transcends the human. Marwick's comments resonate with those of Bradstock and London writing in the 1930s on 'The Psychology of Colour' who comment: 'White is symbolical of purity and innocence, the colour of the brides both temporal and spiritual, approaching the great climax of life' (193–?: 209). These associations are suggestive, and in this figuring of the white female as an exemplar of the serene, the delicate, the fragile, the *light*, the one who graces us with her presence, there is no niche for the black woman who is constructed as the embodiment of the antithesis of those qualities.

These reiterations of the desirability of whiteness and of white women's beauty should alert us to the insecurity that underpins the compulsive assertions of the qualities of 'white' and whiteness. More specifically, examples such as Max Factor's calibrating machine for the measurement and regulation of the female face may be read as another manifestation of the desire to control, and 'bearing in mind the particular ordering principle at work – the synthesis of body parts around a metrical mean – it further presents itself as a privileged instance of the subject's active reaffirmation of his own integrity' (Pacteau, 1994: 93). An affirmation necessary for the futile attempt to make the ego feel secure.

A major problem for the idea of white feminine beauty is that most women do not satisfy the criteria. Thus, on one level, I would accept Patricia Hill Collins' (1990: 79) argument that:

> Race, gender and sexuality converge on this issue of evaluating beauty. Judging white women by their physical appearance and attractiveness to men objectifies them. But their white skin and straight hair privilege them in a system in which part of the basic definition of whiteness is its superiority to blackness.

I would suggest, however, that the system is not quite as complete or as seamless as she suggests. Not all white women are privileged in this respect: there are those who are considered too fat, too tall, disfigured, disabled and so on. Some people are simply outside the ideal with no hope of being able to achieve it because they belong to the 'masses'. Robert Aron-Brunetière (1978: 188), writing on beauty and medicine in terms which suggest he is addressing white women, comments: 'The average standard of looks among white people is not very high: when you look around you on the beach, or on any public place, the spectacle which greets your eyes is hardly edifying.' Evidently, the idea of the great *mass* of European society induces a racialized sense of self-loathing in Marwick (1988: 33) too, who curiously, given his adoration of the blonde, exemplified by Diana Spencer and Twiggy, states: 'I would maintain that among the Arab, Indian and (above all) Chinese peoples are to be found a higher proportion of beautiful individuals than in most Western societies, today as in the past.'

It would be invidious to try and set up some sort of grid or scale on which it was possible to read off how far away from the ideal a white woman has to be before she is surpassed by a 'black beauty' but it would be possible to think this through for a more complex view of what it is that constitutes these differentiated femininities. One key site of difference in regard to the racialized discourse of beauty which I have identified is the link between white feminine beauty, the idea of delicacy and woman's responsibility for the viability of the 'race'. For the black women who have been deemed beautiful and objectified by a white masculinist gaze, their distance from the white feminine ideal has not produced the unambiguous revulsion of Cuvier: rather, it has been a substantial part of their appeal. However, this attraction, based on the exoticism of otherness, is just as problematic as the racism from which it has emerged.

Exotica erotica

In the north [of central Africa], the women are not very good-looking, but farther to the south, where the males approximate a feminine type, there are real beauties among the softer sex. As the traveller goes eastward he observes that the features of the natives become more refined. In some types very few characteristics usually attributed to negroes are found. The black colour, so common on the west coast, is replaced by a soft chocolate-brown, which in certain individuals merges into dark yellow. (Emil Torday, *National Geographic*, 1919)[5]

We stopped to watch three well-muscled young wenches rhythmically battering away at a gigantic wooden mortar of clay with mighty six-foot pestles. Their sturdy shoulder blades rippled pliantly between black satin skin, and they smiled coyly and displayed their clean, white teeth when we told them in sign language what good figures they had. (James Wilson, *National Geographic*, 1934)[6]

Age for age, there is a far higher proportion of men with good physique in some African ethnic groups, and feminine beauty among the Eurasians of Indonesia. (Aron-Brunetière, 1978: 188)

The quotations from the *National Geographic* in particular represent recurring themes in specifically white male discourses on blackness, femininity and sexuality. The sexualized fascination with the other and the fixation with skin colour and other phenotypical features are particularly clear in these examples. The softness of the skin tone and the fantasy of edibility are regarded as positive characteristics especially when the people observed do not conform to the 'negro archetype'.[7] This distance from the conventionalized look of the west coast African – a look designated quintessentially 'African' by white Europeans – leads to a 'refinement' of the features, a word nuanced with judgement of moral and social worth, and notions of 'civilization'. The way in which these accounts are articulated suggests an enthralment with black women that is without the constraints imposed by 'civilized' society. The emphasis on the texture and tone of the skin, the contrast of dark skin with white teeth, the suggestion of a convergence of the masculine and the feminine in the strange environment in which these European adventurers find themselves, all these have their echoes in contemporary culture.

The point about the blurring of the edges of the masculine and the feminine is of particular interest since it suggests the presence of a racialized homoeroticism in the scenario of white men looking at black women. The sense of the otherness of the black female standing in for the sexual other within the white male heterosexual self is echoed in Jean-Paul Goude's appropriation and manipulation of Grace Jones' body in the 1980s: indeed, it would be interesting to examine the extent to which the attraction of androgyny was a key factor in the relative success of some black women performers in the 1980s.[8]

The explicit exoticism of Josephine Baker, the African-American performer who made her name in the Paris of the 1920s, drew mixed responses: 'Was she horrible, delicious, black, white?' (quoted in Stuart, 1994: 139). Similar confusion is articulated in interestingly similar terms by Jean-Paul Goude (1982: 102), famous for his moulding of model and singer Grace Jones' career:

> The strength of her image, then as now, is that it swings constantly from the near grotesque – from the organ-grinder's monkey – to the great African beauty. You are constantly looking at her and wondering if she's beautiful or grotesque, or both and how can she be one if she is the other.

Goude self-consciously uses the black female body as a 'blank space' on which to play out his racialized sexual fantasies of domination and control over otherness. The book *Jungle Fever*, in which he photographically manipulates the bodies of black women such as Grace Jones and Toukie (also a model), is not simply a collection of his images: it also contains a fascinating narrative which, again somewhat knowingly, reveals his enthralment with what he sees as the distinctive properties of women of African descent. Thus of Jones he writes: 'On stage she became the threatening, blue-black, male-female, erotic menace I wanted her to be' (107) and he comments on Toukie: 'I saw her as this primitive voluptuous girl-horse' (41).[9]

Pacteau (1994: 135) observes that Goude is attempting to image the fantasy of the fantastic other whose beauty is 'multiple, excessive, exorbitant'. As doubly other to the white male, it is no wonder that black women disturb and confuse him. Is he meant to be attracted to or repulsed by this abject creature? Goude's confusion is especially acute as Jones highlights his undecided sexuality as a 'heterosexual sissy' who refers to a homosexual audience as 'shrieking gay bobbysoxers' (102).

Pacteau (1994: 21) discusses how writers, artists and philosophers have described woman as beautiful, 'in so far she invokes a painted simulacrum'. This point is exemplified by Goude, who draws or imagines a succession of black females and on finding the ones who do not quite meet his expectations seeks to rework their bodies photographically or through moulding them, or through offering to pay for plastic surgery. Of course, the image is more pliable, less resistant than the person and, once the love affair with otherness is over, the 'artist' turns against her:

> My masterpiece was a vision entirely my own of what was essentially a simple, naive person, holding back to what she [Grace Jones] had always been. Trouble. ... The 'party nigger' had come back to what she knew best, and I would have to find a new vehicle. (Goude, 1982: 107)

Goude's naming of his 'condition' as 'jungle fever' places him at the centre of a set of discourses in which the all-powerful white male seeks the contagion of the other which will liberate him from his colourless white existence. In this respect, it is worth noting some similarities between Goude's work on black women and Robert Mapplethorpe's on black men.

According to Patricia Morrisroe (1995: 233), by 1980 Robert Mapplethorpe was struck by what he termed 'Black fever'. During this period of his life, he went to a bar frequented by black and white gay men at least four times a week, hoping to find what he considered to be the perfect black body. It was said that he calculated with mathematical precision, the ideal measurement for a *black* penis: Mapplethorpe's preferred term for his Platonic ideal of a black man was 'Super Nigger' (Morrisroe, 1995: 234–6).

Although his work is very different, remarks made by Goude suggest a similar search for perfection in black bodies and both used their photographic work as a form of documentation of their artistic projects and sexual conquests. The question of why these white men should seek to locate perfection in blackness is an interesting one. There was apparently little by way of political motivation: neither appears to have been interested in black liberation or political struggles. Goude, in particular, is dismissive of 'Black Power' because, although he grudgingly admits 'I knew its existence was justified', 'as a white, I felt a little left out to say the least' (Goude, 1982: 31).

Both Goude and Mapplethorpe speak of their fascination with black people's sexuality in ways which indicate that they are seeking to redress what they perceive as white people's lack in regard to exotic sexuality (Goude, 1982: 40; Morrisroe, 1995: 234). They both fetishized and eroticized black skin in ways that articulate the desire for control over the other. Writing about Mapplethorpe's photographs, Kobena Mercer (1992: 5) argues:

> The scopic fixation on black skin thus implies a kind of 'negrophilia', an aesthetic idealization and eroticized investment in the racial Other that inverts and reverses the binary axis of the fears and anxieties invested in or projected on the Other in 'negrophobia'.

But it would be misleading to think of this exoticization/ fetishization as in some way a progressive move, even though, as Mercer argues, the images may afford some pleasure to some black viewers of the material. Each refers to his models using animalistic metaphors and sees his lovers/models as simple-minded and lacking in intellectual sophistication, comments which betray the racism at the centre of eroticist discourse (Morrisroe, 1995: 236; Goude, 1982: 41).

The perceived exoticism of black female sexuality has been particularly visible in the fashion industry through the use of black female models. Janice Cheddie (1994: 37) notes that:

> While the initial flowering of black models appeared as a response to the direct pressure of the black political struggles of the 1950s and 1960s summed up most profoundly in the slogan 'Black is Beautiful', their presence was coupled with the fashion establishment's desire for a 'return to nature', as expressed in its commodification of the signifiers of the counter-culture critique of excess and waste. The black woman's body, within these discourses, signified democratisation and the 'return to the natural' as a 'return to the primitive'.

84

The following description from a beauty book concerns one of the first of the 'new' black models, Donyale Luna, and bears out Cheddie's contention. This description of her appears in a chronicle of looks achieved by fashion models, in a chapter titled 'How Black Became Beautiful':

> The oddest woman ever seen in fashion (or out of it for that matter) exploded into the glossy magazines in 1964. Six foot tall, snarling, crouching, hands crooked into claws, eyes rolling – this was Donyale Luna, the first black model girl to become an international star. (Keenan, 1977: 173)

A rather different characterization is given of 'supermodel' Waris Dirie. Described as being 'breathtakingly beautiful', with skin that 'glows like molasses' and 'almond eyes' that 'reveal a mischievous streak' (Johnson, 1995: 9), Dirie's story was written up in the *Guardian* newspaper and shown on BBC2 television. The main headline for the article is 'A Tale of the Unexpected' but above that we read 'Every young girl dreams of being a supermodel. Not every supermodel started out tending camels in the Somalia desert' (Johnson, 1995: 9). The myth of the authentically exotic 'African' model thrives on autobiographical details of living otherwise in some kind of pre-modern, primitive state and is quite a different narrative from that of urban, sophisticated 'party girls' like Grace Jones and Naomi Campbell.

> Dirie has come a long way from the days when she looked after her father's camels, slept under tents and played with other children of her tribe. Her family were nomads who had little connection with the 20th century, but all that changed for Dirie when, at 13, her father decided to marry her off to a man 50 years her senior. She fled and walked barefoot through the desert. (Johnson, 1995: 9)

Dirie's narrative of her family fixing an arranged marriage, an attempt to rape her and being circumcised all feed into a particular set of ideas about this 'natural', 'African' woman, the 'innocent primitive' abroad. A woman who has experienced and been part of nature in the raw comes to represent it. The packaging of this narrative is a form of commodification to which black women's bodies are subject: it makes them emblematic of a particular image through which 'the fashion establishment aims to present itself as an utopian, transgressive, multiracial arena, full of fun, fantasy, frivolity and sexual freedom, outside any relation to the social world' (Cheddie, 1994: 37). The social world of sexual exploitation, economic reality and political principle only intrudes upon the fashion world as a 'product' to be marketed and on which to capitalize.[10]

The success of both Iman – the first Somalian 'supermodel', to whom Dirie reverentially refers – and Dirie is not only dependent on what is perceived as their exoticism and otherness: there is also a sense in which they are comfortingly physically not too different from white norms of physical appearance. Neither woman's face conforms to the western archetype of African features which connote a difference so profound that the bearer has to be either symbolically or literally annihilated: their looks are 'refined' and do not incite the mixture of repulsion and fascination induced by Sarah Baartman, Josephine Baker or Grace Jones.

Given the long history of the unequal cultural exchanges between black and white people under slavery, colonialism and during the current 'post-colonial' period, it is not surprising that white ideals of feminine beauty predominate. Black women have been constantly subjected to derogatory descriptions and been designated ugly without exception. The desire to prescribe the criteria for notions of beauty from a set of specifically white, European preoccupations represents yet another attempt to assume a position of control. The black man represents a troubling absence/presence not only with regard to notions of sexuality, femininity, reproduction and physical attraction, but in terms of this assumption of masculine power and mastery. There are other gaps and absences that I have not dealt with here but which I will address in a forthcoming essay. For now, I would like to indicate that the notion of beauty is equally problematic when the measures for assessing this 'quality' are constructed by black people since in application it is oppressive, particularly for women.

The notion of possessing the beautiful white woman provides the white masculinist with the comfort of status. The pleasure the black woman affords her 'owner', as she has relatively little by way of social status to confer, is that of the illusion of control and mastery. Thus the black woman is an object to be moulded, improved, packaged and sold. The racialized specificity of this process lies in the deployment of historically established primitivist and eroticist discourses to which white women have not been subject. Where white women are concerned, their whiteness is at once valorized and effaced. I would argue that critical approaches which foreground the forms of racial identifications implicit in many texts are needed in order to gain a more nuanced understanding of the complex workings of discourses of 'race', gender and sexual attraction.

Notes

1. See in particular, Gilman (1985) and Goldberg (1993).
2. Quoted in Gould, 1981: 86.
3. Charles White, an English surgeon, quoted in Stanton (1960): 17.
4. Quoted in Lerner, 1973: 610.
5. Quoted in Rothenberg, 1994: 162.
6. Quoted in Rothenberg, 1994: 171.
7. It is worth noting how frequently black women are compared to sweet things: chocolate, molasses, brown sugar.
8. In addition to Grace Jones, a consideration of Whoopi Goldberg (see Young, 1996a; 193–5) and the singer Sade Adu, of whom Liz Jobey wrote in the *Independent on Sunday*:

   I'd read an old interview in which Sade had been described as 'boyish' – something which I'd found hard to imagine until I met her. Despite the beauty, there is something rough and direct in her manner: the absence of a need to please, with no hint of the coquette or the prima donna or the vamp. (*Sunday Review*, 25 October, 1992, 4);

   Also, actor Cathy Tyson in *Mona Lisa* (1986); and the role played by Jaye Davidson in *The Crying Game* (1992).
9. The comparison of black people with animals has too long and ignoble history to be considered as playfully ironic. This linking of the grotesque and the bestial was recently represented in *Star Trek: The Undiscovered Country* (1991) where Iman in her role as a shape-changing character becomes a grimacing beast at the moment when she is about to kiss Captain James T. Kirk.
10. A number of well-known supermodels appeared in an advertisement in which they protested that they would rather go naked than wear fur coats. Now that fur coats have been rehabilitated by fashion designers – partly due to the use of fur to signify the glamour of Madonna/Eva Peron in *Evita* – it is no longer seen as desirable to stick to the original principle of not wearing fur for ethical reasons. Naomi Campbell who appeared in the original anti-fur campaign advertisements recently strolled down the catwalk in

a full-length fur coat and was promptly sacked as a patron by PETA, the organization that sponsored the protest.

References

Aron-Brunetière, R. (1978) *Beauty and Medicine* (trans. by Joanna Kilmartin). London: Cape.

Bailey, E. (1996) What is perfect beauty? *Marie Claire*, November.

Blackwood, S. and Adebola, Y. (1997) Black vs black: the women who hate their own. *Pride*, March: 20–3.

Bogle, D. (1980) *Brown Sugar: Eighty Years of America's Black Superstars*. New York: DaCapo.

Bordo, S. (1993) *Unbearable Weight: Feminism, Western Culture and the Body*. Berkeley: University of California Press.

Bradstock, L. and London, J. (193-?) *The Modern Woman: Beauty, Physical Culture, and Hygiene*. London: Associated Newspapers.

Burke, E. (1990) *A Philosophical Enquiry into the Origin of Our Ideas of the Sublime and the Beautiful* (ed. and with an introduction by A. Phillips). Oxford: Oxford University Press (first published 1757).

Cheddie, J. (1994) Ladies first: race, fashion and black femininity. *Versus*, 2: 37–9.

Dabydeen, D. (1985) *Hogarth's Blacks: Images of Blacks in Eighteenth Century English Art*. Mundelstrup, Denmark and Kingston, Surrey: Dangaroo Press.

Gilman, S. L. (1985) *Difference and Pathology: Stereotypes of Sexuality, Race and Madness*. Ithaca: Cornell University Press.

Gilman, S. L. (1995) *Health and Illness: Images of Difference*. London: Reaction Books.

Godlewska, A. and Smith, N. (eds) (1994) *Geography and Empire*. Oxford: Blackwell.

Goldberg, D. T. (1993) *Racist Culture: Philosophy and the Politics of Meaning*. Oxford: Blackwell.

Goude, J. (1982) *Jungle Fever*. London: Quartet Books.

Gould, S. J. (1981) *The Mismeasure of Man*. New York: Norton.

Hannaford, I. (1996) *Race: The History of an Idea in the West*. Baltimore: Johns Hopkins University Press.

Hill Collins, P. (1990) *Black Feminist Thought: Knowledge, Consciousness and the Politics of Empowerment*. London: Routledge.

Hipple, W. J. (1957) *The Beautiful, the Sublime, and the Picturesque in Eighteenth-Century British Aesthetic Theory*. Carbondale: Southern Illinois University Press.

Hogarth, W. (1955) *The Analysis of Beauty* (J. Burke, ed.). Oxford: Clarendon Press (first published 1753).

Johnson, A. (1995) A tale of the unexpected. *Guardian*, 8 August, p. 9.

Keenan, B. (1977) *The Women We Wanted to Look Like*. London: Macmillan.

Lerner, G. (ed.) (1973) *Black Women in White America: A Documentary History*. New York: Random House.

Lewis, M. (1994) Scenic beauty. *Guardian*, 6 October, p. 14.

Livingstone, D. N. (1994) Climate's moral economy: science, race and place in post-Darwinian British and American geography. In A. Godlewska and N. Smith (eds), *Geography and Empire*. Oxford: Blackwell, pp. 132–154.

Mama, A. (1995) *Beyond the Masks: Race Gender and Subjectivity*. London: Routledge.

Marshall, A. (1996) From sexual denigration to self-respect: resisting images of black female sexuality. In D. Jarrett-Macauley (ed.), *Reconstructing Womanhood, Reconstructing Feminism: Writings on Black Women*. London: Routledge, pp. 5–35.

Marwick, A. (1988) *Beauty in History: Society, Politics and Personal Appearance c1500 to the Present*. London: Thames and Hudson.

Mercer, K. (1992) Skin head sex thing: racial difference and the homoerotic imaginary. *New Formations: Competing Glances*, 16 (Spring): 1–23.

Mercer, K. (1994) *Welcome to the Jungle: New Positions in Black Cultural Studies*. London: Routledge.

Morrisroe, P. (1995) *Mapplethorpe: A Biography*. London: Macmillan.

Pacteau, F. (1994) *The Symptom of Beauty*. London: Reaktion Books.

Rothenberg, T. Y. (1994) The *National Geographic Magazine*. In A. Godlewska and N. Smith (eds), *Geography and Empire*. Oxford: Blackwell, pp. 155–72.

Stanton, W. (1960) *The Leopard's Spots: Scientific Attitudes Towards Race in America 1815–1859*. Chicago: University of Chicago Press.

Stafford, B. M. (1991) *Body Criticism: Imaging the Unseen in Enlightenment Art and Medicine*. Cambridge, MA: MIT Press.

Stuart, A. (1994) Looking at Josephine Baker. *Women: A Cultural Review – Gender and Performance, Women on the British Stage*. 5(2), pp. 137–143.

Verni, M. (1933) *Modern Beauty Culture: A Complete Guide to Beauty*. London: New Era.

Weekes, D. (1997) Shades of blackness: young black female constructions of beauty. In H. Safia Mirza (ed.), *Black British Feminism: A Reader*. London: Routledge.

Weigman, R. (1995) *American Anatomies: Theorizing Race and Gender*. Durham, NC: Duke University Press.

Winship, J. (1987) *Inside Women's Magazines*. London: Pandora.

Young, L. (1996) *Fear of the Dark: Race, Gender and Sexuality in the Cinema*. London: Routledge.

Young, L. (1996a) The rough side of the mountain: black women and representation on film. In D. Jarrett-Macauley (ed.), *Reconstructing Womanhood, Reconstructing Feminism: Writings on Black Women.* London: Routledge, pp. 175–201.

5

Working out with Merleau-Ponty

Jean Grimshaw

From the early years of second-wave feminism, the 'fashion-beauty complex' and the disciplines and regimes associated with it have always been issues of feminist concern. Following the earliest analyses of the apparatuses of cosmetics and fashion, and as women's obsession with dieting and body shape escalated (and anorexia and bulimia began to increase to their current epidemic proportions), feminist writing has also focused on the ideals of slenderness and of the 'fit' and 'well-toned' body, and the exercise regimes frequently associated with this.

In this chapter, the 'body practices' with which I am particularly concerned are those of 'keeping fit', 'working out' and 'staying in shape'. During the 1980s, there was a huge escalation and commercialization of activities such as aerobics and visiting the gym, and a great increase in both the number of private 'health' clubs offering a range of these activities and the number of people employing personal trainers to devise tailor-made exercise programmes. Specific fashions and trends within this sphere have changed quite frequently; the kind of 'high-impact' aerobics presented, for instance, in Jane Fonda's earliest videos has largely gone out of fashion and has been replaced with newer variants such as step aerobics. Clothes have changed as well; the ubiquitous leg-warmers of the early 1980s are now a matter for mirth, and participants in exercise classes are more likely to wear lycra cycling shorts. The environments within which these activities are conducted remain similar, however. The basic formats are: either a gymnasium with machines such as treadmills and exercise bicycles, complemented by a range of machines and weights designed for the development or honing of specific body parts or muscle groups; or a studio with mirrors and equipment to provide the music which is a ubiquitous background to exercise classes. (In what follows the term 'aerobics' will be used in a generic way to mean any exercise class done in this kind of setting.)

While both women and men visit the gym (although not necessarily for the same reasons), exercise classes to music remain a predominantly female preserve; the vast majority of teachers and participants in such classes are female. Popular publicity and promotion for aerobics classes or for going to the gym invoke a range of discourses, of which the three most important are the following. First, these practices may be legitimated by reference to notions of 'health' and 'fitness'. The kinds of health benefits invoked include benefits to the cardio-vascular system and increased stamina and suppleness. Most gyms and healthclubs offer fitness tests, which claim to be able to measure an increase in 'fitness' as an exercise programme progresses. Second, appeals are made to what might be called 'feel-good' factors. Exercise, it is claimed, will increase energy and vitality, improve the quality of life, and enhance self-esteem. Third (and perhaps most problematic from a feminist point of view), classes and gyms offer to female participants a vision of attaining the body shape currently seen as ideal; slim, taut and well-toned, with a visibly developed (though not bulging) musculature.

Aerobics and feminist body politics

In recent years, there has been a significant amount of feminist writing about women's relationship to and investment in such exercise programmes. Susan Bordo (1993), for instance, who has written extensively about the significance of eating disorders such as anorexia and bulimia, has also discussed the cultural significance of ideals of the slender and toned female body which is so often presented as the objective of exercise and fitness activities for women. She argues that the industry and ideology of body-shaping, whether by exercise or by plastic surgery, is fuelled by fantasies of a limitless improvement and reshaping of the body which defy its historicity, its mortality and even its materiality. The contemporary intoxication with freedom, change and self-determination has led to a vision of the body as a kind of 'cultural plastic' which we can shape at will. But the idea of the 'plastic body' which can be sculpted at will effaces the darker side of body-shaping practices. The idea that we can all choose our own bodies, for instance, effaces the inequalities of privilege. money and time needed to engage in these practices. It effaces addictions, obsessions, botched operations and eating disorders. Above all, despite the frequent popular presentation of body change and shaping as a matter of mere individual choice and will, or even as 'fun' and free play, the body that women want is a highly normalized one. It bears witness constantly to the dominance of a racial and gendered iconography. The content of the ideals of beauty and the perfect body are not arbitrary. It is true that these ideals change; thus neither the curvaceous Marilyn Monroe figure of the 1950s nor the stick-thin image of Twiggy represent the dominant ideal of the female body in the 1990s. Nevertheless it remains the case that not any body will do, and that the generalized tyranny of fashion and body shape is articulated differently for different groups. If black women attempt to lighten their skin or straighten their hair, for instance, this has to be read in the context of a still-powerful construction of white women with flowing hair as representing the pinnacle of female beauty. Similarly, perhaps, the perfectly honed, slim and taut 'aerobic body' can be read as connoting the requirement that whatever their class or race, women should above all be *young* and attempt to remain youthful-looking.

Moya Lloyd (1996) has suggested that while there has been a great deal of writing about eating disorders and women's relationship to food, and a considerable amount about general ideals of slenderness for women, less has been written specifically about aerobics (or related exercise practices for women). Aerobics is commonly coded as 'healthy' and concerned with 'fitness'. Lloyd argues, however, that it inhabits contradictory and competing discursive spaces. Whereas the 'healthy' aerobically exercised body might appear to be diametrically opposed to the unhealthy and pathologically starved or abused body of the anorexic or bulimic, Lloyd suggests that aerobics shares an 'axis of continuity' with anorexia and bulimia. Much of the discourse surrounding aerobics is not about 'health' at all. It reveals an antipathy to flesh and to 'fat' similar to that which is visible in eating disorders.

Lloyd notes (as does Bordo) the contemporary prevalence of

the belief among women that they are 'too fat', a belief which bears little relation to health or even to an accurate perception of the body in relation to cultural norms. The connections between aerobics and body shape involve a notion of an 'ideal body', and most particularly a body which is not 'fat'. Much of the publicity addressed to women that surrounds exercise and working out is orientated around notions of fat; fat-burning, fat-busting or 'lean' workouts, for instance. 'Fat' is always inscribed negatively, especially if it is on stomach, hips and thighs. Nearly all classes or workout routines and videos have an explicit goal of toning or fat reduction on these particular areas of the female body. Lloyd argues that underlying all the competing discourses within which aerobics are framed is the overarching imperative that women be slim (and as youthful-looking as possible).

The visual aspect of aerobics is central to its practice. The practice of the class is orientated around mirrors, as in a dance studio, where one can survey one's own body and the bodies of other participants. Lloyd notes the curious displacement of images in the workout video, where the TV screen acts almost as a substitute 'mirror', except that in it one does not see one's own body, but the body of the presenter of the routine. The strong visual element in aerobics and the constant surveying of one's own body might suggest that aerobics can be read in terms of a female internalization of the male gaze, and a dominant heteronormativity.

Sandra Bartky (1990) has addressed the question of female appearance and body image using Foucauldian concepts of power, self-surveillance and processes of normalization in the disciplining of the female body. She notes the 'facelessness' of many of the imperatives of the fashion-beauty industry, which seem to emanate from nowhere and from no one in particular. No one apparently 'makes' women diet, walk in high heels, dress fashionably or wear mascara. But the power of these imperatives, she suggests, derives precisely from their facelessness; it is easier to regard them as purely self-chosen and the discipline involved as self-imposed. Like Bordo, she also notes the constant processes of 'normalization' involved in what is presented as a free choice to 'make the most of yourself', whether it be through fashion and beauty, exercise, or cosmetic surgery. She also suggests that despite the increases in autonomy which some women have achieved, the increasingly overwhelming power of the visual image means that women are ever more tightly imprisoned in the heteronormative trap of constant self-surveillance. Because of its strong visual elements, aerobics too might be seen in this light.

Aerobics, however, involve not merely images, but techniques. These are normally detailed and highly ritualized. And the very term 'workout' suggests that they involve effort and dedication. Hilary Radner (1995) discusses the way in which Jane Fonda's 1981 *Workout Book* articulates a technology of the self, to be achieved through the workout. A strong contrast is presented, in both images and text, between Jane's mother, Frances Fonda, and her latest stepmother, Shirlee Fonda, who is at the centre of the illustrations of aerobic exercise. Frances Fonda feared and loathed becoming fat; she committed suicide in her forties. Shirlee Fonda is also pencil-thin; but (it is implied) this is the result of her exercise programme. A contrast is suggested between the 'bad' body, which is controlled by drugs, surgery or eating disorders, and the 'good' body which is controlled by self-discipline and exercise. This contrast is exemplified by the narrative of Jane's own life, which chronicles her progression from anorexia, bulimia and reliance on drugs such as dexedrine to the discovery of exercise in her forties. In the workout book, as Radner notes, Fonda comments on the ways in which women have been judged by their looks and men by their accomplishments. But she tries to resolve this antinomy by making looks into an accomplishment, something that one does actively and autonomously. This accomplishment is anchored in a vision of 'authentic' woman-hood as strong, autonomous and self-reliant. In that sense, it conveys Fonda's own reading of feminist politics.

In the 1981 *Workout Book*, Radner notes, the models are varied (and include black women). They vary in age, though they are mainly of a physical type often associated with dancers – taut and slim, with small breasts and a narrow pelvis. They, and Fonda herself, are often portrayed as absorbed in the workout in a way that does not appear simply posed for the camera, and does not construct them as obvious objects of a male erotic gaze. In the later workout books, however, there is a shift towards the use of sleeker, younger and better groomed models, and Fonda herself tends to appear in more obviously 'glamorous' poses. The kind of feminist politics that was seen to legitimate earlier versions of the workout has largely disappeared, and Fonda's own marriage to billionaire media mogul Ted Turner in her fifties appears as the ultimate reward for the strenuous years of effort and dedication. Thus, perhaps, is heteronormativity reinstated.

My account of these feminist approaches to women's aerobic exercise makes it clear, I hope, that it is a highly complex phenomenon, and that feminist writers have approached it from somewhat differing standpoints. I think it is possible, however, to summarize the main elements of recent feminist critiques as follows, though it is important to note that not all writers agree with all of them, or articulate them in identical ways.

Discourses about exercise and fitness for women, it is suggested, convey the following messages:

1. It fetishizes the youthful body, and reinforces in women a panicky desire to hang on to the youthful body (and contemporary ideals of sexual attractiveness to men) as long as possible.
2. It fetishizes the thin or hard body, seeing any female softness or fleshiness as disgusting 'flab' which has to be worked off. The ideal body shape is lean and hard, with visible muscle definition. Lean and muscled hips, thighs and arms should ideally be complemented by rounded breasts, not visibly damaged by the ravages of time or childrearing.
3. It destroys the 'unity' of the body. The body is broken into 'parts' which have to be worked on. Underlying the apparent ideology of 'loving' your body or caring for it is a profound somatophobia which focuses, often with a language of quite virulent hatred, on the inadequacy of body parts.
4. It is premised on the illusory attempt to imagine that in the end the body can be controlled and the processes of ageing defeated.
5. It suggests that controlling the body somehow means that one's life is in control. This fetishization of body control may be read not only as a denial of the material realities of ageing and death, but as symptomatic of the lack of control most of us have over other aspects of our lives.
6. It epitomizes the need, in a capitalist and consumerist society, for the *presentation* of self to be constantly worked on. What matters above all is how one looks. And although there is evidence that men are becoming increasingly aware of appearance, issues concerning how one looks are still heavily gendered. The sexual 'market value' of a woman, for

instance, is far more dependent than that of a man on retaining a youthful appearance.

Re-evaluating the feminist critique

Feminist praxis

It is interesting, first, to note that views of the implications for feminist praxis of critiques of aerobics or other exercise and fitness practices vary. Despite her critique of ideals of the slender female body, Bordo reveals in *Unbearable Weight* that she undertook a national weight loss programme and lost twenty pounds. She notes that while the weight loss brought her benefits (which she does not specify), it also left her feeling ambivalent, and with a regret that she could no longer provide a 'role model' for her students of a woman who was happy to be larger in size than the current norm. Bartky does not explicitly say that women should resist fashion and beauty practices as far as possible but given the nature of her critique, which sees women as profoundly colonized by the faceless imperatives of the fashion-beauty complex, it is hard to see what form of resistance there could be other than to try to opt out of as many relevant practices as one can. Given the extent to which Bartky sees women's own motives and desires as colonized by these patriarchal imperatives, one might also be pessimistic about the extent to which this could be possible.

The most explicit recommendation comes from Lloyd. Lloyd argues that feminists should be just as concerned about 'normal' practices such as aerobics as they are about others widely perceived as 'pathological' such as anorexia. In fact, precisely because aerobics is perceived as normal and commonly publicized through apparently 'neutral' discourses of health and fitness, it is all the more insidious, since it makes it harder to perceive the insistent normalizing pressures which pervade the practice. Lloyd suggests that any participation which doesn't visibly or publicly challenge the conventions of aerobics – perhaps by forms of parody or subversion – is all too easily recuperated.

Bordo, Bartky and Lloyd all take issue with those who would prefer to see beauty or fitness practices in a more postmodern vein as a mere play of 'difference' or changing and elusive subjectivity. Madonna, for instance, who reshaped her body by a strenuous programme of exercise and weight reduction, is often seen (and has presented herself) as a paradigm of a playful, autonomous and chameleon-like process of constant self-reinvention. Bordo argues that such a view effaces both the pain and obsession involved in the praxis by which Madonna reshaped herself, and the way in which the more 'unruly' body of her earlier years, when she seemed to refuse to conform to dominant ideals of thinness or fashion, has been replaced by a body that, however self-chosen, insistently reinforces the ideal of a slim and taut body for women, with all 'fat' ruthlessly eliminated.

While most critics of fashion or fitness practices distance themselves from making prescriptions about what women should or should not do, the logic of the kinds of arguments they deploy does seem to suggest that, if women engage in these practices, they risk reinforcing both their own colonization by suspect and dangerous norms of what the female body should look like, and a kind of public collusion with these norms which will serve to undermine any feminist critique.

A *new repressive hypothesis?*

Lloyd asks whether it is possible to disarticulate aerobics from the tyranny of slenderness, or recuperate it as potentially liberating or empowering for women. Her answer is no; but the pessimism with which this conclusion is articulated, and the suggestion that women should only engage in aerobics if they consciously intend to subvert its conventions, reveals, I think, an ongoing tension in a number of feminist critiques.

Lloyd, like Bordo, is at pains to stress that the body is always culturally mediated; there can be no such thing as a 'natural' body. But in what she writes there is also an implicit suggestion, which is in tension with the idea of the culturally mediated body, that only if motivation could be completely 'pure' could we be happy about feminist engagement in aerobics. To be 'liberatory' or 'empowering', any form of praxis for women must, apparently, be totally free of patriarchal pressures.

The obverse of the idea of a practice which is uncontaminated by processes of normalization is that of women's consciousness as 'false consciousness', wholly colonized. Such conceptions tend to lead to what Hilary Radner suggests can be seen as a new form of the 'repressive hypothesis'. But what is seen as 'repressed' is not so much sexuality, as the female body. Foucault argued that there was no 'sexuality' that could be 'outside' discourse, nor could there be 'resistance' which was not itself implicated in and discursively constructed by that which it is resisting. Neither can there be a female body which is outside discourse, or a resistant body that can stand as a simple exception to forces of normalization or domination. From a Foucauldian perspective, there can be no binary opposition between resistance and normalization. Such an opposition runs the risk, despite the strong disavowals of this by the writers I have mentioned, of implicitly reinstating ideas of a 'natural' body with which a woman might have an entirely comfortable and unmediated relation. There are hints of this in Bordo's writing at times. She quotes, for instance, a transcript from a TV talk show in which a participant noted that women are never happy with themselves (1993: 251). But the idea of being totally 'happy with oneself' is a hair's breadth from supposing an 'authentic' or 'real' relationship with one's body which is free of cultural norms and pressures. Bordo is absolutely right to note the dangers in the ways in which the stress on mere 'difference' or 'play' loses sight of the pressures of normalization. She is right, too, to note that the degree of women's misery and unhappiness about their bodies is a problem with which it is crucial that feminists engage. But it is also a problem to offer a critique premised on too simple a notion of being 'happy with one's body'. This tends to deny the ways in which bodies are *always* problematic in one way or another, and issues concerning shape or appearance *always* have to be negotiated in some way, whatever the cultural context. To suggest, simply, that women should be 'happy' with their bodies is in its way as problematic as aiming to tackle issues concerning age or disability simply by saying that the old or those who are not able-bodied should be 'happy' with their bodies as well.

Radner also notes that if the binary opposition between resistance and normalization is discarded, so too must we discard a binary opposition between feminine and masculine. This latter opposition does not define the body as such. There is a danger in seeing the female body simply as the dominated body, and a tendency, within feminist critique, implicitly to compare a repressed and dominated female body with an unrepressed male body which is not subject to discipline. (This tends to occur in de Beauvoir and Young, whom I shall discuss later.) Foucault has rightly been criticized for his failure to adequately consider the *specific* ways in which female bodies have been disciplined. But his delineation, in *Discipline and Punish* (1979), of the emergence of the body of the modern citizen was justified, in a sense, in concentrating on men, since it was men, unlike women, who were paradigmatically citizens. Despite the important differences between male and female forms of bodily discipline, and despite the persisting imbalances in power relationships such that certain sorts of pressures are far more insidious and far-reaching on the bodies of women than on those of men, nevertheless, in so far as women too become 'citizens', their bodies are subjected to forms of discipline which, while gender differentiated in many ways, do not owe all of their characteristics simply to gender. (One might instance here the ways in which forms of discipline and normalization which affect the disabled are not always clearly differentiated by gender. An interesting aspect of disability, for instance, are the ways in which the non-able-bodied are frequently desexualized.)

I think that it is this tendency to consider the processes of discipline and normalization of female bodies in more or less complete abstraction from the processes to which either male bodies, or both male and female bodies are subjected and by which they are shaped, which has led to some significant absences in feminist theorizations of exercise and fitness practices. There can be no guarantees that any practice is free of normalizing pressures; no assumption of ideological 'purity' in any motivation; no clear dividing lines between what is internally or externally imposed. And no body practice, in all of its manifestations, can be understood wholly in terms of subjection or capitulation to normalizing pressures. But this raises the interesting question of how else they can be understood. And it is here that there seems to be a 'gap' in most contemporary feminist theorizations of exercise and fitness practices. Writers such as Bordo make it plain that they do not wish to deny that there may be 'benefits' associated with such practices and programmes. But the benefits remain shadowy and untheorized. Both medical and popular discourses stress the health benefits, such as decreased risk of heart attacks or osteoporosis. Simply to spell out the benefits in terms of health, however, is problematic for a number of reasons. First, the health benefits are themselves frequently contentious, and 'expert' opinion about them varies. Second, the simple means-end model of exercise as a means to health is plainly inadequate to capture the variety of reasons why people exercise. It is arguable that most people are remarkably resistant to undertaking any regime on health grounds alone, if no other form of motivation is in play. An abstract concern with health alone rarely provides adequate motivation for continuing with an exercise programme, even if it provided some reasons for embarking on it in the first place.

Publicity for exercise and fitness practices commonly stresses 'feel-good' factors such as renewed energy, revitalization of one's life, or increased self-esteem and self-empowerment. But it is of course precisely these sorts of claims which have been viewed with most suspicion by feminist critics as irredeemably tainted with the kinds of normalizing pressures which help lock women into a dangerous fetishization of a thin and youthful body and a constant reinscription of heteronormativity.

Nevertheless, the countless thousands of women who go to the gym or go to exercise classes include many who would count themselves as feminist, and many who are also lesbian. There is a need to think more deeply about the kinds of reasons why women who in other aspects of their lives consciously and constantly resist heteronormative pressures and oppressive paradigms of the young and thin female body nevertheless give priority to exercise, and sometimes also to practices of body shaping or sculpting. And if we are to discard the binary opposition between resistance and normalization, we cannot depict such women merely as 'exceptions', whose motivations must be understood as radically different from those of 'ordinary' women.

My project therefore is to ask whether and how it might be possible to offer a phenomenological analysis of the kind of pleasure and empowerment gained through fitness and exercise practices which occupies a different kind of theoretical terrain. In the attempt to do this, I want to draw on Merleau-Ponty's account of the lived body in *Phenomenology of Perception* (1990) and to outline some central relevant themes from the book.

Merleau-Ponty

'I think that' and 'I can'

Merleau-Ponty argued that the ground of human action was not thinking, conceived of as a purely mental activity. The primary origins of human action lie not in thinking, conceived of in this way, but in movement and motility. The *body* is our general medium for having a world. Consciousness is in the first place not a matter of 'I think' but rather of 'I can'.

In normal action, Merleau-Ponty argues, people immediately 'come to grips' with the relation between tasks or goals in a spontaneous way; they do not have to *work out* how to move their arms or legs, nor calculate the location of their limbs. My own body is not *in* space for me in the same way as other objects. It *inhabits* space. The space around me, the objects in it and the possible movements of my body are integrated for me in an overall orientation, and they all gain significance from each other. There is a kind of primary bodily orientation towards action in the world, a basic motor function, which is more fundamental than and essential to other abilities. Human consciousness and human action are rooted in an ability to *move* in the world, in a 'body schema' which allows us to inhabit space and to move and act in integrated ways.

Habit

Merleau-Ponty writes that understanding habit is a key task in revising our thinking about the body and about what we mean by 'understanding' itself. Habit, he says, is a renewal and rearrangement of one's body schema; it expresses our power of dilating our being-in-the-world or changing our existence by appropriating fresh instruments. There are many things which we 'know how to do' which can never be put fully into words; riding a bicycle, for instance, or driving a car, or playing a musical instrument; learning to walk with a stick, or knowing one's way around one's own house. We do not do these things simply by a process of intellectual synthesis, nor do we learn them by any kind of mechanistic association. Rather, these skills and abilities become integrated into our body schema and integrated with the world around us. So, he writes (153):

> Whether a system of motor or perceptual powers, our body is not an object for an 'I think', it is a grouping of lived-through meanings. ... Sometimes a new cluster of meanings is formed; our former movements are integrated into a fresh motor entity, the first visual data into a fresh sensory entity, our natural powers suddenly coming together into a higher meaning.

Our body schema is not static but constantly adapting and changing. And skills and abilities can not only be acquired but also lost through disuse. So I may need to keep 'in my hands' or 'in my legs' the orientation towards specific movements or distances or directions.

The 'intentional arc'

Merleau-Ponty writes that the life of consciousness is subtended by an 'intentional arc'. The arc is the span of our projects, past, present and future, the settings in which we live and are situated, and the integrated bodily orientations which we have towards the world. The body is a nexus of lived and related meanings, related not only to present positions and intentions but to past and possible future ones as well.

Merleau-Ponty's analysis is not restricted to actions which consist merely of concrete physical tasks in relation to objects immediately to hand. Consciousness, he says, also projects itself into a cultural world. The way he expresses this in *Phenomenology of Perception* might lead to the accusation that he gives an ontological priority to certain kinds of immediate bodily movements and actions and fails adequately to recognize the ways in which the meaning of *all* actions, however immediate, is always mediated by culture. But the supposition of some kind of ontological priority is not necessary to most of his central arguments. All human action involves dispositions of the body and a 'body schema' of some sort, even when the task aimed at cannot be achieved merely through bodily movement.

We sometimes make a commonsensical distinction between kinds of human actions which do or do not involve bodily movement. But while some human enterprises, such as intellectual work, do not involve 'gross' bodily movements, they nevertheless involve dispositions of the body; the gaze, the focusing of eyes or ears, the physical as well as mental efforts involved in concentration. And here as well, habit is important – the ability to endow such dispositions of the body with 'a little renewable action and independent existence', such that we do not have to painstakingly reconstruct or recall them every time that we deploy them. If one is engrossed in intellectual work, the 'tools' one is using, such as paper, pen, book or word-processor, and the bodily movements involved in making use of these, become subsumed in the 'arc' of one's current intentions. To borrow a phrase from Merleau-Ponty, there can be a kind of 'melodic' flow, a circuit in operation between hands, gaze, thoughts and the objects being used. An *environment* can have what Merleau-Ponty calls a certain 'physiognomy'; the tasks and goals it suggests, and the bodily positions and movements that these require, can easily be summoned up.

Merleau-Ponty and 'the normal'

Central to Merleau-Ponty's writing about the body is a concept of 'normality'. He constantly contrasts 'normal' human action in the world, where bodily movements are integrated into a schema which allows for spontaneous and unreflective action, with the actions of people who suffer from motor disturbances or disabilities which affect their capacities to act or to move. A great deal of *Phenomenology of Perception* is devoted to a discussion, derived from the work of various physiological and clinical specialists, of people who for instance cannot touch their noses with their eyes shut, or who do not know how to obey an order to move their arm.

Beyond the consideration of disorders such as aphasia and apraxia, Merleau-Ponty does not problematize the concept of 'the normal'. It is, however, raised in a very interesting way by Iris Marion Young (1990), in her paper 'Throwing like a girl'. In this paper, Young uses, but also adapts, Merleau-Ponty to offer an analysis of the ways in which *women's* movement and motility in the world may often be inhibited. Following Merleau-Ponty, she argues that 'it is the ordinary purposive orientation of the body as a whole toward things and its environment that initially defines the relation of a subject to its world' (143). But, she suggests, the modalities of typically *feminine* movement in the world are commonly different from the masculine. Young's analysis focuses primarily on movements of the body undertaken in order to accomplish specific tasks (such as throwing) which entail gross movement and the body's encounter with the resistance of objects in the world. Drawing both on de Beauvoir's account of woman's existence in the world as defined by a tension between immanence and transcendence, and on Merleau-Ponty's account of the 'normal' relationship between human bodies and their environment in action, Young suggests that female goal-directed bodily action in the world is commonly distinguished by three features. She labels these 'ambiguous transcendence', 'inhibited intentionality' and 'discontinuous unity'.

The body is the locus of intentionality in the world. 'The lived body as transcendence', writes Young, 'is pure fluid action, the continuous calling forth of capacities that are applied to the world' (148). But women (unlike men) typically refrain from throwing their whole bodies into a movement. One part of the body reaches out for a task, while the rest of the body remains relatively immobile. Women, Young suggests, often 'live' their bodies in *ambiguous transcendence*; the body moves towards a task, yet is also a burden, which has to be both dragged along and protected.

Merleau-Ponty locates intentionality in motility. But typically, Young suggests (148), the feminine body may underuse or underestimate its physical capacities. Thus:

> Feminine bodily existence is an *inhibited intentionality*, which simultaneously reaches towards a projected end with an 'I can' and withholds its full bodily commitment to that end in a self-imposed 'I cannot'. [emphasis in original]

Finally, Merleau-Ponty writes of the way in which the body creates a 'unity' with its environment, and organizes the surrounding space as an extension of its own being. But the third modality of feminine bodily existence which Young identifies is *discontinuous unity*. Women not only tend to draw back from full physical engagement with a task; in addition, the space that is available to them is commonly less than the space they inhabit. And while Merleau-Ponty suggests that in the enactment of intentions the body is not an *object* to itself, for women there is commonly a sense that the body is indeed 'object' as well as 'subject': the object of the gaze of others, and an object which is frequently experienced as limited and limiting.

The idealization of male bodies

Earlier in this paper I noted a problematic tendency in some feminist critique implicitly to compare a repressed female body with an unrepressed male body. I think it can be argued that Young, in a way reminiscent of de Beauvoir, tends to idealize masculine movement.

In the chapter on childhood in *The Second Sex* (1983: 307) de Beauvoir writes:

> The great advantage enjoyed by the boy is that his mode of existence in relation to others leads him to assert his subjective freedom. His apprenticeship for life consists in free movement towards the outside world; he contests in hardihood and independence with other boys, he scorns girls. Climbing trees, fighting with his companions, facing them in rough games, he is aware of his body as a means for dominating nature and as a weapon for fighting; he takes pride in his muscles as in his sex; in games, sports, fights, challenges, trials of strength, he finds a balanced exercise of his powers; at the same time he absorbs the severe lessons of violence; he learns from an early age to take blows, to scorn pain, to keep back the tears. He undertakes, he invents, he dares.

De Beauvoir does note briefly that this may at times be problematic for adults and other children. But this kind of idealization of the male body and male movement appears elsewhere in the text of *The Second Sex* (406). She writes as follows about sexual initiation:

> True, the male organ is not a striated, voluntary muscle; it is neither plough-share nor sword, but only flesh; however, man imparts to it a movement that is voluntary; it goes back and forth, stops, moves again while the woman takes it submissively. ... It must not be forgotten that male and female adolescents gain awareness of their bodies in quite dissimilar fashion; the male assumes his easily, and with pride in its desires; for the female, in spite of her narcissism, it is a strange and disquieting burden. The sex organ of a man is simple and neat as a finger; it is readily visible and often exhibited to comrades with proud rivalry; but the feminine sex organ is mysterious even to the woman herself, concealed, mucous and humid as it is.

Alongside de Beauvoir's powerful analysis of the kinds of restrictions to which girls were subjected in provincial France in the 1940s (which have by no means all disappeared), there is also a powerful strand of idealization of the male body and masculine movement which ignores two things. First, it tends to sideline the ways in which male bodily movements can be oppressive to women, and male 'freedom' of action can sometimes be bought only at the price of female restriction. Second, it seems to offer a problematic conception of a 'free' and 'unrepressed' male body. It is important to recognize the specific and historically changing kinds of restrictions that have been placed on female movement (including such things as restrictive clothing and constraining conventions about feminine deportment and demeanour). But while it is true that restrictions on female movement and motility have operated in a context of power where women have consistently been at a disadvantage, it is certainly not true that men do not see their bodies or their sexuality as a problem. Neither is it true that conventions of masculine movement always and in all circumstances allow men greater 'freedom' than women.

Young notes what she sees as the tendency of women not to 'reach, stretch, bend, lean or stride to the full limits of their physical capacities'. Possibly it is right to say of certain specific activities, such as throwing, that women tend to hold back and not immerse themselves bodily in throwing in a way that is typical of men. But this may be just as much to do with the fact that throwing is so closely related to the kinds of sports which are paradigmatically or exclusively male, as related to any feminine tendency to 'hold back' from immersion in all forms of physical activity. It is interesting to compare women's throwing with male participation in aerobics classes (which is in fact considerable). Commonly (and in my experience), men are ill at ease, inhibited in their movements, and above all stiff and rigid; they often find it very hard to engage in the kinds of co-ordinated or flowing movements which characterize parts of an aerobics class.

But in addition, Young fails to note the ways in which men's full occupation of the maximum possible amount of space around them may be oppressive and inhibiting to others. A discussion of masculine movement in a seminar of my own produced a *frisson* of recognition about the ways in which men frequently occupy space in public spaces such as pubs or bars in a way that excludes and inhibits others. The Australian sociologist R. W. Connell (1983) suggests that the occupation of as much space as possible is coded as masculine; the fascination of young men with motor bikes (and perhaps noisy or fast cars as well) is a way of amplifying space and putting one's impress upon it. There have indeed been conventions and dress codes which at times have limited women's capacity to stride, bend, lean and reach. But when the 'task' involved is walking along a crowded pavement or through a busy store, the propensity to occupy as much space as possible or to stride and reach to the maximum of one's physical capacity is likely to be perceived as a form of harassment of others.

While I agree with Young, then, that feminine bodily movement has often been inhibited, I would want to add three important riders to this. The first is that feminine bodily inhibition should not be premised in implicit opposition to a 'free' or unrepressed male body. The second is that the extent to which masculine bodily movement *is* 'free' and uninhibited (in the manner suggested by Young) may often depend on the gender coding of activities, rather than on a more generalized propensity to move in uninhibited ways. The third is the importance of recognizing that in certain circumstances moving in ways that reach the limit of one's physical capacities can oppress or terrorize others.

What Young's analysis rightly suggests, however, is that Merleau-Ponty's conception of the 'normal' needs problematizing and that it can be revised and adapted. *Within* his category of the 'normal' there may be different 'modalities' which cannot be identified simply with 'disorders' such as aphasia or apraxia. While I have raised some questions about aspects of Young's analysis, the idea that there are gendered modalities of bodily existence and movement is a very important one, although certainly not one that is considered by Merleau-Ponty himself. There may also be other modalities – inflected by class or by race (see Bourdieu, 1984). And while the idea of black 'rhythm' and rhythmic movement has been used in patronizing, demeaning and oppressive ways (to suggest the 'jungle' origin or primitive animality of black people), there are unquestionably different cultural norms of movement and ranges both of expression and of inhibition.

But perhaps there are also other ways, intersecting with gender, but not reducible to it, in which Merleau-Ponty's analysis of bodily existence might be adapted to allow for the idea of 'modalities'. In fact, there are hints of this within his own work, although they are never spelled out. In his analysis of habit, for example, there are suggestions (never developed) that *within* the category of the 'normal', bodily action may be more or less integrated; habits can deteriorate or lapse; bodily dispositions can wax and wane; the 'melodic flow', when there is an integration of the body with the surrounding environment, can be more or less effective.

Young's primary concern is with the modalities of bodily movement and action involved in specific goal-directed tasks or sets of movements. My own interest lies, rather, in asking whether it is possible to theorize or give an account of a more *general* kind of bodily orientation in the world which is connected to one's engagement with a wide variety of tasks. It is important again to remember the 'bodiliness' of all human action; everything we ever do involves dispositions and movements of the body, and my own analysis is not restricted to specific tasks involving 'gross' bodily movements.

I would like now to tentatively suggest some ways in which one might 'think' the effects of bodily movement and exercise on one's life as a whole. Two points should be made at the outset. On some occasions, when I have discussed these issues with friends or colleagues, they have suggested that the kinds of effects which I wish to delineate can be explained quite simply by appeal to scientific concepts such as endomorphins, and their effect on the human body during exercise. I should therefore make it plain that I do not wish to challenge such theories, and do not in any case have the competence do so. But what I am interested in is the phenomenological effects of exercise and the relation between it and other aspects of life.

I should also note that my remarks have an autobiographical core. They are partly an attempt to make a kind of phenomenological sense of aspects of my own experience, and to address some issues for which there has seemed to be little space in contemporary feminist critique of women's body practices. Autobiographical narratives are constructions which cannot lay claim to 'the truth' about one's own life, let alone about anyone else's. I would simply note that the absence I have noted in recent feminist writing has found recognition and struck a chord on a number of occasions when I have presented earlier versions of this paper. There is, at the very least, something here to explain. So I shall now give an account of some ways in which Merleau-Ponty's view of the body, adapted through a notion of 'modalities', might be used to address this absence.

Inhabiting one's body

Merleau-Ponty writes a great deal, as I have said, about people who have lost the capacity to move their bodies in 'normal' ways.

In normal action, as he describes it, the body is not an 'object' for itself in the same way as other objects in space; rather, there is a 'body/subject' for whom intention and bodily movement are integrated in a continuous flow. But he also notes the ways in which the body schema can become extended, when movements are integrated into a new unity. His own analysis of the development of new body schemas does, in fact, suggest that even within his own terms, his concept of normality needs modifying not merely to deal with disorders such as aphasia and apraxia. If, for instance, I learn a new skill involving bodily co-ordination, such as riding a bicycle, there is likely to be a progression from a situation where my limbs and my movements are not well integrated (I might need to find out what my body will do, how my legs need to move in order to achieve balance), and a situation where I no longer need to go through any consciously reflective processes in order to ride, since a body schema has developed which allows me to ride a bicycle 'spontaneously' and unselfconsciously.

Transcending previous limits to bodily action and developing new body schemas may therefore involve a prior stage of 'objectification' of the body and its movements where aspects of it may be experienced as an obstacle and where new movements or postures have to be consciously learned or practised. Young contrasts flowing, unselfconscious and spontaneous movement and engagement of the body in action with the kind of 'objectification' where my body becomes an 'object' for me because it is the object, or potential object of the gaze of others. And she sees this kind of 'objectification' as constraining women's abilities to move freely in the world. But my body may be an 'object' for me in senses other than that in which it is objectified by the gaze of others. It is arguable that this kind of 'objectification' is involved as a transitional process whenever previous bodily limits are extended in some way.

Young writes of the ways in which 'normal' feminine movement may be inhibited or limited (and I have noted myself the ways in which this may also at times be true of masculine movement). But the question of limits is an interesting one, in which gender is not the only variable. Sedentary or inactive lifestyles lead to a lack of much realistic knowledge of one's own body. There is a sense in which certain kinds of knowledge *about* my body (about what it can or cannot do, or what it could be trained to do), may be necessary for me to be able to develop new kinds of body schema in which I can unselfconsciously do certain things and move my body in certain ways, instead of regarding them with an air of distanced horror or terror (running up a flight of stairs, or moving and stretching in certain ways).

So acquiring a new kind of knowledge *about* one's body – a realistic understanding of what it can or cannot do or how its capacities can be extended – can lead to the development of new body schemas in which certain kinds of movement are entered upon in an unselfconscious and spontaneous way which transcends the knowledge on which they rest. Merleau-Ponty writes that we can 'dilate' our being-in-the-world by developing fresh bodily skills or appropriating fresh instruments. In my own case, starting to engage in activities such as aerobics (in my forties), learning to move my body in new ways and acquiring a far more discriminating knowledge of its capacities and limits led me, phenomenologically, to feel that I 'inhabited' it differently. I acquired a new bodily orientation, which felt more integrated and mobile, and which led me to project myself differently into the world. This new and relatively unselfconscious orientation was connected to new forms of knowledge. I could look at an exercise video, for instance, and instead of regarding the whole of it with vague terror, be able to discriminate clearly between those things which I could do easily, those which would be harder, and those which would be beyond me.

For much of my life there was a real phenomenological sense in which 'I' and 'my body' pulled against each other. (This kind of feeling is well captured by Young in 'Throwing like a girl'.) I did not want to 'be' my body; I frequently experienced it as an obstacle; I often felt as if I 'carried it around' under sufferance. I think that this struggle between 'me' and my body was over-determined. Part of it was indeed due to various gender-related phobias about size and appearance, which afflicted me acutely. Part of it was, I think, also due to a kind of bodily fear and unease resulting from a somewhat inactive lifestyle.

The forms of exercise I have mostly engaged in have been aerobics and going to the gym. Why did I choose them? There were many reasons. Questions of accessibility and availability were important. I had friends to go with, and friends who were exercise teachers to whose classes I went. But aerobics in particular resonated with my existing enjoyment of music and dancing, and the exhilarating discovery that I could learn to do certain dance-like movements quite well and easily. The focus on stretching and bending showed me how much I valued and enjoyed suppleness and flexibility, as well as a better general level of 'fitness'. The kinds of exercise that people enjoy vary widely, some really like running or jogging alone on foggy wet November mornings. I do not. The interesting thing is that although the forms of exercise which I have undertaken have mostly been those which have particularly been the target of feminist critique, in my own case it was precisely the experience of doing them which helped me to feel 'comfortable' in my body for the first time in my adult life, and helped me, albeit precariously, to begin to jettison phobias about size and appearance which had dogged me since adolescence.

'Habit' revisited

In his analysis of habit, Merleau-Ponty notes that there is a habituation of the body to tasks which leaves what can be called 'traces' in the body schema – knowledge that is 'in my hands' or 'in my legs'. The sorts of tasks he had in mind were skills such as riding a bicycle or playing a musical instrument or knowing one's way around one's own house. I would like to extend this analysis of habit, and suggest that physical activity (including that undertaken 'for its own sake') can leave 'traces' of a kind of outwardness or outgoingness of bodily disposition which is closely involved in feeling that one can cope with any task or project at all.

Merleau-Ponty notes that there may be close connections between 'mental' illness or distress and bodily disturbance. Things such as depression, panic or anxiety attacks are integrally related to dispositions of the body. Tasks such as walking down the street or going out of the house, normally done in an unreflective and unproblematic manner, may become insuperable hurdles. There may be an inability to move in normal ways, and rigidities and lack of flow in bodily movements. In acute cases of panic or anxiety, *no* situation has a physiognomy which suggests action or involvement, and a person may locked into a 'frozen' kind of state where doing anything seems almost inconceivable. Now while it would be common to see the mental distress as the 'cause' and the physical manifestations as 'effect' or 'symptom',

Merleau-Ponty's analysis of the body suggests that a cause-effect model is inappropriate, and that the 'mental' and the 'physical' are more like aspects abstracted from what is experientially a total situation into which they are dovetailed.

I want to suggest that bodily movement and exercise can leave 'traces' of a more generalized outwardness of bodily disposition, or engagement with tasks that lie to hand, and immersion in the physical demands that all human activity makes on one's life (including intellectual activity). The 'mental' and the 'bodily' are always, as I have said, experientially dovetailed. And the second autobiographical root of this paper lies here. In situations in my own life which involved, for example, coping with terminal illness and bereavement, I have frequently found that physical movement and exercise has been the *only* thing that has helped me to break out of a feeling of frozen inability to do anything at all, and to feel that perhaps I could, after all, be able to immerse myself in the world and cope again. Scientific explanations (in terms of endomorphins, for instance) might be given for this. But even if true, a scientific explanation is not a substitute for a phenomenological account, and does not render such an account redundant.

Conclusion

My aim in this chapter has been to suggest, like Iris Marion Young, that it is possible to adapt Merleau-Ponty's view of the body to give an account of differing 'modalities' of bodily existence and the role of physical activity in human life. These modalities are heavily inflected by gender but are by no means reducible to it. They are also plainly culturally specific in many ways. Thus the importance of the idea of exercise and physical activity 'for its own sake' rather than in relation to a specific task is highly culturally variable. In a society in which, for everyone, there was a closer integration of more strenuous physical activity into the tasks and projects of life, a concept of 'exercise' anything like our own would be unlikely to exist. There are also paradoxes and problems surrounding our own concept of 'exercise'; the paradox, for instance, of driving one's car to an aerobics class!

But my analysis does suggest, I think, that models of exercise and physical activity which see these just as a means to an end (whether the end is apparently desirable goals such as 'health' or ideologically suspect ones such as thinness or the ideal body) cannot by themselves give a rich or even adequate account of the kind of importance bodily activity may have in human life. It may be related to much more general orientations, to modes of being-in-the-world whose importance extends far beyond their aptness for limited or specific goals.

The idea of 'modalities' of bodily existence might be further used or adapted in the following ways. Both the gendered restrictions on feminine bodily movement described by Iris Young, and the extraordinary lack of bodily motility prevalent among many people in our relatively sedentary culture which is dependent on the motor car might be seen as disabling in some ways. Young writes about the ways in which the female body is sometimes experienced as a burden or as an 'object' in ways that can impede its unselfconscious projection into the world in action. But it is also important to consider the modalities of bodily existence involved in more conventionally labelled 'disabilities', including such things as being paraplegic, having a severe asthmatic condition, or experiencing forms of terminal illness which involve the severe deterioration of the body and the attenuation of its normal capacities.

In the context of these disruptive forms of illness, the body may be experienced as 'betraying' the person. Simon Williams (1996: 23) discusses the need to look at the problems of *dys*-ease and *dys*-order they raise. He writes:

> The typical course of the chronic illness trajectory involves a shift from an initial state of embodiment, one in which the body is largely taken-for-granted in the normal course of everyday life, to an oscillation between states of *dys*-embodiment (i.e. embodiment in a dysfunctional state) and attempts at *re*-embodiment.

The vicissitudes of chronic illness and the coping strategies deployed may vary widely. One response, for instance, to the problems of a painful terminal illness where the body will not 'work' as usual is an attempt to construct a sense of oneself as 'disembodied': I *am* no longer my body, and its dysfunctional aspects are no longer a part of *me*. Since I can no longer project my body into the world in the former relatively unselfconscious ways, I might attempt to disinvest my body of its normal significance in my life, and see it as no longer a part of my 'self'. It is simply an 'object' to be managed and controlled as far as possible. A very different kind of response in the case of paralysis might be to attempt to reorganize one's bodily mode of being-in-the-world and to articulate one's 'embodiment' in new ways compatible with the restrictions imposed. Both of these responses involve a profound modification of one's sense of self, of the narrative of one's own life, and of the relation between embodiment and the projects one might hope to undertake.

Responding to terminal illness or disability, whether one's own or that of other people, involves understanding that the body can never be understood simply as a means to an end. Coping with illness or disability is always more than a practical question of how to achieve certain ends despite the limitations of the body. But if there are different modalities of bodily existence in 'normal' life, and if forms of physical activity can at times change the kinds of orientation of one's self towards the projects one has in the world, this suggests that one can learn a great deal about 'normal' embodiment, and about the phenomenology of change within that, from a phenomenological approach to the experience of illness or disability. Conversely, recognizing the close relationship between one's sense of self and the vicissitudes of changing bodily orientations and engagements can provide an approach to understanding the experience of people for whom the body has suddenly become a problem in wholly new ways.

The body can never be wholly unproblematic, something with which one can be 'happy' in in a simple, stable or permanent kind of way. Apart from the fact that it is always subject to vicissitudes such as ageing and illness, there is a continuum between the kinds of modalities which might form part of the pattern of a 'normal' life and those which come into being in more extreme circumstances. These modalities do not stay constant. They are culturally variable. They are subject both to changes that are beyond our control and to unpredicted effects born of changing circumstances or lifestyle. Our bodies are also the object, from time to time, of conscious interventions. The kinds of interventions that women make, and the practices in which they engage (including those of exercise and 'fitness'), may indeed at times need analysis and critique. But their effects and the motives for which women undertake them cannot be adequately understood simply in terms of capitulation to ideological pressures to conform to a particular norm of the feminine body.

References

Bartky, S. (1990) Foucault, femininity and the modernization of patriarchal power. In S. Bartky, *Femininity and Domination*. London: Routledge.

Bordo, S. (1993) Material Girl. In S. Bordo, *Unbearable Weight*. Berkeley: University of California Press.

Bourdieu, P. (1984) *Distinction: A Social Critique of the Judgement of Taste*. Cambridge, MA: Harvard University Press.

Connell, R. W. (1983) Men's bodies. In R. W. Connell, *Which Way Is Up?* Sydney: Allen and Unwin.

de Beauvoir, S. (1983) *The Second Sex*. Harmondsworth: Penguin (first published 1949).

Foucault, M. (1979) *Discipline and Punish*. Harmondsworth: Penguin.

Lloyd, M. (1996) Feminism, aerobics and the politics of the body. *Body and Society*, 2(2), 79–98.

Merleau-Ponty, M. (1990) *Phenomenology of Perception* (trans. Colin Smith). London: Routledge.

Radner, H. (1995) Speaking the body: Jane Fonda's *Workout Book*. In H. Radner, *Shopping Around: Feminine Culture and the Pursuit of Pleasure*. London: Routledge.

Williams, S. (1996) The vicissitudes of embodiment across the chronic illness trajectory. *Body and Society*, 2(2), 23–47.

Young, I. M. (1990) Throwing like a girl. In I. M. Young, *Throwing Like a Girl: And Other Essays in Feminist Philosophy and Social Theory*. Indianapolis: Indiana University Press.

6

'Doing Looks': Women, Appearance and Mental Health

Liz Frost

By exploring a number of connections between the issue of women's appearances and their well-being, I will argue in this chapter that 'doing looks' is a potential source of pleasure and even power and may contribute positively to women's mental health.

For many centuries and across seemingly diverse value systems women's involvement with their own appearance has consistently been ascribed a set of negative meanings. From a traditional Christian view in which it has been understood as embodying the sinful states of pride or vanity, through scientific pathologization of looks-related activities, to a strand of modern feminism which would see it as trivial, unsisterly or proof of a colonized consciousness, 'doing looks' has been cast as 'a bad thing'.

The passive, other-defined state of being beautiful has of course been differently valued, but the processes and outcomes of an active engagement with their own appearance has often led to women being criticized, and may have made it extremely difficult for women to experience anything other than at best a profound ambivalence and at worst shame at the self construction of their visual identities. In this chapter I seek to re-evaluate the available meanings of doing looks from within a feminist perspective, while also challenging some traditional feminist positions in relation to women and appearance.

First I will consider how feminist critiques of psychiatry have interpreted women patients' looks-related activities as indicative of their oppression within a patriarchal psychiatric system, and suggest some alternative meanings. I will then briefly examine how the process of pathologizing women's various engagements with their looks, discernible in some contemporary psychology, is another potential source of negative interpretations. I will go on to suggest that the blending of the psychoanalytical notion of narcissism with the more traditional criticism of vanity has served to invest the former with a far from objective set of value judgements, and that much second-wave feminism has served to reinforce this negative valuing. I will consider whether this may have served to deny women a discursive space for self-appreciation of the skills, knowledge and outcomes of their doing looks. Instead of potential pleasure, denial, guilt and shame may have become the only possible feelings women can ascribe to this range of activities. This would, of course, be very bad for women's mental health.

There is now a considerable body of literature which takes as a central tenet the oppression of women within a patriarchal psychiatric system, and indeed in medicine more generally (Chesler, 1972; Ussher, 1991; Russell, 1995). Under this generalized notion of gender oppression a variety of specific issues has been explored, frequently focusing on the ways in which sex-role stereotypes are reinforced. The application of this happens in both general and specific ways, some of which connect importantly with issues concerning appearance.

Anne Davis writes (Brook and Davis, 1985: 82)

> It is by no means rare, for example, for a psychiatrist or nurse to describe a female patient to colleagues primarily in terms of her appearance, to judge her progress to 'health' by her feminine dress and make-up, and to evaluate the outcome of her treatment in terms of her adjustment to a traditionally acceptable female role.

Make-up and skirts, a hair-do and not 'letting yourself go' are the correct attributes of the sane woman, the necessary tools to construct sane identity. Cultural norms are crucial here. For example, in the UK only a certain degree of looks engagement is an indicator of mental health. 'Too much' make-up, clashing colours or wild applications, clothing that is too girly or too sexy, may well be interpreted as a symptom of manic reactions, a kind of hysterical well-being expressed in over-beautification. Equally spending 'too much' time in the process of constructing appearance might be suspected as indicative of an obsessional disorder.

The history of the ways in which 'proper' femininity has been applied as a guide to and prescription for women's mental health, and the sometimes cruel limitations this has imposed on women, has become a firm part of feminist demonology. Feminist social constructionists have proposed that 'madwoman' is simply another label, like witch or nymphomaniac, through which men seek to control women's social and sexual behaviour, and women's valid anger and rebellion against their inferorized social position.

Appearance has always been implicated in this analysis. Witches were ever ugly, gentle maidens ever beautiful. Patriarchal approval went to the appropriate demeanour, shape and size, and women have undergone various forms of physical abuse to achieve acceptable femininity. From foot-binding through corset-lacing to crash-dieting women are compelled to suffer within a misogynist hegemony, the argument goes. If women cannot or will not placidly accept these confines then their abnormality will be punished by various forms of incarceration, torture or humiliation. Psychiatry, with its compulsory detention, its seclusion rooms and electric shock treatments, its lobotomies and chemical strait-jackets, is one system through which women are forced to conform. Alternatively the feminist social constructionists would argue that the very pursuit of physical standards imposed by patriarchy may actually cause depression, lowered self-esteem, eating disorders and, generally, poor mental health.

From Charlotte Perkins Gilman in the nineteenth century (1892) to Sylvia Plath (1963) and Janet Frame (1961), the autobiographical and semi-autobiographical literature of psychiatric repression has moved and angered successive generations of feminists. Jane Ussher (1991: 175), for example, writes of the central women in the work of Frame, Plath and Antonia White (1954):

> The women are incarcerated in monstrous and frightening institutions, as they are incarcerated in their rigid, feminine roles. They are naughty if they disobey, they are punished for misbehaving, they are washed, watched and wronged through their treatment as objects. The codes of femininity to which they must conform in order to escape are rigid, defined and decreed from above by those in control. Artificial beauty (successful

application of cosmetics) was applauded, passivity and gentleness are to replace the anger, the rantings, the depression for which these women are condemned.

And unless we conclude from this that, of course, it was a long time ago, and fictionalized and 'real' life, including gender oppression, has moved on, autobiographical work such as Kate Millett's (1990) and mental health survivors' contemporary accounts would tend to suggest that little has changed. Louise Roxanne Pembroke (1992), talking about what she called her 'psychiatrisation', found that, still, 'care with make-up and hair style were seen to be clear indicators of getting better' (Pembroke, 1992). Dianne Harrison, speaking in 1995 at a women and self-injury conference, reported an incident whereby she was physically dragged into the charge nurse's office and spent an hour being humiliated about her lack of self-care. She was told she would look prettier, better, if she plucked her eyebrows and put on make-up. These women share an unambivalent, feminist perspective on women's madness: that it is the expression of distress at the limitations and injustices of women's roles within patriarchy, frequently reinforced by further oppression within the system they had turned to for help.

In almost complete contrast, however, some work has been undertaken, mostly hospital-based and not specifically critical of the medical model, which attempts to consider the impact of mental illness on self-image. Its concern is with the fragmentation of a sense of self that such distress can bring about, and how the relationship with the self can be repaired. And within this medical discourse a quite different interpretation of the link between looks and mental health is offered: the use of beauty practices as treatments. Perutz (1970: 73), working in this area in the US in the 1970s and without apparent gender differentiation, identifies the overall aim of such therapies:

> By bringing the patient into the beauty culture, one hopes to restore his sense of self-respect and give him a public personality that will allow interaction with others and with his private self. Clothes, make-up, grooming offer control over role-playing; they permit the patient to put his antic disposition off because he can now be identified as a member of society.

In the USA at this time hairdressers were common and beauticians not unheard of in psychiatric hospitals. (Hairdressers were also standard in UK facilities.) Attendance was voluntary (as much as anything can be voluntary in settings of such intense and rigid power differentials), though this does not preclude the interpretation of this action entering into diagnostic and treatment decisions. Whether a woman attended beautification sessions or not may well be interpreted as indicative of her state of mental health. As well as this kind of *service* to patients, there also seem to have been active beauty therapy strategies for the *treatment* of patients. Beauty programmes, fashion groups, performance arts teaching that includes costume and make-up – a wide variety of activities seems to have been going on to help what were then called mental patients, supported by the general ideology that beauty therapy offered patients some kind of access to improving their self-image and a crack at 'repudiating unattractiveness, the badge of outcasts' as Perutz describes it.

Hospital hairdressers, though always popular, are a relatively rare phenomenon these days, but workers at institutions such as Rampton Special Hospital report that if the hairdresser is there women do not turn up for other activities, and any groups to do with issues of appearance are massively over-subscribed. The Mental Health Act Commission (MHAC), a UK special hospital authority established to protect the interests of compulsorily detained patients (and consequently making regular visits to psychiatric hospitals), was critical of how few opportunities there were for women to 'do looks'. It has gone on to advocate that 'one of the major needs is to enable women to feel they have some degree of control over their appearance, by being able to choose clothes, having access to cosmetics and hairdressing facilities' (Mental Health Act Commission, 1996: 88). Clearly the subject being referred to here is both gendered and active, exercising choices and controlling her appearance. Doing looks is conceptualized as a self-determining experience, of benefit to women suffering from mental health problems and in stark contrast to notions of a repressive and forced engagement which both furthers and symbolizes the gender oppression inflicted by patriarchy on a powerless subject.

The essence of the whole debate within second-wave feminism about the relationship between women's appearances and women's selves is encapsulated in these two contradictory positions, which in turn are underpinned by implicit differences in beliefs about the nature of female agency and subjectivity. For many early second-wave feminists, for whom the issue of looks served as symbol and rallying cry (picketing the Miss World competition and binning restrictive clothing were the inaugural demonstrations of the movement), women's appearances were not part of their subjectivity but a created image and essentially not the real woman who lay hidden underneath this mask. That there was a happy, almost utopian state in which women did not have to have any thoughts of appearance was a theme from the 1970s which is still potent in feminist argument, for example:

> The pleasure to be had from turning oneself into a living art object is some kind of power when power is in short supply, but it is not much compared to the pleasure of getting back forever inside the body; the pleasure of discovering sexual pride, a delight in a common female sexuality that overwhelms the divisions of 'beauty'; the pleasure of shedding self-consciousness and narcissism and guilt like a chain mail gown; the pleasure of freedom to forget all about it. (Wolf, 1990: 285)

Women's engagement with their looks is interpreted as imposed by patriarchy for men's gratification, as alienating of the potential alliance of woman with woman, and as a distracting diversion from a woman's real self, located internally. After centuries of looks being seen as reflective of women's personalities (Marwick, 1988), their looks can, within this strand of argument, be interpreted as some kind of external opponent, or even enemy, which may actively hinder women from finding their real selves. Just like the 'Caroline' of the dedication in Germaine Greer's *Female Eunuch* (1971), who 'jumped up from the dinner table in tears, crying that she wanted to be a person, went out and was one, despite her great beauty', women's looks are not conducive to active and satisfactory personhood.

It is possible to understand why there was an investment in this position. Worth being equated with physical attractiveness can be a very cruel and damaging system for many women (and all women over a certain age), and in 1970 the look was far more rigid and standardized with far less access to the tools to achieve it. However, there seem to me to be two major difficulties in adopting this approach. First it cannot explain any pleasure that women may take in their own engagement with their appearance, other than by resorting to implied notions of false consciousness or brainwashing, and second it assumes that appearance is detachable, something women can simply not have anything to do with if they choose to.

I would argue that women cannot exist as pure spirit. They have to live in real and visible forms called bodies (components: face, hair, skin, body shape and size). Only the most profoundly disturbed women experience themselves as detached and separate from their bodies, a state theorized as a psychotic dissolution of self, in, for example, the work of Melanie Klein (1946). For most women in this culture, the construction of gendered subjectivity involves necessarily engaging with the external, which usually means the visual (though other senses would be used if the subject was, for example, visually impaired). When Sophie, in *Sophie's World* (Gaarder, 1995), the teen philosophy best-seller, poses herself the question 'Who am I ?' she goes first to her mirror for an answer, which, I think, rings entirely true. Women looking in shop-windows to catch their own reflection are looking for something far more profound than instant ego-boosting, and it connects to their overall definition of who they are.

And if I 'do looks' because I cannot disconnect from my looks, and if the visual aspects of myself are implicated in identificatory processes (which I consider further later), then meanings which offer me some sense of choice within this set of givens become very important. If, as some feminist writing suggests, there is only the pain and humiliation of being the object of other's judgement to be had in this situation, then clearly women must suffer badly. Or if, as I considered above, mental health is judged on passive good-girl femininity which necessarily involves looking 'nice' in some stereotypical way, women will experience this as demeaning.

An analogy with something like intelligence or intellect is possible. I can 'own' my looks as mine, first and foremost, and not the property of someone else. In the same way, my intelligence is mine. My intelligence may be frustrating and limiting to me, but I may also have a sense of pride in it from time to time. It can be used to occupy me, to define things about me, to communicate who I am to other people, in ways more or less chosen by me. This applies equally to looks. And if this model is adopted then it does not immediately suggest that women will always be contented with their looks, but that a whole range of possibilities exist within which the active, female agent can manoeuvre. Of course, in the case of both looks and intelligence, being judged within someone else's system of meanings is also inevitable. Their meanings may reinforce, contradict, slightly dislodge (or any variant of these) my own, in an ongoing process of symbiotic meaning construction.

In the MHAC version, doing looks becomes a normalizing state. It seems to me to be grounded in the relatively modern view that the psychiatric experience should reflect as far as possible the 'real life' situation for the patient, and be as empowering as possible. Clearly they believe that women having opportunities to 'do looks' fits both these criteria. Women's mental health is best served by linking to this crucial self-driven identificatory process. And what seems at first an extraordinarily anachronistic suggestion on the part of the MHAC resonates with the rediscovery in feminist analysis of the active agency of women, either as well as or instead of the passivity of the victim.

It is not just from within the psychiatric institutions themselves that obvious links between women's looks and their mental health are evident, but within the discourses that have a substantial role in reinforcing the notion of normal and abnormal mentality/personality, particularly the proliferating discipline of psychology. The range of psychological explanations in this field may offer some helpful insights with which women can give meaning to their own actions and activities, but may also, via the implicit demarcation of what is a deviation from the normal, threaten and even pathologize women's relationships with their looks.

The underlying 'symptoms' of those who have cosmetic surgery, for example, have attracted much psychological research activity. The ever-increasing list of mental illnesses includes monosymptomatic hypochondriacal psychosis (Munro, 1988), neurosis and anxiety (Slater and Harris, 1992) and body dysmorphic disorder (Phillips *et al.*, 1993). The social psychological damage inflicted by childhood sexual abuse and family dysfunction are also seen as possible underlying causes (Bradbury, 1994).

Similarly the psychopathology of those who attempt to control their weight has become a topic for medical, psychological and popular dissection (Smart *et al.*, 1976; Orbach, 1978). Whereas once only the extreme and occasionally fatal condition of anorexia nervosa excited psychological and medical responses, the ever-broadening category of 'eating disorders' ensures that almost any weight control activities are likely to be defined as abnormal. And of course these kinds of definitional activities build on a whole tradition of medicine and psycho-medicine interpreting and intervening in women's involvement with their own bodies. The danger of this is that in the end labelling such activities as losing weight or having liposuction as 'abnormal' or even 'ill' may invalidate positive feelings and instead make women feel guilty, isolated and deviant.

Such pathologization may ignore the link between control of appearance and overall sense of identity for women. For some women it may well be the case that putting themselves under the surgeon's knife is due to body hatred based on past traumatic experiences. But the alternative explanation, that the decision to have cosmetic surgery may be the rational choice of an active, thinking (female) adult, aware that she is living in a highly visual consumer culture needs more serious consideration. Kathy Davis, in her recent study (1995) of women undergoing cosmetic surgery, found that it was the desire to perceive themselves as ordinary and normal that precisely drove their decision to have the operation. Certainly they spoke with considerable unhappiness of the particular feature of their bodies, but it did not appear to be pathology or generalized body hatred driving their actions. Nor, interestingly, did it seem to be a quest for super-beauty, or a desire to hang on to or attract a man.

Similarly, for some women the issue of losing weight may well be no more psychologically significant than the issue of quite consciously eating to excess over Christmas or a holiday period which preceded the diet. The intake of calories in rich Western cultures is defined by social practices of excess, not just individual psychology, though the negotiation of this can become highly personal. This is of course a problematic area. Dieting and serious eating disorders such as anorexia and bulimia have often been uncritically assumed within much feminist writing to be the same kind of phenomena with different degrees of severity. And although there may well be some overlap and some grey areas, the notion that a grown-up woman dieting (perhaps not eating sweet things for two weeks because her jeans are too tight after some period of celebration) is engaged in the same kind of project as a teenager weighing five stone and eating nothing because she wants to starve to death is not convincing. In psychiatric wards now there are young women being compulsorily detained so that they can be force-fed to stop them dying from chronic eating disorders. It seems almost insulting to suggest that trotting off to Weight Watchers once a week can be considered in the same way.

But because they do share the activity of controlling food intake it is tempting to see them as similar phenomena. Theoretical explanations such as that of Orbach (1978), which focuses on eating as women's attempt to heal the pain of both the early experiences of a disturbed mother-daughter relationship and the ongoing situation of inferiorized female status and consciousness within patriarchy, or that of Chernin (1986), which looks at the impact of Western mind-body dualism, the connection between women and the denigrated 'body' and the need then to demonstrate control (mind) of this to be approved in a male world – both offer universal explanations that cover all kinds of eating control, and incidentally leave one questioning why all women in the West do not have eating disorders.

Some recent writing on the subject, though, has challenged this kind of universalism. Gimlin (1994), for example, suggests that Orbach's and Chernin's cultural explanations tend to see women with eating disorders as holy martyrs to the feminist cause, symbolic of and representing the suffering of all women within patriarchy. She proposes instead the notion of anorexics as overconformists to patriarchal notions of appropriate femininity, using extreme strategies to deal with their difficulties with the female role. This does offer some way of differentiating 'usual' strategies, such as dieting, and extreme strategies, such as starving, while allowing that the overall project has the same context: the active negotiation of 'doing woman'.

I would argue, then, that some forms of dieting are most usefully interpreted as women actively negotiating embodied personhood, part of constructing a gendered identity – 'making themselves up' – and precisely in tune with the late twentieth-century *Zeitgeist* of making every part of life an ongoing, active project. The tendency to 'make' rather than 'have' or 'be', as in making and then constantly improving relationships, subjecting our homes to ongoing DIY, enlisting expert advice on how to be better parents, better lovers, better at our jobs, more fulfilled, more sorted-out, etc., etc. is so all pervasive that it would be quite noteworthy if women (and men) did not approach their bodies in exactly the same way. As Giddens (1991: 7) comments:

What might appear as a wholesale movement towards the narcissistic cultivation of bodily appearance is in fact an expression of concern lying much deeper actively to 'construct' and control the body. Here there is an integral connection between bodily development and lifestyle ...

The body as the infinitely improvable ongoing project of the active gendered subject then, or as the site of oppression in a patriarchal society? It is of course an unhelpful dichotomy. For any particular woman it could be experienced variously as both these things, and a whole range of other meanings may also be available. Looks engagement/body alteration may be rebellion in minor or major ways, a strategy for re-identifying self at periods of major life transition, or even an art form, for example in the work of the French performance artist Orlan (1994). Other meanings may be equally important. The tendency to equate looks with either oppression or psychopathology is simply too limited.

The critical label of 'vanity' and its psychoanalytical counterpart 'narcissism', and the widespread condemnation of forms of self-love and self-appreciation, is, I would argue, of considerable importance to how women feel about themselves and how they feel about their feelings about themselves. If women internalize this society's highly critical views of 'doing looks' then they will inevitably feel confused and unhappy. Although appearing as young and beautiful as possible could be seen as the Holy Grail of the late twentieth century, this culture has an historical, Christian and misogynist tradition of condemning women's interest in their looks as pride and vanity, while still making strong links between being beautiful and being good. Research by Dion *et al.* (1972), for example, showed that the personal attributes ascribed to photographs of stereotypically 'attractive' people were mostly positive (kind, friendly, successful) and those ascribed to 'unattractive' people were negative (lazy, unfriendly, unsuccessful). This builds on an inheritance from fairy stories and folk-tales from the past, whereby it is evident that a beautiful face confirms a good, kind and generous nature; ugly is always evil, like Cinderella's sisters and all wicked witches. But the catch was, and perhaps still is, that you had to be naturally and unselfconsciously beautiful. To resort to mirrors or any contrivance indicated an evil heart. Witness the wicked Queen in 'Snow

White', whose corrupt nature is manifest in the unforgivable sin of self-appreciation.

To return to Davis's cosmetic surgery research (1995), it is quite noticeable that the women she interviews all condemn the notion of having plastic surgery to try to be beautiful, and are scornful of women who engage in this and other activities just to improve their appearance. They do not interpret their own activities in this way, and Davis suggests that the influence of Dutch Calvinism in the USA is such that obvious or excessive vanity is unacceptable; such a motive would be inadmissible to self or others. Looks cannot be 'just for pleasure' a situation which, I would suggest, is entirely replicated in other northern European cultures with Protestant and, in England's case, Puritan heritages.

As far as any empirical research in this area goes, a dilemma is immediately opened up. One suspects that women are unable to express appreciation of their own appearance, at least in the present tense, and indeed my own experience of running a pilot group session to examine the issue of women's subjective experience in relation to 'doing looks' entirely reinforces this. The eight women could only discuss themes, such as how their looks impacted on other aspects of their lives by distancing themselves from the discussion, by generalization, or by discussing their teenage self, not the current version. My attempts to focus the discussion in the here and now of our appearances were politely side-stepped.

The inability to have open discussion and debate can lead to a very narrow range of interpretations. For example, interviews with younger women about their looks (especially weight) are a recurring feature of women's 'pages', programming and magazines. The interviewees inevitably express discontent with their bodies. The usual feminist and increasingly popular interpretation of this is that this reflects the damage caused by the mass circulation of images of impossibly beautiful and skinny models. (Coward, 1984; Winship, 1978). However I would suggest an equally valid interpretation. It could be that for a young woman to voice the notion that she has a great body, lovely hair, good skin or whatever, is out of the question. There is no language of physical self-appreciation, no discursive space for self-admiration.

Vanity is unacceptable. White, heterosexist northern European cultural baggage expressed in various ways by various means, including peer-group pressure, makes self-criticism and discontent the only available position women can take in relation to their own looks, although there are suggestions that this may be a different experience in other cultures where there may be room for women to celebrate their bodies (Leeds, 1994).

But even if, standardly, I cannot admit it, do I actually like looking at myself and generally 'doing looks'? Perhaps I need to look at myself to identify myself? Could it be perhaps that it is in relationship to this surface, this exteriorized version, that a kind of integration of self happens? How best can this be understood?

One possible area of inquiry may focus on women looking at each other, and at the objectified women that have some representative resonance with self. Women consume images of women; they are bombarded with them but they also seek them out. Countless women buy women's magazines, almost invariably with a picture of a woman – dressed-up, made-up and looking good – on the cover. Women watch other women in public places and social situations. Some watch beauty competitions. Young women often idolize female pop stars and models. Women look at themselves in all kinds of mirror surfaces, and in photographs. This has been variously theorized as the active internal male subject in our being watching the passive female object, or as us identifying with this position. It has also been taken as women identifying with the women they are watching, to measure themselves against and/or to learn how to be like them (Betterton, 1987).

The third and most recent strand of this debate, which is perhaps applicable to consuming images of other women and of self, addresses the issue of women's visual pleasure. Stacey (1995), for example, in considering women viewing 'movie stars' considers the various kinds of active pleasure available via the consumption of images of glamorous women. She also positions her interviewees not just in front of film screens but also in front of their mirrors using these images in a process of ongoing identity construction, broadening out considerably the notion of 'identificatory' processes in relation to women viewing women. In front of the screen identification encompasses the perhaps homoerotic pleasures of fantasy and idealization:

> Thus the processes here involve the negotiation between self and other, but also between self and the imaginary self which

temporarily merges with the fictionalised feminine subject [the star] to test out new possibilities. The recognition of a potential self in the fictionalised situation, based on some similarity between star and spectator, is operating simultaneously with a desire to maintain the difference between self and ideal.

In front of the mirror identification takes on a meaning more akin to copying:

> The impact of the film on the spectator caused her to desire to resemble the ideal physically. In front of a reflection of herself the spectator attempts to close the gap between her own image and her ideal image, by trying to produce a new image, more like her ideal.

The idea that women not only take pleasure in looking at women, but use these images to take pleasure in engaging with their own appearances perhaps offers some substance to the possibility of an enjoyable, allowable and creative engagement with the only self we can see. This of course stresses only the visual aspects of identification and indeed 'doing looks' in all its ramifications entirely negates the crucial embodied identification standardly undertaken by those for whom vision is unavailable. Tactile pleasures and identifications as well as the primarily visual may offer identificatory pleasure via literal and metaphorical mirrors, and indeed various literary and artistic encounters underline a highly self-contained, absorbing and rewarding encounter, particularly in relation to the intense identificatory period of adolescence (La Belle, 1988).

This takes my argument into a theoretical overlap with the psychoanalytical concept of narcissism. It is a rather slippery theoretical area, with some quite fundamental issues, such as why women rather than men sustain these tendencies into problematic adulthood, not easily amenable to a condensed and comprehensive analysis within Freudian discourse. The basic mechanism at work here though, of the split that allows the subject to take their ego as a love object offering the duality of object and subject within one person, and hence allowing a theoretical space between the internal and the external, and between the viewer and viewed, has proved to be fruitful ground for work on women and their appearance in cultural studies and philosophy, as well as the social sciences. That there is a relationship between the visual and the construction of subjectivity is crucial to this, as is some notion that an integrated female identity necessitates the incorporation of the external, the vision, into the identity. 'Men have faces but women are their faces', Susan Sontag (1972: 34) has famously suggested, offering an interpretation of this relationship at once both indissoluble and unequivocal. Others have seen this as a far more problematic and hazy situation. Just who it is lurking about in there (in here) appraising whom is far from settled.

In the tradition of Freudian psychoanalysis, Simone de Beauvoir (1949: 361) and some later psychoanalytical theorists have suggested that at least in adolescence this 'doubling' of self is an important process, but that the inevitable outcome of these feelings of no longer coinciding with oneself is the realization that 'the stranger who inhabits my consciousness is really me'. The mirror-based knowledge of and love of self undergone in adolescence is a healthy, indeed necessary phase of self-love and self-construction, though de Beauvoir is equally definite about the destructive pathology of the adult female narcissist, whom she ultimately condemns.

This is not without challenge within feminist Freudian psychoanalysis. For example, Kofman (1987) offers a far more positive interpretation of narcissism as conferring on women an independence which men are ultimately desirous of. Grounding her analysis in Freud's *On Narcissism: An Introduction* (1914), Kofman suggests that the differential development, intensified at puberty, which allows a woman to take herself as her love object (unlike men who must love 'the other') gives women distinct advantages, 'particularly should beauty develop'. She argues, extrapolating from Freud, that this confers not only a compensatory self-sufficiency on women, as she can offer love to herself, but also a high degree of desirability:

> Such women exert the greatest charm [*Reiz*] over men, not only for aesthetic reasons ... but also because of some interesting psychological constellations. Indeed it seems quite evident that a person's narcissism exerts a great attraction over those who have relinquished their own narcissism and are in quest of object love. (211)

Kofman's analysis is, however, very unusual, and work such as de Beauvoir's has been far more influential in setting what seems to me to be a far from neutral tone in feminist discussion of the issue of narcissism.

Following a tradition, grounded in psychoanalytic thought, which always assumes that the subject of the gaze is male and the object female, contemporary feminist philosopher Sandra Bartky (1990) interprets narcissism in a way which moves it even closer than de Beauvoir did to its critical, popular usage. Knowing that as a woman she is going to be judged on her looks, Bartky argues, she learns to appraise herself first, and it is this that produces a duality of female consciousness; the gaze of the other is internalized. Woman becomes see-er and seen. But like Berger (1972) and Mulvey (1975) and later theorists of representation this see-er must necessarily be male, and this other a generalized male other, in the form of the (internalized) fashion beauty complex (a patriarchal/capitalist structure using ideology to enforce consumption), an interpretation that finds its substance outside psychoanalytic discourse and grounds the notion of 'other' in a value system which rates it negatively, rather than the 'that which is not I' neutrality of de Beauvoir and the psychoanalytical theorists.

Bartky's women are under constant scrutiny from an internalized representative of the fashion-beauty complex, objectifying them and subjecting them to impossible standards and criticisms, allowing not for narcissistic pleasure but only for shame and narcissistic damage. But must an internalized other who constantly scrutinizes one's appearance necessarily be some manifestation of the beauty-fashion complex? Must it inevitably be a negative message that I am offered? Could the internalized other of this version of gendered subjectivity perhaps be instead the introjected loving parent, adoring boyfriend, benevolent woman friend or friendly mirror telling me I look great, and hence offering a considerable degree of narcissistic pleasure? This may be worth speculating on, though the tone of moral disapproval seeping out from both de Beauvoir's and Bartky's discussion of narcissism may incite even more women to deny their own possible pleasure in themselves than seventeenth-century religious attitudes.

Some strands in feminism – from the philosophical work I have just briefly considered to the populist polemic of Naomi Wolf (1990) and spanning fifty years of feminist writing (though with a concentration in the early 1970s) – may have reinforced the message that active engagement with appearance is unacceptable. During early second-wave feminism, the politicization (in the sense of exposing the politics of) of issues concerning looks, women were offered the opportunity for a re-interpretation of being 'feminine': looking 'pretty' was not just some natural by-product of neutral mating behaviour but one more highly gendered and oppressive feature of Western Patriarchal Capitalism.

Having had this pointed out to them, feminists came to believe that the cessation of make-up and high heels, of frocks and hairdos, was the liberated response. And some even managed it, but many did not, or did not for long. The personal may well have become political but this did not stop it also being personal, and for some feminists the sense of shame and failure of nerve at still wanting to 'do looks' despite its oppressive nature was experienced at a personal and isolating level. What had seemed perfectly straightforward turned out to be very complicated.

As I discussed earlier, there had been an assumption that doing looks was a rather trivial pastime that women could easily, and would want to, get rid of. That women were divisible into 'real' selves, located somewhere non-specific inside their bodies, and that their bodies were inauthentic, compromising, misleading and distorting this real self was the ontological underpinning. The critique of this kind of mind-body dualism is now well established within feminism, fuelled by postmodern feminist thought. That body and mind are not so easily detachable, indeed that the dualism itself is implicated in limiting women's ways of being is frequently voiced. One popular strand of this may be the newly privileged status of all things holistic, in which feeling good about your body is inseparable from feeling good about yourself. Similarly a generation's understanding of the process of representation allows no space for women to delude themselves with the notion of invisibility. Their appearance will not simply go away. Meanings will be made, signifiers will be signified, whether the 'author' wishes them to be or not. Inevitably women (and of course men) must project a visual self and indeed throughout the duration of second-wave feminism the value of the visual presentation of self has massively increased, not receded.

However, the kind of approach that argues that Wonderbras and red lipstick present no contradictions for feminists seems equally reductionist. To simply collude with the equating of women's social value with their ability to create a version of themselves that approximates a studio-constructed fantasy vision of womanhood, which I would argue is pretty much the context within which we are struggling, is basically disengaging with any feminist principles or practice. If women are to gain anything positive from the activity of 'doing looks', an activity which cannot be avoided, then they must be given every encouragement to value their knowledge and skills, and indeed the outcomes of this range of activities as highly as possible. A whole range of meanings need to be acknowledged and credited, meanings that could be appropriate for women of fifty as well as those of twenty.

A new language of self-appreciation, not based on approximation to Munroe or Moss, or whoever is 'the face', and certainly not self-deprecating and critical, would in itself be liberating. If women could ascribe various meanings to doing looks they might not then automatically feel forced and demeaned by patriarchal systems (like psychiatry) to prove a traditional gendered passivity by traditional gendered presentation of self. For women to feel powerful and in control, to feel a sense of agency and competence (all, I would argue, essential for mental health), doing looks can no longer be viewed as an optional extra but rather as a central identificatory process which can offer meanings such as pleasure, creative expression and satisfaction provided that women can appropriate a discursive space in which to contradict the silencing discourses of vanity, abnormality, superficiality and unsisterliness.

References

Bartky, S. L. (1990) *Femininity and Domination: Studies in the Phenomenology of Oppression*. London: Routledge.

Berger, J. (1972) *Ways of Seeing*. London: Penguin.

Betterton, R. (ed.) (1987) *Looking On: Images of Femininity in the Visual Arts and Media*. London: Pandora.

Bradbury, E. (1994) The psychology of aesthetic plastic surgery. *Aesthetic Plastic Surgery*, 18: 301–5.

Brook, E. and Davis, A. (eds) (1985) *Women, the Family and Social Work*. London: Tavistock.

Brownmillar, S. (1986) *Femininity*. London: Paladin.

Caskey, N. (1986) Interpreting anorexia nervosa. In S. R. Suliman (ed.), *The Female Body in Western Culture*. Cambridge, MA: Harvard University Press.

Chernin, K. (1981) *The Obsession: Reflections on The Tyranny of Slenderness*. New York: Harper.

Chernin, K. (1986) *The Hungry Self: Women, Eating and Identity.* London: Virago.

Chesler, P. (1972) *Women and Madness.* New York: Avon.

Coward, R. (1984) *Female Desire: Women's Sexuality Today.* London: Tavistock.

Davis, K. (1995) *Reshaping the Female Body: The Dilemma of Plastic Surgery.* London: Routledge.

de Beauvoir, S. (1949) *The Second Sex.* London: Pan (1988).

Dion, K., Berscheid, E. and Walster, E. (1972) What is beautiful is good. *Journal of Personality and Social Psychology* **24**(3): 285–90.

Edholm, F. (1988) Beyond the mirror: women's self-portraits. In F. Bonner (ed.), *Imagining Women: Cultural Representations and Gender.* London: Polity Press/Open University Press.

Frame, J. (1961) *Faces in the Water.* London: Women's Press (1980).

Freud, S. (1914) On narcissism. In S. Freud, *On Metapsychology.* Harmondsworth: Penguin (1984).

Gaarder, J. (1995) *Sophie's World.* New York: Pheonix.

Giddens, A. (1991) *Modernity and Self-Identity: Self and Society in the Late Modern Age.* Cambridge: Polity.

Gilman Perkins, C. (1892) *The Yellow Wallpaper.* London: Virago Press (1981).

Gimlin, D. (1994) The anorexic as over-conformist: towards a reinterpretation of eating disorders. In K. A. Callagher (ed.), *Ideals of Feminine Beauty: Philosophical, Social and Cultural Dimensions.* New York: Greenwood Press.

Greer, G. (1971) *The Female Eunuch.* London: Paladin.

Harrison, D. (1995) Women and self injury. Unpublished paper, Women and Self Injury Conference, Bristol.

Klein, M. (1946) Notes on some schizoid mechanisms. In M. Klein, *Envy, Gratitude and Other Works.* New York: Delta (1975).

Kofman, S. (1987) The narcissistic woman. In T. Moi (ed.), *French Feminist Thought.* Oxford: Blackwell.

La Belle, J. (1988) *Herself Beheld: The Literature of the Looking Glass.* Ithaca: Cornell University Press.

Leeds, M. (1994) Young African-American women and the language of beauty. In K. A. Callagher (ed.), *Ideals of Feminine Beauty: Philosophical, Social and Cultural Dimensions.* New York: Greenwood Press.

Marwick, A. (1994) *Beauty in History: Society, Politics and Personal Appearance, c1500 to the Present.* London: Thames and Hudson.

Mental Health Act Commission (1996) *Sixth Biennial Report, 1993–1995.* London: HMSO.

Millett, K. (1990) *The Looney-bin Trip.* New York: Simon and Schuster.

Mulvey, L. (1975) Visual pleasure and narrative cinema. *Screen,* **16**(3): 6–18.

Munro, A. (1988) Monosymptomatic hypochondriacal psychosis. *British Journal of Psychiatry*, **153**: 37–40.

Orbach, S. (1978) *Fat Is a Feminist Issue*. London: Hamlyn.

Orlan, H. (1994) *The Body as Site*. Seduced and Abandoned Conference. London: ICA. (AV).

Pembroke, L. R. (ed.) (1992) *Eating Distress*. Bristol: Survivors Speak Out.

Perutz, K. (1970) *Beyond the Looking Glass: America's Beauty Culture*. New York: Morrow.

Phillips, K. A., McElroy, S. L., Keck, P. E., Pope, H. G. and Hudson, J. I. (1993) Body dysmorphic disorder: thirty cases of imagined ugliness. *American Journal of Psychiatry*, **150**: 2.

Plath, S. (1963) *The Bell Jar*. London: Faber and Faber.

Slater, R. and Harris, D. L. (1992) Are rhinoplasty patients potentially mad? *British Journal of Plastic Surgery*, **45**: 307—10.

Smart, D. E., Beaumont, P.J.V. and George, G.C.W. (1976) Some personality characteristics of patients with anorexia nervosa. *British Journal of Psychiatry*, **128**: 57–9.

Sontag, S. (1972) The double standard of ageing. *New York Times: Saturday Review of Society*, 23 September.

Stacey, J. (1995) *Star Gazing*. London: Routledge.

Russell, D. (1995) *Women, Madness and Medicine*. Cambridge: Polity Press.

Ussher, J. (1991) *Women's Madness: Misogyny or Mental Illness?* Hemel Hempstead: Harvester Wheatsheaf.

White, A. (1954) *Beyond the Glass*. London: Virago (1979).

Winship, J. (1978) A woman's world. In The Women's Studies Group, Centre for Contemporary Cultural Studies, *Women Take Issue*. London: Hutchinson.

Wolf, N. (1990) *The Beauty Myth*. London: Vintage.

7

Revolting Women: The Body in Comic Performance

Jane Arthurs

My focus will be on Jo Brand in *Through the Cakehole* (Channel 4, 1994–96) and Patsy Stone in *Absolutely Fabulous* (BBC2, 1992–94 and BBC1, 1995–96) as examples of grotesque performances which are both idiosyncratic and culturally determined. My attention was drawn to these two performers by the extremes of adulation and revulsion which their performances have provoked. In trying to explain these emotional reactions, which go far beyond a simple appreciation or rejection of their humour, I wanted to understand the cultural violations these women represent and how the intensity of pleasure or revulsion can be understood in relation to the social and psychological processes of repression involved in the maintenance of bodily decorum and the pleasurable release of bodily desires. In relation to the body, knowing how to behave is both a question of controlling bodily posture and movements and also controlling the language used to refer to bodily activities and processes, which together constitute bodily decorum. Differences in the rules of decorum between the nations and cultures of the modern world and the traceable changes which have occurred in the course of modernization in Europe point to a flexibility in the particular forms which these conventions take. Yet part of the power of transgressing these rules of decorum lies in the depth of feeling with which these codes of behaviour are maintained. Indecorum invokes disgust and revulsion in non-comic contexts. The transformation of disgust into humour is the provenance of the grotesque, and it is the use of the grotesque body in women's comedy which will inform much of my analysis of contemporary women performers.

I want first to consider the more general question of why the transgression of bodily decorum makes us laugh and what this means in social and cultural terms. Freud's explanation is that joking, and the laughter it stimulates, is one way in which we retrieve and enjoy infantile pleasures (Freud, 1991). The erotic and narcissistic wishes of the infant have been repressed into the unconscious in the course of adapting to the moral and social codes of the adult world. The infant's unorganized polymorphous sexuality, including oral, anal, autoerotic and incestuous desires, has to be organized into the norms of bourgeois sexuality, and defined by an orientation to heterosexual genital sex conducted in private. Similarly, the narcissistic wish to be all powerful, in control and the centre of attention gradually gives way to the demands of reality and a greater sense of humility in a world which demands that we fit in with other people and a set of pre-ordained rules and prohibitions. Thus Freud explains the pleasure of jokes as arising from the momentary release of the psychic repression which maintains these prohibitions. Jokes are a socially acceptable way of expressing those infantile wishes, wishes which originate in the bodily drives and which precede language and rational thought. It is a theory which emphasizes that there is a universal experience involved in the processes of maturation in which the learning of bodily control is fundamental, which is why it is of relevance to the kind of 'body' humour I am considering here. This is not to say that the forms in which this takes place are the same in all societies, or for different groups within each society. The formation of the specific rules governing bodily decorum in modern European societies can be traced as one of the historical processes of modernization.

Freud was writing at the end of the nineteenth century, by which time the 'civilizing process' which attached shame to bodily indecorum was firmly in place. Elias, in tracing the historical transformations in attitudes to bodily decorum from the medieval to the modern age in Europe, attends to the minutiae of changing codes of behaviour within a broader explanation of the political and social significance of those changes (Elias, 1994). Increasing emphasis was placed on the rational control of emotion and the pacification of the physical expressions of emotions, particularly the expression of aggression and sexual desire. Bodily functions such as eating, sleeping and excretion became increasingly regulated so that individuals in general were much more physically separate from each other. Communal eating with the fingers out of a central dish and communal sleeping ceased to be the norm; increasing emphasis was placed on keeping sexual activity hidden from children. Activities which in the medieval period would have been performed quite openly on the street or in a room full of company (such as urinating, farting, defecating, spitting or clearing the nose) were privatized completely or made more discreet. The maintenance of bodily decorum became a sign of being 'civilized'; to break the rules was to be subject to external approbation and disgust which then became internalized as shame. At another level there were rules of bodily decorum which were developed to differentiate the barely 'civilized', the mass of the population, from the upper classes. Their superiority was signified through their manners which demonstrated delicacy of feeling and heightened aesthetic sensibilities. Gracefulness demanded conformity to a set of aesthetic norms in dress, in movement and in speech which indicated a total 'ease' born out of an assured sense of superiority.

These distinctions between the civilized and uncivilized, and between the upper and lower classes, were important in structuring the culture of the newly emerging middle classes of the industrial revolution. Unrestrained indulgence in the pleasures of the body became associated with a subordinated culture of the people that was increasingly separate from the respectable culture of the middle classes. And even for the lower classes industrialization meant that the body became subject to the disciplined regimes of the factory. It was only the increasingly marginal aristocracy who escaped the bodily disciplines of industrial society in a hedonistic lifestyle which required both leisure time and material resources to maintain.

According to Elias, the transition from a feudal society to a modern state required the suppression of the immediate expression of physical aggression, partly because the greater interdependence of people demanded more restraint between them and partly because the right to use violence became centralized in the state. The monopolization of physical force reduces the fear one man has for another but at the same time reduces the possibility of pleasurable emotional release. Life becomes less dangerous but also less emotional and pleasurable and the tension between people is internalized as a tension between the superego and the unconscious. Films, books and dreams provide a vicarious

139

substitute but this only partly satisfies the drives. The inhibited drives may emerge in neurosis and compulsive behaviour, or in laughter.

Bakhtin, like Elias, was interested in how, in the change from a medieval to a modern society, distinctions in class have transformed the culture of the people in a process which progressively represses the expression of spontaneous bodily drives and simultaneously diminishes the communal celebration of the ambivalence of the physical world, subject as it is to the natural cycles of birth and death (Bakhtin, 1984). He looked back to the medieval carnival as a utopian expression of the communal desires of the people expressed through masquerade and their unrestrained participation in the pleasures of the flesh: feasting, drunkenness, sexual licentiousness, violence – all were allowable within this licensed space of a few days. Unrestrained laughter at the inversions of the masquerade, the vulgarities and the clowning was part of the loosening of bodily restraint. But as the new regulation of bodily habits became more widespread this culture of the people became progressively marginalized and condemned by the emerging middle class, backed by the church; the low corporeal humour of carnival lost its social inclusiveness and became instead associated with all that was to be excluded from the polite, legitimate culture of the bourgeoisie. But the exclusion of carnival from the dominant culture did not do away with the desires which carnival expressed.

> As Stallybrass and White argue, the repression of the boisterous margin goes hand in hand with an unconscious desire for exactly the activities which are being repressed, and the more they are subjected to this marginalisation and repression, the more tainted they are with the 'dirt' of their origins, the more attractive they become ... those who adhere to respectable morality are obliged to condemn what they most want and want what they most condemn. (Palmer, 1994: 130)

Thus we can explain the potent mixture of disgust and desire produced by the transgression of bodily decorum and the relegation of body humour to 'low' forms of popular culture which offer a 'licensed space' for the expression of these desires.

These histories of the transformation of the cultural meanings of the body and the consequent relegation of 'body' humour to a marginalized culture of the people say relatively little about how this process affected women. Elias's non-gendered account fails to differentiate the way in which emotional repression operates in men and women. Where men have to suppress the expression of emotions signifying 'weakness', such as fear or sadness, women have had to repress the expression of their sexual and aggressive drives more fully than men. Not only have men had greater freedom to express physical aggression in the privacy of their own homes (there is still widespread domestic violence which escaped, until recently, the public prohibition on aggressive behaviour) but they have also had access to a wide range of representations of male aggression which, in Elias's view, is the modern form through which these fundamental bodily drives are released. This has not been true for women except through their ability to identify with the behaviour of male protagonists. Whether in sport, feature films or comedy the prevalence of male aggressive behaviour, whether amongst men or directed at women, has left women without much space for the vicarious pleasures of identifying with a female aggressor. Where fantasies of female violence have been shown in feature films there has been a huge public outcry based on the assumption that women are above such behaviour, even above the desire for aggressive fantasies, and must remain so to protect civilization from descent into barbarism. This is a measure of the extent to which women are still regarded as the moral guardians of society whose behaviour must set the standard for men, acting as a kind of generalized super ego for the unruly id of the masculine psyche.[1]

This is why comedy is an important arena for the expression of female fantasies of physical aggression. The ambivalence of the 'licensed transgression' institutionalized by comedy – a cultural form within legitimized public spaces, where the unthinkable and the undoable can be thought and done without retribution either from society in general or the individual psyche – has allowed for a growing cultural expression of women's anger, especially the anger generated by their experience of subordination. Dressed up in jokes and comedy, this aggression can find a place in popular culture which is sufficiently unthreatening to gain a space in the mainstream without much controversy. For a while, in the early nineties, Friday nights on Channel Four was taken over by stroppy, unruly women who literally and metaphorically 'took up space' in the schedules.[2] In one sense this is women claiming the same rights as men to let their hair down on a Friday night, indulge in unrestrained expressions of bodily pleasure in the company of their own sex, as traditionally has been men's right on a Friday night as a release from the constraints of the working week. But it could be seen, more depressingly perhaps, as a recognition that while the men are down at the pub having a good time there's a captive audience of women ripe for jokes which go some way towards expressing their sense of grievance and hostility towards men. Whichever way, it is a refusal to let men have all the fun, leaving the women with the less immediate compensations offered by moral superiority.

The female grotesque

For Bakhtin, whereas men transgress in their actions, women transgress in their very being by challenging any notion of a body with fixed boundaries. In the secretions of menstruation, and the processes of pregnancy, childbirth and lactation any clear distinction between inside or outside is lost. Women's bodies are always in process. The maternal body in particular is the grotesque body par excellence. The word grotto-esque (like a cave) also refers to the womb. Bakhtin's analysis, though reinforcing cultural assumptions about women's identification with the biological processes of their bodies, has formed the basis for work in feminist cultural studies on the trope of the 'unruly woman' and the transgressive potential of the female grotesque.[3] The pre-modern carnival is referred to as a source of images for contemporary women's refusal of the constraints imposed by the social and cultural hierarchies of modernity. The masquerade of carnival created a space within which the social hierarchies of the everyday world were inverted, in which beggars could be kings and women could be men. The unruly woman inverts the power relations of gender by breaking the codes of bodily decorum. These codes in modern societies construct an ideal of bourgeois femininity that demands of 'respectable' women an even greater restraint than men in the expression of spontaneous bodily desires. Women's femininity depends on bodily decorum even in the privacy of family relationships. In public, any indecorum is a sign of lack of respectability which, for women, is always a sexual category associated with promiscuity or prostitution. In transgressing these codes of femininity, the unruly woman demands the right to the satisfaction of her own bodily desires; she eats in excess and has unbridled sexual appetites. She demands attention by making a spectacle of herself, talking loudly, dressing flamboyantly and taking up space with her size and loose, energetic movements.

In adapting carnival theory to a modern context where mass participatory carnivals have given way to the privatized consumption of spectacle, for example in the experience of watching television, the body is an object of spectacle, not part of a physical experience where all the senses of touch, smell and kynesics are involved. Here then the body is experienced as an object of sight and as an object to be spoken about. The female body as grotesque spectacle is analysed by Russo (1995: 23) in the context of a consumer market economy in which one female body or body part is differentiated from another in a quest to maximize market potential. In that differentiation we have at one end of the spectrum the female grotesque who is marginalized because she is fat and low class. This is the female body as monstrous and lacking, the 'stunted' body who transgresses in her being. She is the passive repository of all that is denied by the sleek and prosperous bourgeois.

> Heavier with projections than with flesh she siphons off guilt, desire and denial, leaving her idealised counterpart behind: the kind of woman one sees on billboards, sleek and streamlined like the cars she is often used to advertise, bathed in the radiance of the commodity. (Ellman, quoted in Russo, 1995: 24)[4]

At the other end of the spectrum are female grotesques who transgress the norms of femininity by denying the limits of their female bodies, embracing the ambivalent possibilities of carnival through masculinization. Here she takes the figure of the female philobat[5] as exemplary, the aeroplane pilot or the trapeze artist, who transgresses feminine decorum by leaving the earth, traversing space, risking her body in the performance of daring stunts. This differentiation between the 'stunted' body of the passive female grotesque who transgresses in her being and the 'stunting' body of the active female grotesque who is 'up there, out there' (Russo, 1995: 17–51) transgressing in her actions has been used here to analyse the grotesque performances of women comics on television.

In doing so it provides a way of thinking about the interaction between a number of contradictory forces in the construction of feminine modes of performance. The demands of a market economy for individuation and originality in performance, the creation of a unique comic persona, is partly dependent on the differentiation of body types through anatomical difference and partly on characteristic ways of using and of referring to the body in performance.[6] Working against this process of differentiation is the dependence of humour on relatively stable cultural expectations, the conventions of genre and gender which form the ground-rules against which humorous deviation can be recognized.[7] However, this stability is always in interaction with forces for change, thus giving importance to the historical specificity of the cultural context in which 'jokes cluster around points of rupture in the social order where the dominant discourse is already giving way to a counter-discourse' (Tulloch, 1990: 250). These contradictory forces are readable in the comic performances of female grotesques as they negotiate the ambivalent possibilities of the 'unruly woman' image in a context where feminism is a well established, though contested, counter-discourse.

Patsy in *Absolutely Fabulous*

Any performance will be read in relation to an already established set of generic conventions; generically, *Absolutely Fabulous* is a farcical domestic sitcom in which the outrageous and the deviant are the expected norm. What creates the difference, and what marks this sitcom as of significance in the development of the genre, is that the family grouping at the centre of the comedy is entirely composed of women. Already then the basic premise marks the women as 'unruly'; they are economically independent and live outside and beyond the control of men, who exist only as walk-on parts when needed for plot purposes. This comes at a time when anxieties over single mothers and absent fathers have reached a crescendo in the media more generally as the number of women-headed households continues to rise. This development in the basic scenario of the domestic sitcom is a significant aspect of the context for interpreting Edina and Patsy's grotesque performances. These women are not funny because of temporary subversions of patriarchal control, they are funny (or for some people horrifying) because they are permanently beyond control. The demand for greater decorum comes from a teenage daughter,

Saffie, who by definition has no ultimate power in the household and who can only comment from the sidelines. In yet another inversion, her youthful but sensible presence provides a contrast which accentuates the fact that Edina and Patsy have patently failed to become more respectable with age.

Although both the two main characters can be regarded as grotesques, it is Patsy I want focus on as an example of Russo's second category of female grotesques, the embodiment of female exceptionalism, who performs daring stunts 'up there, out there', and who denies the limits of her female body in a process of masculinization. Patsy is an ambivalent performance which can be appropriated in different ways by differently situated audiences (a prerequisite for all mainstream television comedy). This is demonstrated by the way in which the character of Patsy has entered into the culture more generally, with people holding Patsy fancy-dress parties, buying birthday cards and T-shirts with photos of Patsy on them, gay pride marches in Australia featuring Patsy clones (all carnivalesque occasions). But the intensity of many people's investment in the Patsy persona is matched by the revulsion of others who find her performance unreadable as comedy. It is simply too bizarre, too divorced from the norms of their everyday experience, to have any plausibility at all; it seems merely silly and, at times, monstrous, for example, in her behaviour towards Saffie. She expresses her absolute hostility to Edina's daughter in grotesque, witch-like gestures and facial expressions behind Saffie's back as well as in unrestrained verbal insults and asides. In doing so, she completely undermines the cultural norm of women as nurturers and endless fountains of love for children. This is completely shocking for anyone who is not in the right state of emotional arousal to find it funny. For example, in one episode ('Morocco') she burns the back of Saffie's hand with a lighted cigarette because she wants to stop her coming on holiday with them and so spoiling their fun.

The creation of an original comic persona which accumulates value as a commodity within a differentiated consumer market depends on the development of characteristic ways of using and referring to the body as well as having a recognizable 'look'. With Joanna Lumley taking the part of Patsy Stone we are simultaneously aware of her star image, an already established range of connotations, in contrast with this performance which consciously works against type for comic effect. This creates an

Figure 7.1 Patsy, hard-faced, after burning Saffie on the arm with a cigarette. (Still from *Absolutely Fabulous*, BBC2)

ambivalence and instability in the meanings conveyed; her performance embodies layers of contradictory meanings in oscillation. The resulting incongruities enhance the humour because we are not just contrasting her grotesque performance with an abstract idea of feminine norms of bodily decorum but with her previously established star persona as the epitome of upper-class, classical beauty. Her success in serious roles is never quite forgotten, even where she explicitly undercuts them in the way she moves and dresses and speaks in this show. She is known in particular for her role as Purdie in *The Avengers* where she took an active role 'up there, out there' performing her own stunts with agility, grace and skill.[8] Nor do we forget her early career as a model and her frequent appearances in contemporary advertisements; she does indeed come 'bathed in the radiance of the commodity' (Russo, 1995: 24) as a model of female exceptionalism. Rather than inviting a belief that what we are now seeing is a distortion of her 'real' self, with its origins in an upper-class colonial upbringing in India, this layering is more easily understood and appreciated as a series of skilful performances. It is one more masquerade in which the notion of a 'real' self is put in question, an interpretation reinforced by the camp excess of her performance. Thus she embodies the ambivalence of carnival in which masquerade does not merely invert the power relations of class and gender but unsettles the categories on which they are based. She is simultaneously upper-class and lower-class, masculine and feminine, respectable and unrespectable. She is both a figure to emulate and a figure to condemn, an object of reverence and revulsion.

This ambivalence in class, gender and status has a social and historical specificity in the forms of their representation. The comic transgression of codes of bodily decorum depends on a precise recognition of the prevailing cultural codes which vary across contemporaneous social groupings as well as across historical time. The locating of Patsy within a metropolitan upper-middle-class milieu with a job as fashion editor of a women's magazine is inflected by the fact that she grew up in the 1960s. The attention to high fashion in clothes and design, combined with a bohemian lifestyle with its origins in the hedonism of the Sixties, produces an orientation to bodily decorum which is determinedly anti-bourgeois.[9] Patsy is offering a critique of bourgeois manners not from below but from above; she is 'up there, out there' looking down on those 'respectable' people who, in their concern to differentiate themselves from the lower classes, maintain tight rational control over the expression of their emotions and bodily desires. She has no qualms about extravagant spending sprees on clothes, jewellery and make-up or on skipping work to shop at Harvey Nicholls. She represents a post-war generation whose orientation is towards a hedonistic enjoyment of conspicuous consumption, rather than the hard work and thrift of the pre-war generations.

In her excessive attachment to style and hedonism she has become a figure of camp appropriation by gays and a figure to be imitated by cross-dressing males. This highlights the ways in which Patsy can be read as a drag performance. Her clothes, make-up and hairstyle have the exaggerated glamour of the drag queen which tips into a parody of femininity. For instance her hair-style is a parody through exaggeration of an early 1960s peroxide 'bouffant' style in which its status as natural hair is undermined by its elaborate architecture. The idea that she could be a man in drag is reinforced by the masculine connotations of aspects of her behaviour such as her use of the phrase 'I'm going for a slash', or her movements as she swigs from the bottle, stands with her hands on her hips, or leers at men's bottoms. It might be argued that there is nothing particularly new here; there has long been a drag-queen tradition in British comedy and there is currently a proliferating number of mainstream examples of cross-dressing and 'queer' performances in cinema and television. But here, rather than a man playing a woman, we have a woman playing a woman who can be appropriated as 'really' a man. What was initially only a potential reading of her performance was given further credence by a flashback sequence in the 'Morocco' episode which revealed that Patsy had had a sex-change operation on a previous visit. 'What happened?' asks Saffie wide-eyed. 'Oh it fell off after a year', replies Edina nonchalantly, as we cut back from a scene in which Patsy is shown playing a guitar with long hair and moustache in a uniform reminiscent of the front cover of *Sergeant Pepper's Lonely Hearts Club Band*. Is this a radical de-stabilization of sex and gender categories or does the idea of her biological maleness explain away her transgression of feminine decorum leaving the norms of gender intact?

Patsy's conspicuous consumption includes drugs and alcohol as well as high fashion. The transgression of bodily decorum in comedy is usually motivated either by reference back to the physical incompetence of childhood in the clowning tradition of the 'prat-fall' or to the chemically-induced loss of physical control in the figure of the comic drunk. In Patsy's case inebriation is just as likely to be induced by cannabis or cocaine, another shift in generic convention for a mainstream TV sitcom which indicates the shifting social context for drug use in contemporary British society; it is no longer merely sub-cultural, though still illegal and therefore subterranean. Substantial sections of the audience are able to recognize and enjoy watching the specific bodily effects of drug use with the enhanced enjoyment of it being an illicit knowledge. The comic effects are intensified in the case of Patsy by the incongruity of watching this figure of immaculate elegance disintegrate to a slumped and dishevelled inebriate who at various times has found herself waking up in a rubbish tip and being transported down the Thames to be dumped out at sea, or crouched on the bathroom floor sharing a joint with Edina and wallowing in emotional outpourings about their friendship, or in

Figure 7.2 A flashback sequence showing Patsy as a man after having had a sex change in Morocco. (Still from *Absolutely Fabulous*, BBC2. Copyright © BBC)

Morocco finding they have slept for several days and missed most of their holiday after smoking from a hookah, or most shockingly, falling drunk into an open grave at Edina's father's funeral. In these scenes, Patsy is brought 'low' both literally and metaphorically, her grotesque behaviour having connotations of the 'freak'.[10] Her 'freakiness' is also connoted in her close relationship with Edina; Edina's mother refers to them as being 'joined together at the hip'. They are shown as such in the 'Final Ever Episode' (BBC1, November 1996) where we see them as Siamese twins in a cage displayed for all to point and laugh at in a fairground show.[11]

As with all comedy, we can simultaneously reaffirm our sense of superiority by looking down at her, recognizing that she has failed to conform to bourgeois standards of respectable behaviour, while also enjoying the pleasure of letting go of bodily repression through a sudden outburst of laughter induced by the momentary acknowledgement of our transgressive desire to be like Patsy. In this sense, these are stunts of daring which we can look up to in admiration and envy. Not only is the cavalier disrespect for the rules of acceptable behaviour risky in a general sense, it is doubly so in the case of Joanna Lumley, not just because she is a woman, but also because she has re-framed her whole persona as a performer in the construction of her role as Patsy.

The undermining of Lumley's image as an icon of refined and elegant femininity is interesting in the ambivalent meanings it generates within the contemporary context. As discussed above, in many ways she talks and behaves like a man when it comes to her body and its appetites, and in doing so she risks being labelled a slag within a traditional discourse of gender. This is still a real term of abuse for women but it is being challenged by a proliferation of representations of women in which active sexuality is celebrated rather than condemned. As a grotesque figure she is quite distinct from the maternal grotesque who signifies fecundity and who is identified with the female body. She has sex in a kind of detached way, quite outside bourgeois family norms. She is so detached from her bodily processes and natural functions that when she is asked to go for a smear test she has to go to Saffie, Edina's daughter, to find out what it means and then reveals she has no idea what her cervix is. The idea of giving birth is to her disgusting and unthinkable; this is accompanied by a blind terror of ageing and death. She is no female symbol of the natural cycles of birth and death and rebirth. Perhaps that is why she is able to speak to the kind of feminist sensibility which wants to disconnect female identity from their bodily functions, that doesn't want that reduction to the natural as a matter of course. The great power (and weakness?) of comedy, though, is that we can have it both ways. She makes us laugh because she is incongruous. She doesn't fit our traditional image of woman-hood, but at the same time she expresses a deeper ambivalence about our relation to maternity and fertility, an ambivalence which contains both strong attachment and rejection.

She also expresses the social demand on women to be thin but takes it so far that in its excess it is able to express the critique of that cultural requirement. The female grotesque is either too fat, transgressing in her excessive appetites, or she is too thin, her leanness expressing her ambivalence to womanhood. Patsy is revolted by food. When trying to eat a salad she has to force a lettuce leaf down even as she is gagging. There is an excess in Patsy's revulsion for food which speaks to the current cultural malaise of anorexia as a form of female resistance, a delusion of control. Here it is made comic by a complex nexus of joking around food in which the delusions we live with are exposed to full view through Edina's struggle to lose weight. We laugh out of recognition of the impossible contradictions in our desires which are confused by the simultaneous encouragement to eat and to look as if we don't. But Patsy isn't like Edina, struggling to deal with these conflicting demands and forever oscillating between bingeing and guilt-induced attempts to slim. Patsy's slimness expresses her lack of maternal feelings and her hostility to domesticity. Being able to look good in designer clothes far outweighs any other calls on her femininity. It is an expression of her class superiority.

Jo Brand in *Through the Cakehole*

The performance of stand-up comedy sets up a different relation between the persona and the performer than in a comic fiction with actresses playing characters. There is a perceived lack of gap between the two which make the ideas of role-playing or masquerade less pertinent. This is particularly true of the 'autobiographical style' of comedy which has emerged from the 'alternative' clubs in Britain where women comedians have developed personae grounded in their own subjectivity rather than having to pretend to be a man or offering themselves up as objects of ridicule as they did in the harsh setting of the working-men's clubs.[12] One of the most successful of this new generation of female stand-up comedians is Jo Brand, who after several years on the club circuit has now completed two series on Channel 4 Television which combined her stand-up routine with interspersed sketches. From the opening moments of her show it is clear that Brand's comic persona is entirely dependent on her body; its size is the fact from which all of the performance ultimately derives, both in her use of the body in performance and the jokes she tells. Hers is the 'stunted' body of the passive female grotesque who transgresses in her being, the abject body of the fat woman who is the repository of projected shame and guilt. But as a comic performer she has to avoid being perceived as a powerless victim; she has to find a way to transform disgust and pity into laughter. This she does through a refusal of the social norms of femininity, a display of female exceptionalism which appropriates the masculine, not least in her daring to perform at all in à genre of comedy long dominated by men. She is 'up there' on the stage, willing to risk herself in a public display of comic virtuosity. In doing so she has to negotiate a persona which incorporates both these active and passive modes of grotesque spectacle.

Physical immobility characterizes her performance style; she scarcely moves except to make small gestures with her hands, while her facial and voice expression is deadpan. But this repression of affect in her demeanour and voice does not signify powerlessness; on the contrary it matches the lack of expressiveness demanded of men in the bourgeois world of suited businessmen, a style of decorum which Elias associates with the rise of the rationalized bureaucratic middle classes in the course of industrialization (Elias, 1994). Repression of affect in gesture and in voice became associated with powerful men in public arenas. It conveys a confidence in the right to speak and be listened to as well as signifying control over irrational and emotional impulses. In the masculine world of stand-up comedy, where control over a separate but participating and possibly hostile audience is integral to the context, deadpan is often used by male comics to establish their authority.

While authority is essential, female stand-up comics have the additional task of negotiating their right to speak 'as a woman'. Jo Brand's performance incorporates small gestures which can be read as a need to be placatory as well as authoritative, for instance in the hint of a smile on her lips, the sideways tilt of her head and the occasional scratching of her temple with a finger. Her placatory approach is also there in the structuring of the jokes in the show. She starts with self-deprecating jokes in which her size and unattractiveness are the butt of the joke, before launching into her more aggressive jokes directed at men.[13] This can be interpreted as a 'tactic' adopted out of necessity from a position of relative powerlessness: she has no right to the stage and therefore has to find ways to placate a potentially hostile audience in order to establish the space in which to challenge their assumptions in the rest of the performance. A recent starter joke was 'Thank you for that lovely ironic whistle there, I'm sure you're not that desperate' ('Crime and Punish-men', *Through the Cakehole* Series 2). She then tells us that her boyfriend's pet name for her is 'eclipse'. She takes on the negative attitudes to fat women and uses them (in the same way as Jewish comedians use self-deprecation) to say something like, ' I know fat women

Figure 7.3 The hint of a smile on Jo Brand's face as she performs her act. (Still from *Through the Cakehole*, Series 1, Channel 4)

disgust you all, I know that I am a social outcast, but I'm going to use that set of attitudes to forge a bond with other fat women and all women who feel oppressed by the control they are expected to maintain over eating.' Then she moves into a more abrasive, challenging position by taking it all to excess and saying, 'I'm going to indulge myself as much as I like and I don't care what you think.' There is a narcissistic drive being expressed here in the refusal to bow to social norms.

Although in the past the primary focus for repression of women was sexual desire, so that, for instance, Mae West's unruly persona was premised on the fact of her frank acknowledgement of lust and sexual enjoyment, today this is only a fruitful area for comedy where there are remaining areas of taboo. So, although in many forms of popular media women's active sexuality is acknowledged and celebrated, it goes along with an assumption that only women who look a certain way are able to fully explore and enjoy their sexuality. It is in this area that Brand's humour works. She's the wrong shape and size for heterosexual sex because her appetite for food is greater than her appetite for sex. There are complex interrelationships between these areas of bodily desire and pleasure which mean that the overall theme of Brand's show is to do with the relationship established between her fatness, which is the fact from which all the rest of the jokes follow, and her sexual desire. In a context where awareness of women's eating disorders is rising there is more cultural anxiety around eating than sex. To admit in public to unrestrained greed is far more potentially shameful than to admit to promiscuity. Indulging our appetite for food is something that can only be done in private, as a secret activity. Brand breaks this taboo and goes one step further in celebrating food as an alternative to sex.

There's a knot of contradictions here which her humour skilfully negotiates. She is very insistent to establish her heterosexuality, with frequent anecdotes about her various boyfriends. Thus she establishes a complicity between herself and an assumed heterosexual audience. For example in 'A Load of Old Bollocks' (*Through the Cakehole*, Series 2) she tells a series of anecdotes which depend on an acknowledged intimacy with men as well as some hostility to them. As she says 'I've got a reputation as a man hater – but I don't. I love them', before going in to a string of anecdotes about the type of men she does hate. One thread in these is disgust at men's lack of hygiene, jokes which could be perceived as a straightforward reversal of male comedians' misogynist disgust at female bodies, as in the sketch where her friend is surprised at her eating onions before a date and she replies 'if you think this is bad you should smell his penis'. Or the time her boyfriend gets NSU and has difficulty giving a urine sample for testing. 'Just wring out the mat in front of the toilet, that should do it,' she tells him. But she doesn't tell these jokes from an assumed position of superiority based on the heightened fastidiousness on which traditional ideals of femininity depend. Rather it is based on a more contemporary feminist egalitarianism within which women claim the right to be just as 'uncivilized' as men. When she tells a joke about bad habits becoming a problem in intimate relationships, 'gobbing in the ashtrays, pissing in the bath', we laugh when she reveals that 'I just had to stop doing it, he didn't like it', because we assumed it was him, not her. She is getting a laugh here from playing on our cultural assumptions about gendered standards of bodily decorum, but she is also capitalizing on the central contradiction in her comic persona, namely that she is simultaneously associated with anti-men jokes in which she asserts her own subjectivity, and with self-deprecating jokes in which she articulates the general hostility and disgust with which her fat body is regarded. This allows for a lack of predictability in her jokes because we are never quite sure which aspect of this persona will be activated in any one instance. The comedy is thus enhanced through surprise.

The jokes which depend on an assumption of intimacy with men exist in contradiction to another major strand of jokes in which she is just too fat for men ever to want to have intimate relations with her. Examples include an anecdote in which her boyfriend leaves her waiting in the car on their first date in order to go to a prostitute. We collude with her in accepting the plausibility of the joke – that she is so revolting that this is likely and understandable behaviour – but it is only funny, rather than sad, because we also recognize that this is implausible and outrageous: however unattractive she is, only a monster would treat her in such a way. Yet even here plausibility matters. The joke depends on us acknowledging that men are capable of this kind of behaviour, and the real work of the joke is the exposure of men's capacity for hurting women in the pursuit of their sexual appetites. This meaning is reinforced by its juxtaposition with a preceding joke in which she refers to the recent highly publicized prosecution of Hugh Grant for breaking the rules of sexual decorum by being caught in public having oral sex with a prostitute in his car. 'Well, you can't blame him, can you?' she says. 'That Liz Hurley – she's let herself go, hasn't she?' This depends on our knowing that Liz Hurley, his girlfriend, is a superstar model and film actress known for her flawless beauty. In that phrase we have the dual acknowledgement that men behave badly to their girlfriends and that beauty doesn't save women from that fate. The promise which is implied in the demands made on women to strictly control their food intake and cultivate a thin body, the promise of beauty leading to love and happiness, is exposed as a delusion. Jo Brand presents an alternative, a refusal to accept the kind of self-denial involved and positing a more achievable route to pleasure in guilt-free eating as a satisfying and more autonomous substitute for sex. She gives women a sense of control over their own happiness which doesn't depend on men's approval.

This orientation is signalled in the title sequence to the first series, which begins with close-up shots of a cake being made, with a deadpan voice-over giving recipe instructions. Imperceptibly we slip into the realm of the grotesque when the third huge dollop of cream goes one step beyond the bounds of what seems reasonable, acceptable behaviour. This is then intensified in the instructions to 'Serve with custard, ice-cream and no friends' as a chair is jammed against the door, thus simultaneously undercutting the accepted relationship of women to food (that they make it for other people to enjoy), while acknowledging the reality of secret bingeing experienced by many women. 'Garnish with bars of chocolate and a large pork-pie.' This final touch invites laughter at the incongruous combination but it is also an unconsciously appropriate choice given the central place held by the pig in carnival feasting. But unlike the communal excesses of carnival feasting we have the banality and neurosis of the modern equivalent: secret solitary bingeing behind closed doors on unlikely combinations of food which we just happen to have in the fridge. It is one manifestation of the continuing process of privatization in the pursuit of leisure and pleasure. There's no one to please but yourself; there's no one to depend on for your happiness and the fulfilment of your desires. It is the very antithesis of the medieval carnival's grotesque celebrations of the interdependence of all humanity. It could be deeply depressing and for some viewers it is so. That it succeeds as comedy for a large number of people, especially women, is a measure of the anxiety and repression which surrounds the consumption of food in our culture, where women's appetites are simultaneously aroused and denied. Thus a fetishistic response is encouraged in which the desire to eat is disavowed and instead projected onto the guilty 'other' who is punished for her desire.[14] Instead of being depressed by the hostility expressed towards fat women derived from these fetishistic processes, Brand refuses the position of victim. Her self-deprecating acknowledgement of these negative attitudes which manifests itself in some of her jokes and sketches, is offset and in contradiction to her defiant celebration of the joys of eating.

A comparison of the title sequences of the first and second series of *Through the Cakehole* indicates a repositioning of Brand's show following the success of the first series. This repositioning is partly a matter of production values, with an

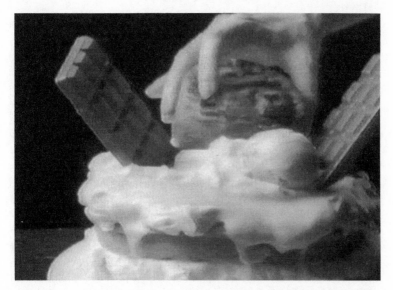

Figure 7.4 'Garnish with bars of chocolate and a large pork pie.' (The final shot in the title sequence for *Through the Cakehole,* Series 1, Channel 4)

obvious escalation both in the sumptuousness of the set and the complexity of the filming signifying Brand's increased market value as a performer. It also highlights a shift in emphasis away from a celebration of excessive eating towards an aggressive street-wise persona which places her within the current populist vogue for 'girls with attitude' or 'ladettes' as they have come to be known in the media. In this aspect of her persona, her position as victim is countered by aggression. The low-angle shot of Brand as she strides across the screen places us below her feet. As she walks over us she drops a women's magazine whose title announces: 'BLOKES WHO NEEDS THEM: A magazine for today's modern woman' over a picture of Jo Brand's face and a centrally placed strawberry flan. As in the title sequence for the first series, she invites women to indulge themselves with cake, the most taboo of all foods, but here it is visually subordinated to the image of Brand looming over us as a physical threat.

The first episode of the new series is entitled 'Crime and Punish-men', the crime theme allowing for the development of anecdotes and sketches which focus on Brand's aggression

Figure 7.5 Jo Brand towers over us as she stubs her cigarette out with her boot. (From the title sequence for *Through the Cakehole*, Series 2, Channel 4)

towards men or emulation of the aggressive licence they enjoy. But this is never a straightforward celebration of physical power; it is always undercut by the knowledge that women aren't really supposed to behave like this and to see them do it is therefore funny because it is incongruous. The incongruity is made sufficiently plausible to be funny by inserting women into scenarios where if it were men involved we would expect a certain level of aggression and physical violence. So we get the Littlecock (all-ladies) Amateur Players' version of Tarantino's *Reservoir Dogs* in which a group of respectable middle-class ladies mouth obscenities at each other as they build towards the shoot-out at the end. This is funny as a parody both of amateur dramatics and of *Reservoir Dogs*. It draws attention to the extreme differences in the codes of performance between these two contexts and the cultural codes of decorum on which they are based. Similar in some ways is the coachload of Westwick Ladies Amateur Netball Team on their way to a match, acting like lads on a rampage. Brand, as their referee, encourages their violent tactics on the pitch and takes a flying kick at a group of supporters who object. In this sketch the rather heavy-handed irony is underwritten by an old-fashioned sports commentator referring to 'the gentle touch of woman' and the 'tradition of sportswomanship'. Again it is women acting aggressively in a situation where we would normally expect to see men. But as parody it isn't related closely enough to an original text or genre to be effective so its main referent is the real-life behaviour of male sports teams. This sketch left me unsmiling because it seemed merely to be inviting us to enjoy the idea of women behaving as 'ladettes' in a rather formless sketch which lacked either the wit or skilled comic performance at a visual level which would have compensated for my lack of emotional engagement in the prohibited behaviours depicted. I really don't want to be a 'ladette', whereas I am fully involved in the aggressive behaviour depicted in *Absolutely Fabulous* because I enjoy the expression of aggressive emotions within the family which in real life I have to keep repressed. It also points to one of the limitations of Jo Brand as a comic performer. She is much better at stand-up, where she tells us a joke about aggression which is funny because of the structure of the joke, than she is at doing sketches where she has to perform the story and use her body as a comic actor. In this sphere her limitations are more apparent than her skill; her lack of physical mobility, her limited range of gesture, her deadpan voice and facial expression, which in her stand-up act reinforce a sense of control, confidence and power, lose that connotation in the sketches and instead connote lack of skill as an actor. She is always Jo Brand, the stand-up comedian, performing a sketch because the medium demands it, rather than from any intrinsic talent for that form of comic performance.

Autobiographical anecdotes about violence are scattered through the stand-up sections; typically we are told of situations where Brand is in potentially threatening situations but is able to get out of them because of her size. There's one where she's been cornered by a car full of angry blokes whose car she has damaged. She tries to get out of it, ' "Look, this isn't fair, it's five to one," and they said, "Well, pound for pound, we reckon it's about even." So I thought I'd brave it out, so I said "Right, come on then, I'll have the lot of you" and they all ran off crying – I think they must have thought I meant sexual intercourse – but – um – I did.' This joke is a good one to end on, I think, because it illustrates so well the constant oscillation in Brand's performance between self-deprecation and unruly defiance, both of which are grounded in her 'too fat' body and its appetites.

Conclusion

In seeking to answer the question of why there are such extreme responses to comic performances by female grotesques such as Jo Brand and Patsy Stone I have argued that this is a consequence of the body orientation of the humour. They depict areas of behaviour in which standards of taste and decorum set the boundaries. These trivial-sounding concerns are in fact very deep-seated in that they function as external signs of what it means to be civilized within a differentiated hierarchy based on race, class and gender. The internalization of external rules means that we project onto the 'other' the desires we deny in ourselves. It is only if a performance is 'funny' enough to overcome the censorious processes described that we can laugh instead of turning away in disgust. That perception of funniness depends in turn on the degree to which we recognize the plausibility of the impulses displayed. If it is too implausible it appears trivial and inconsequential, just childish silliness. At the other extreme, if the plausibility is too great we may feel threatened by the power of our own transgressive desires. It will be frightening, monstrous, a performance to condemn as potentially dangerous.[15]

Both Patsy and Jo Brand have developed a presence in the culture beyond the parameters of their 30-minute television shows which demonstrates the difficulty in sustaining a transgressive impulse within a market economy. Jo Brand has her own column in the *Independent* newspaper and is an occasional panellist on the BBC political discussion programme *Question Time*, indicating that she has now become a figure whose 'brand' of popular feminism can be used in serious as well as comic contexts. But in these contexts the rules of rational discourse diminish the potentially disturbing, grotesque ambivalence of her stand-up performance. She is recuperated into the respectable middle-class culture from which she originated. Patsy's image has been recuperated in other ways. The advertising industry has capitalized on her popularity by trading on her image as a camp celebration of superficiality in the service of consumption. In the spin-off programmes following the series itself, Patsy's status as really a man in drag, which was just one of the potential meanings of her performance, is now accentuated as the clue to her identity and behaviour. In March 1997 I watched an in-flight video quiz programme about *Absolutely Fabulous*, presented by Edina and Patsy, in which attention was focused on the sex-change scenario in Morocco. In that same month Patsy and Edina appeared as guests on an episode of *Roseanne* in which Patsy[16] was assumed to be a man by other guests at a party. In the process, the radical ambivalence of her performance is reduced. She is fixed in a more stable set of cultural relations in which her masculine behaviour is explained away by her biological maleness, thus reducing the impact of her image as an unruly woman. In a capitalist society, where an 'image' has accumulated value, its meanings will tend to be circulated in ways which diminish the transgressive potential of the original 'risky' performance, minimizing the danger they pose to existing cultural norms.

Notes

1. Leonore Davidoff and Catherine Hall discuss this nineteenth-century development in ' "Lofty Pine and Clinging Vine": living with gender in the middle class' (Davidoff and Hall, 1987: 397–415). They argue that whereas men's power and status was ultimately dependent on their economic position as owners of property, 'Middle class women had no such power. The minutiae of everyday life, their personal behaviour, dress and language became their arena to judge and be judged' (398).
2. I am indebted to Helen Kennedy, a former undergraduate and now a PhD student at the University of the West of England, for pointing this out to me in an essay. Jo Brand was scheduled immediately after *Roseanne* at 10.30 p.m.
3. Mary Russo's analysis of the female grotesque first appeared in 'Female grotesques : carnival and theory', Teresa de Lauretis (ed.), *Feminist Studies/ Critical Studies* (London: Macmillan, 1988), 213–19.
4. Russo is quoting from Maud Ellmann, *The Hunger Artists: Starving, Writing, Imprisonment* (Cambridge, MA: Harvard University Press, 1993), 3–4.
5. Russo uses this concept from Michael Balint's *Thrills and Regressions* (New York: International Universities Press, 1959). Balint defines the philobat as an individual who seeks thrills and danger away from the security of home and its familiar objects. The philobat pushes off in a stance of independence and autonomy, psychoanalytically figured as walking away from the mother's body, but simultaneously as a return to the free-floating

environment of the womb in which the body is supported in space. Philobatic activity as spectacle is exemplified by the acrobat who generates admiration, awe and envy in the spectator because of the sense of danger and excitement generated. Balint's philobat is male, performing death-defying feats of daring while in an ambivalent relation to mother earth, who is both a threat and a place of safety. The female philobat is both attractive and frightening because of her oddity; she is in that sense grotesque (Russo, 1995: 34–40).

6. James Narremore refers to this as the performer's 'ideolect' (Narremore, 1988).

7. Steve Neale and Frank Krutnik (Neale and Krutnik, 1990: 176–208) draw attention to the individuation of comic performances on television in the context of the particular conventions of the genres of television comedy. It is worth noting that all their examples are male.

8. Contemporary audiences have access to these earlier performances in current repeats of *The Avengers*, as well as in programme publicity which provides details of Lumley's past career.

9. Jerry Palmer comments that 'the set of activities now known as "the sixties" was an attempt to recreate at least some aspects of "world we have lost", and the fact that this attempt dwindled into consumerism should not blind us to its meaning'. The 'sixties' counter-culture can be viewed in some ways as a critique of the bourgeois repression of the spontaneous expression of bodily desires and emotions (Palmer, 1994: 129).

10. 'Freak' was used in the 1960s as a term of membership of the counter-culture, that is, as a statement of identity and lifestyle. Russo comments on this usage as an appropriation designating 'an identification with otherness within the secret self'. This was at a time when 'freaks of nature', the fairground curiosities of dwarfs and Siamese twins, were being withdrawn from display. It was a move to 'steal the magic of their specularity' (Russo, 1987: 76).

11. In Russo's bifurcation of the term, the fairground freak is an instance of the stunted, passive grotesque who transgresses in her being (1995: 22). In a recent article in the *Guardian*, headlined 'Welcome to the Freak Show', another unruly woman, the stand-up comedian Jenny Eclair, says ' Sometimes I feel like a dancing bear. Being a comedian, it can feel like you're a member of an asylum, brought out to dance for all the normal people to laugh and point. Comedy is a travelling freak show' (4 July 1996, p. 4).

12. See Francis Gray's analysis of the development of women's stand-up comedy in 'Making it on your own: women in the new comic traditions' (Gray, 1994: 133–60).

13. This insight into her tactics derives from Helen Kennedy's essay, cited in Note 2, which was instrumental in raising my interest in Jo Brand's performance because it challenged the prevailing feminist evaluation of her as simply in the tradition of female self-deprecation. See, for example, 'Gender and Humour' by Lisbeth Goodman, 1992).

14. Lorraine Gamman and Merja Makinen argue that food fetishism is widespread amongst women (Gamman and Makinen, 1994: 145–70).

15. This analysis of the structure of jokes as necessarily combining plausibility and implausibility is drawn from Jerry Palmer's model of the 'logic of the absurd', which he outlined first in *The Logic of the Absurd: On Film and Television Comedy* (London: British Film Institute, 1987). He expands on the ideas presented there in his subsequent book (Palmer, 1994) where he also considers the reasons why in some circumstances jokes fail to provoke laughter and instead cause offence.

16. I owe this interpretation to a conversation with my colleague, Liz Frost. As a fan of *Absolutely Fabulous*, she was infuriated by the move to diminish Patsy's transgressiveness in this way.

References

Bakhtin, Michael (1984) *Rabelais and His World*. Bloomington: Indiana University Press.

Davidoff, Leonore and Hall, Catherine (1987) *Family Fortunes: Men and Women of the English Middle Class 1780–1850*. London: Hutchinson Education.

Elias, Norbert (1994). *The Civilising Process: Vol. 1: History of Manners*. Oxford: Blackwell.

Freud, Sigmund (1991) *Jokes and Their Relation to the Unconscious*. London: Penguin.

Gamman, Lorraine and Makinen, Merja (1994) *Female Fetishism*. London: Lawrence and Wishart.

Goodman, Lisbeth (1992) Gender and humour. In Francis Bonner *et al.* (eds), *Imagining Women: Cultural Representations and Gender*. Milton Keynes: Oxford University Press/Polity Press, pp. 286–300.

Gray, Francis (1994) *Women and Laughter*. London: Macmillan.

Narremore, James (1988) *Acting in the Cinema*. Berkeley: University California Press.

Neale, Steve and Krutnik, Frank (1990) *Popular Film and Television Comedy*. London: Routledge.

Palmer, Jerry (1994) *Taking Humour Seriously*. London: Routledge.

Russo, Mary (1995), *The Female Grotesque: Risk, Excess and Modernity*. London: Routledge.

Rowe, Kathleen (1995) *The Unruly Woman: Gender and the Genres of Laughter*. Austin: University of Texas Press.

Tullock, John (1990) *Television Drama: Agency, Audience and Myth*. London: Routledge.

8

Talking Dirty in *For Women* Magazine

1993-1995

Clarissa Smith

Since the mid-1980s the content of women's magazine publishing in the UK has changed almost beyond recognition. Where once the discourse of love and romance reigned supreme, sex has become the primary focus of articles, problems and stories in a whole range of titles aimed at a diverse readership that crosses age and class lines. One consequence of this increasingly sexualized focus of mainstream magazine publishing was the proliferation, in the early nineties, of magazine titles which aimed to move beyond discussions of relationships and sexual activity towards the erotic arousal of their women readers. Titles like *Ludus, Bite, For Women, Women Only* and *Women On Top* attempted to offer women the kinds of sexual arousal and pleasure made possible for male readers through their use of top-shelf magazines.[1]

The only surviving title is *For Women*, from the stable of pornographic publisher Northern & Shell. Sold through high street newsagents, the magazine features many of the staples of traditional women's magazine publishing alongside photosets of nude male models. In offering up male bodies to the female gaze, the magazine can be seen as transgressive of the codes of representation which insist that the appropriate object of the sexualized image is female.[2] But the photographic imagery of the magazine is not necessarily its most transgressive feature. In this article I want to examine the ways in which the magazine's textual elements invite its women readers to experience the pleasures of pushing against the boundaries of normative female

165

behaviour, especially against those rules and codes of decorum which constitute part of what it means to be feminine in our society.

In looking at *For Women* magazine it is important to recognize that it belongs to two relatively despised genres: alongside the devaluing of women's culture in general and women's magazines as a specific genre within that culture[3] run the value judgments about the place of pornography in our society. Sexually explicit material is often divided into two categories: the erotic with its pretensions to mutuality and artistic merit; and pornography which supposedly exploits and distorts 'natural' human sexuality with its tawdry images and cheap production values. *For Women* began its career as a hybrid using the traditional formats of women's magazines plus some of the more 'brazen' attributes of the pornographic genre. Unfortunately for its ability to attract sales,[4] the magazine was deemed sufficiently explicit to be relegated to the top shelf, an area of the newsagent's traditionally considered off limits to and by women. While more conservative observers might consider other women's magazines overly explicit, for their readers (and, importantly, for distributors like Menzies and W H Smith)[5] they appear to have maintained a sufficiently diverse mix of sexual material and more 'appropriate' items for their sexual function to remain undeclared: entertainment and education still form a considerable chunk of the 'pleasure zone' made available by the mainstream titles. The 'pleasure zone' of *For Women* was to be different:

> The whole *For Women* concept is not just to take the clothes off the models, the other idea is to address sexual issues in a candid way. I look at *Cosmopolitan* and it promises all kinds of things on its front cover, but then fails to deliver all of those things once you open up. This is a good time for us to launch the magazine because other women's magazines have been successful with their sex supplements but we aim to push the boundaries further than they have done, we're trying to demystify the whole sexual process, the whole interaction and we try and do it in a way which has humour, we try and take away the fear of it. Other publishers tend to promise the earth and then fail to deliver. With *For Women* I think we do deliver because we can be very explicit – look at the guide to semen – it's all there. (interview with Jonathan Richards, Managing Editor, *For Women*, 13 January 1994)

Richards' comments suggest that the character of the magazine will appeal to a 'reader personality': women he described as 'bold, intelligent, tough, horny and not afraid of talking about their pleasure in sex'. In appealing to this kind of reader some articles highlight the fun aspect of sexual activity with condom flavour tests and dressing to tease. But *For Women* is not always confident about its ability to contain sexuality within a safe and fun framework. The issue of safety, both in terms of buying the magazine and acting on any of its suggestions, is important to an analysis of the magazine. I will show later that this is a central concern of *For Women* and that such concern is reflected in the editorial imposition of limits and boundaries on women's sexual activity at the same time as more morally and aesthetically inflected boundaries are transgressed.

A brief outline of the magazine's contents will offer some insight into the various kinds of 'conversation' offered within its pages. I have focused on the magazine in its late 1993 and early 1994 incarnation for a number of reasons: firstly, during the course of a lengthy correspondence with a number of readers of the magazine, the period late 1993 to the beginning of 1995 appears to be the time when the magazine was at its best, at least for them. Through a textual analysis of some forty issues, it also seems to be a time when the magazine featured a high proportion of written material: it had a lot to say about sex and therefore appears at its most confident. This confidence did not convert into increased sales or more advertising revenue. Consequently in late 1994 the magazine underwent the first of its major reworkings with the removal of full frontal photographs and the sealing of the sex directory pages (a group of advertisements from mail-order sex-aid retailers and phone lines). Budget cuts in 1995 led to many of its more mainstream features – the problem page, the 'expert' page and lengthy articles – being dropped in an effort to streamline the magazine and perhaps push it in a more 'hard-core'[6] direction. Thus 1994 can be characterized as a period of relative stability.[7]

My analysis begins by trying to identify the ways in which *For Women* creates a woman's world of sex.

The invitation to the *For Women* world

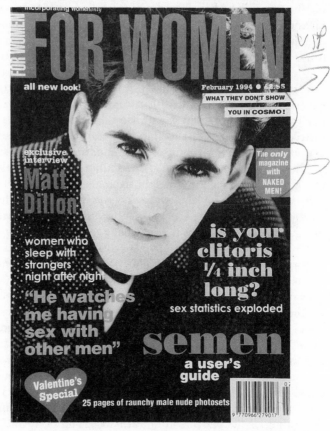

Figure 8.1 The invitation to the *For Women* world. Front cover of *For Women* magazine.

For Women is a glossy, relatively 'up-market' magazine. Each issue features an editorial outlining the month's contents; Girls' Talk and product reviews featuring gossip about celebrities; luxury consumer items; health reports; film, TV, music and book reviews; and a Hollywood interview. Further into the magazine there are fashion and beauty spreads, two further celebrity interviews and a two-page travel feature. These items are standard features in most glossy women's magazines. What is interesting, however, is the fact that they should have been included at all in a magazine which sells itself on its sexually explicit content. The inclusion of this 'soft-sell' of femininity suggests a recognition of the uneasiness some women might feel in buying a magazine whose content is entirely sexual. Thus the reader is eased into the magazine through the instantly recognizable elements of more traditional women's magazines.

The limiting of these items to the front quarter of *For Women* also indicates a desire to make the magazine itself 'safe' - these are elements which can be perused on the bus, so the magazine does not have to be hidden away in a bag until the reader reaches the safety of her home. This hiding of 'naughty' material behind an 'innocent' façade is further indicated by what is perhaps the main difference between *For Women* and other women's glossies: the distinct lack of advertising within the main body of the magazine. Advertising is limited to pages of sex toys, phone-lines and contact ads strictly confined to two sections in the back half of the magazine; the back cover is usually occupied by a vitamin advertisement and the front cover features the face of the male celebrity interviewed within. This may have been a deliberate ploy to ensure the magazine does not have to be hidden inside a brown paper bag.

The items outlined above proffer the magazine's invitation to join in a saucy, sexy world, to pamper yourself with 'safe' sexiness: sexy dresses, sexy chocolate, sexy make-up, sexy men. But fantasy and sexual allure are not just located in consumer products or the unobtainable Hollywood idol – feature articles contribute to the possibility of 'ordinary' women as sexual personae.[8] These are the areas which mark *For Women* as different to other magazines and in which tensions and contradictions are located.

The sexual world of *For Women*

For Women includes a number of lengthy articles, usually at least three pages long. In contrast to the short snappy pieces of Girls' Talk, the length of these articles suggests that they are to be lingered over in private. They can be divided into various themes which I have called techniques, peeping-in, conversations and problem-sharing. It should be stressed that the features of these themes are not exclusive and often one article will include elements of more than one theme.

Techniques

Sexual techniques are largely covered in the 'How to do ...' articles: how to give good head, make your orgasms last longer, get your man to perform oral sex, etc. The articles suggest ways of being happier, sexually and emotionally, and are written by various contributors. *For Women*'s role as 'teacher' is stressed but there are tensions here. These techniques often involve practice and the magazine recognizes the tedium of this, so while it suggests readers try them out it also mocks the need for working at getting them right. For example: 'With these sort of claims, the ESO programme can't fail to get everyone's attention – that is, until you take a gander at what they want you to do' (May 1994). And, from the same article: 'Of course, if the thought of making like a Buddha mid-clinch is a little off-putting you could always concentrate on telling yourself you're having a good time.'

Many 'How to ...' articles stress that any problems experienced are often universal:

> Sound familiar? I thought so, it's happened to the best of us, and those who have escaped such a scenario will undoubtedly have witnessed and/or helped someone else through it. (No. 9, p. 41)

and use personal testimonies as a back-up for the efficiency of the sexual technique outlined. Testimonies also serve as a way of ensuring that the article does not become too prescriptive - for and against verdicts are given allowing the reader space to accept or reject the practice discussed.

'Peeping-in'

These articles focus on the activities of other people. Typical topics have included people who swing, who practise S&M, and who sleep with their friends (male, female, gay, lesbian, bisexual).[9] These articles foreground the experiences of ordinary women, 'women like us'. Testimonies also make up a large part of these features. At least two positive and two negative experiences of the practice under discussion are described. *For Women* asks 'What is going on here?', offering readers the opportunity to peep-in on other women's lives and understand what pleasures are possible for women who want to experiment. Such features do not insist that a practice must be a part of everyone's sexual repertoire, it is much more about seeing what other women are doing and why might it be good or bad for them.

Both the 'How to ...' and peeping-in articles offer multi-narratives which suggest the magazine expects its readers to appraise the subject under discussion for themselves. This seems to be particularly true of those articles which deal with the arguably more contentious issues of anal sex and 'three-in-a-bed sessions'. In fact, much of this material allows space for women to reject certain practices as not for them without incurring the censure of the magazine. *For Women* offers a chance to expand horizons without making those horizons compulsory. This doctrine is sometimes made explicit:

> We're not trying to force you into one pattern of sexual behaviour; if you want to experiment with the idea of multiple orgasms, feel free. But if you really don't want to get into the anal sex play which is usually involved, or if you find that prostate caresses don't give you any kind of pleasure, then don't worry. Sex should never be some kind of contest, but a place where physical enjoyment can be both given and shared. (1(6), p. 46)

Aided and guided by more knowledgeable contributors, readers are invited to take part in explorations of sexual matters. However, there are other kinds of relationship available to readers, where readers are asked to participate as equals. These are the articles I would label 'conversations'.

Conversations

Regular contributor Kitty Doherty often takes a tongue-in-cheek look at a specific area of sexual manners. In the February 1994 issue, Doherty writes 'Semen – a user's guide', which examines the question of whether to 'swallow' or not.

> What is it about semen? All of my friends have healthy, nay excessively healthy, sexual appetites. Why do they spend so much time doing it when they view the obvious outcome with the same distaste as something you brought in on your shoe?

Inviting readers to puzzle about this question with her, she joins a group of friends in a restaurant discussing the pros and cons. A call for agreement is made when Doherty offers all the reasons for not swallowing semen and then dismisses them: 'Most of my friends describe the taste as "salty". Is salty enough reason for disgust? How do they manage crisps?' (p. 49). Such questions invite readers to laugh at 'the friends' and perhaps question their own hang-ups.

This is a topic which may well be of interest to readers but would be difficult to approach from a 'How to do . . .' standpoint. Here readers are invited to eavesdrop on a private conversation and, while the overall tone seems to suggest that dislike of semen is really rather silly, the article is written throughout as a round-the-table discussion enabling readers to position themselves anywhere on the issue. The use of first-person testimonies allows readers to get in close to the subject, to marvel at the sexual freedom of some women, and to laugh at the inhibitions of others. The primary concern of this article seems to lie not in the question of whether to swallow or not, but in having the space to discuss an intensely private issue without fear of recrimination.

Sharing problems

The problem-sharing theme includes the problem page and resident 'sexpert' Dr Andrew Stanway's page. It features almost the entire spectrum of sexual positions, methods and problems from how to use your tongue, make your own video, choose a vibrator, have safe anal sex, to female ejaculation. Stanway's articles often reflect male concerns, offering insight into the 'complicated male psyche'. In both these sections *For Women* is anxious to outline the credentials of their experts:

> Jan Birks is Deputy Editor of *Forum* magazine and has been giving advice professionally on sexual matters for the last five years. (No. 1, p. 9)

and

> Andrew Stanway MB MRCP is the author of more than fifty books, many on his specialist subject, sex and relationships. Dr Stanway has a thriving psychosexual and relationship practice and is the creator of the pioneering *Lover's Guide* video series. He lives in Surrey with his wife and three children. (August 1994, p. 114)

(Note the nice touch of respectability in the last sentence.)

It is important that readers recognize the legitimacy of these contributors' claims to pronounce upon specific problems.

Although these pages also offer multi-narratives it is unlikely that readers are given the same opportunities for appraisal as in the previous sections as both these items reflect a more authoritative voice within the magazine. For example, Stanway uses terms like 'From where I sit as a therapist all this is quite important' and 'A common question I'm asked by couples is . . .' so that his expertise is always prominent but, as his title 'sexpert' suggests, his is supposed to be a non-threatening expertise and one it might be safe to trust.

These themes reflect the intimacy that *For Women* wishes to create and share with its readers, giving a sense of a direct communication between women.[10] The magazine offers a variety of 'conversations' to its readers, all focusing on sex, sexuality and sexual behaviour. In labelling the stance of the magazine as conversational I am moving away from those accounts of women's magazines which stress the one-sided-ness of the relationship between text and reader. It is through its format of informal conversations between women that *For Women* offers ways of transgressing dominant codes of feminine behaviour.

In order to illustrate the complex ways in which *For Women*'s sexual world is articulated I want to use two articles (November, 1993: 36–8; February, 1994: 34–8) focusing on three-way sex, a sexual practice which features regularly in the magazine. Peeping-in articles are similar to the problem-sharing pages: in offering the opportunity to gaze on a closed world, they provide readers with information about how to do something, why they might like it and, via authorial comment, ways of doing it safely. For example:

> Room for One More On Top. The do's and don'ts for those seeking a trois to join their menage. We explore threesomes in all their explicitness. (November 1993, p. 36)

Kitty Doherty invites readers to join in her personal exploration of troilism:

> I now find myself strangely attracted to the idea of a threesome. But before I take the plunge and put the trois into the menage, I have decided to find out why three isn't always a crowd.

Most of the scenarios in this article involve women with two men and the emphasis is on the acting out of fantasy, fun and mutual attraction. Doherty tells us about the various ways of meeting a third person for sex and allows the interviewees to 'speak for themselves' in a way that opens up a direct communication between subject and reader. This might also point to the possibility of readers using the material as a spur to masturbation or trying this practice for themselves, for these are ordinary women acting out their own fantasies. The magazine clearly states that this activity is not an abnormal fantasy although reality might be somewhat different:

> Two's company, but three can be even better – sometimes. A sexual menage a trois is a popular fantasy, but what about the reality?

The juxtaposition of fantasy and reality is an on-going theme within the article and it is quite clear that the motivating fantasy for the couples interviewed is one which is shared, not the exclusive property of either the male or female partner. Despite this, the first three experiences outlined are entirely negative, two because they involved advertising for a partner and the other because the woman participant was 'outsider' to the core relationship (two bisexual men) and instead of being a major player she responds to male initiation. The first positive experience takes place on holiday in Thailand where the exotic location contributes to the 'erotic experiment'. The female participant's testimony is given first-hand:

> I've always wanted to try a three-some and I thought three sexually unconnected people would be the best mix. ... This may seem obvious, but the secret of a successful threesome is to think about it in terms of what three people can do at once. What is the point in having sex in the missionary position with two people consecutively – it's a wasted opportunity.

Thus the scenario should be well-planned, desired and taking place within the context of a mutually respecting relationship (platonic or sexual). A further example of the pleasures of group sex is outlined and then the author asks,

> Apart from the logistical problems involved in three-way sex and the disasters when the third person is undesirable, I wonder if it is always possible under such circumstances, to keep your emotions locked in a bedside cabinet?

We then enter an exploration of emotion and both testimonies point to the negative conclusion of these affairs, especially when they become regular occurrences (though we are only told about experiences with a regular third partner rather than multiple partners). However, despite the negative outcomes (relationship break-up and jealousy), the positive side of exploring fantasy in reality is also stressed:

> For me, the liberating thing about the threesome is that it let me explore same-sex sexuality with the safety net of a heterosexual partner present ... I really learnt a lot about myself as a woman – how sensual I was, how liberated I was.

Experimentation can be positive, so long as the need for desire (for the activity and the others involved) and the significance of jealousy, as a pointer to emotional danger, are recognized. The article finishes on an up-beat note:

> In retrospect, I think a successful union can be achieved between three people, without resorting to rope burns. The recipe for success seems to be one-part spontaneity, one-part choreography, and one-part emotional reserve. Stir well with a liberal splash of alcohol, and you could be onto a sexual winner. Sounds like a recipe for sexcess, to me!

Comparing the conclusions of Doherty's article with the one on the same subject written by Tuppy Owens (February 1994: 34–8), illustrates that there are a number of ways in which acting out fantasy is related in the magazine (Figure 8.2). Instead of the up-beat introduction that characterized Doherty's article we have:

> As a columnist for a men's erotic letters magazine, I have come across the same phenomenon from a different perspective. Letters arrive from husbands who sound as if they sincerely care for their wives, but as the story/fantasy/wishful thinking evolves, what he really cares about is seeing her being shafted silly by some muscular dude, usually black, with an enormous dong. And she's loving every minute. (p. 34)

This article, entitled 'He wants to watch me with another man', was one of the few articles where I felt *For Women* took a less celebratory view of its subjects. Given that the subject matter is again group sex, it seems quite strange that the tone should be so different. Whereas the previous article showed how female motivation led to sex that was 'safe, sexy and deeply satisfying', Owens' article relates a depressing set of experiences.

Figure 8.2 'Peeping-in' with Tuppy Owens.

The introduction sets the scene for the interviews to follow:

> Out at clubs, you sometimes see some unbelievable things. Take this, for example. A couple arrive together, appear to be enjoying each other, and then he moves to the side and looks on while she flirts with other men. Is this some kind of sex game? Is he her pimp? Is he impotent? Is she greedy? Is he bisexual? Are they into blackmail? What, you might wonder, is going on?

Very clearly readers should recognize the scenario played out by others, but there is no suggestion, as often happens in other 'peeping-in' articles, that we have actually had first-hand experience of this practice. Readers may have *seen* it but it is presumed they haven't *done* it. So this is an introduction to a 'strange world', one which readers might be forgiven for disbelieving.[11] A number of questions are foregrounded:

> Are there really all those horny housewives out there, who need to advertise to get laid, whose husbands really want to watch? And if so, what on earth are they getting out of the situation?

Despite the implied scepticism about the men's role, we might expect to find an upbeat and appreciative discussion of women acting out their fantasies in this article. Yet this is not the case.

Again personal testimonies are used. On the surface, two of them appear positive but they are framed in such a way that it is clear the magazine perceives things rather differently: the women concerned were not in control. The first testimony describes Suzanne as 'an incorrigible show-off' who discusses her fantasies with her husband and, in the beginning, it is her desire which is foremost. However, in the narration of her encounters we find the major difference between the two articles: Owens' subjects are not allowed to speak for themselves. Their voices and experiences are mediated through the writer. For example,

> surrounded by men, [Suzanne] became more and more flirtatious. Sooner or later, she found herself in an eight-man-one-girl gang-bang.

The use of the word 'found' is intriguing; it suggests that Suzanne had no active role in the 'sooner or later' but this is not to say that the experience has no positive connotation for the magazine. The protagonist is given the chance to explain that herself:

> That night ... Derek 'reclaimed' me as his own. ... It was as if something deep inside me had surfaced.

This is standard stuff: breaking-down-barriers and letting out your true sexual self. However, the up-beat moment does not last long. Various other women are introduced and it becomes clear that what is being acted out owes little or nothing to autonomous female fantasy:

> Betty lives on the east coast and is quite matter of fact, lacking sparkle. ... The men who come along do absolutely nothing for her ... [she says] 'The men who come are sex objects. They penetrate me which Philip likes to watch.'

This scenario is firmly attributed to Betty's husband's desire and her wish to keep him happy. She is allowed to say that it gives her pleasure to make him happy but it is a very depressing tale. The only male interviewee – he was the third partner – confirms the thrust of the article:

> he ... realized the whole thing wasn't worth all the travelling and scheming. It was, in fact, unerotic and pathetic.

Overwhelmingly, the message is that this is an activity which lacks spontaneity and a true depth of sexual feeling, precisely because it is driven by the husband's desire to see his wife being fucked by another man. Implicit in this is a disapproval of male direction of the fantasy event and the coercion of women. There is no sense of these women feeling sexual arousal for both men. All the scenarios stress the anonymity of the third partner (they are respondents to advertisements or strangers picked up in bars). This is completely different from those in Doherty's article who were, with one exception, known to and desired by the 'couple'. The magazine is not criticizing the women for indulging in anonymous sex, rather disapproval is voiced at the way in which it is practised. In Owens' article there can be no mutuality in the couplings and, more importantly, they do not allow the women involved to practice even the most basic forms of self-protection.

It is this emphasis on safe sex or lack of it that indicates the magazine's disapproval:

> Alarmingly, when I asked about safer sex, she said that most of the men are respectable husbands who don't have diseases. I remind her that anyone can be an HIV carrier especially people who go in for unprotected sex with strangers. She doesn't want her fantasy nights spoilt by harsh realities.
>
> I suspect that Shirley *is* very worried, but prefers to keep her head in the sand. There are probably thousands like her.

Obviously this hints at the dangers for all in indulging in unsafe sex, reminding readers that they could meet one of the thousands like Shirley or one of her partners, but it also suggests that in their failure to recognize danger these women are powerless: 'Of course, we'll never know how many do it, and how many enjoy it.' The implication being, of course, that it is unlikely many of them do like it. Where it might be usual to find an upbeat summation, this article concludes with an hypothesis about the kinds of pleasures available in this activity for the husband and wife, further distancing *us* – the readers and the magazine – from *them*. It is interesting and significant that the husbands are given no voice in the article, it places them firmly outside *For Women*'s discourse, for they have no interest in the magazine's idea of acceptable sex.

Safety and embodiment

The setting-up of an 'us' and 'them' scenario in this article suggests that the women interviewed are not *For Women* readers, although this division has nothing to do with liberation as such.

What this points to is an implicit suggestion that acting out fantasy cannot be separated from the body and that women must remember where sexual activity impacts on their health – emotional, sexual and physical. *For Women* locates female sexuality firmly within a material body. Criticism is not levelled at the women because they want to please their men, rather it is because they fail to recognize the autonomy of their bodies and protect themselves by using safe-sex methods. It is problematic for the magazine that these women are not talking about their own desire but it recognizes the pleasure available in pleasing a male partner and would see this as positive, if the women showed awareness of the need to protect themselves.

The concern for safety is illustrated further and more explicitly in the editorial section of the February 1994 issue. 'Can we talk?' (p. 2) dispensed with the usual catalogue of this issue's contents, instead focusing entirely on Owens' article and containing what amounts to an attack on its interviewees:

> Have these people got a death wish? Can there still be people out there who don't know that unprotected sex can kill?

A very close relationship between the magazine and readers is implicit here and excludes those women who do not practise safe sex. While this item primarily relates to the unsafe practices of the women in Owens' article, the magazine is quite clearly taking on a teaching role. With its exhortation for all women to use condoms to stop the spread of AIDS, the magazine calls for readers to question their own complacency about their sexual activities. But why might *For Women* have felt it necessary to make this plea?

The safer sex message in the magazine is firmly linked to the autonomy of the female body and female sexual desire: knowing what you want sexually includes knowing how to protect yourself. If the issue of safer sex is ignored then that amounts to a refusal to acknowledge the embodiment of sexuality. Sex for *For Women* includes bodily fluids, for example semen and vaginal lubrication. These are not revolting in the magazine, they are what makes sex sexy, but recognizing their sexiness means remembering their danger. It does seem to be the case that women are expected to take responsibility for safety – on one level, this seems eminently sensible but on another it places women back in the role of gatekeeper of men's less responsible desires.

For Women is an odd mixture of the 'erotic' and the everyday. Unlike UK magazines for men (some of which are published by the same company as *For Women*), the sexual explicitness of the magazine is related as real-life experience rather than fantasy. By that I mean that topics which would be used in, for example, *Men Only* as a basis for a narration which owes much to fiction genres, are here confined to relatively serious articles. The reader of *For Women* is not given an extended narrative which runs from a meeting, through recognition of mutual desire, to sexual activity, to orgasm. Instead we have small snippets of dialogue arranged in much the same ways as a discussion of work experiences might be laid out in *Cosmopolitan*. Thus I sense that the magazine is not predicated, as one might expect, on the relation of fantasy for the sole purpose of masturbation, but on information and sharing experiences which might then tap into fantasy and masturbation. This points to the ways in which the magazine is located at a very precarious site between sexual pleasure and sexual danger for women.

For a magazine which advertises itself as a publication for the sensual woman and labels its contents as sexually explicit, *For Women* does, in fact, devote a lot of space to 'ordinary' lives. On one level this establishes sexual activity as something experienced by 'all' women and therefore 'normal' (even at its most perverse). For this reason it is actually quite expected that the question of male sexual coercion or violence should figure within the magazine, despite these surely being the antithesis of a 'fun' sexuality. There have been articles on date rape, stranger rape, women's reactions to male pornography and women's disastrous experiences of sex (funny or depressing as well as violent). The inclusion of these subjects suggests that *For Women* is attempting to manufacture a space in which women can be sexually free. For example, a four-page article on date rape and tactics for avoiding it[12] was featured in the first issue of the magazine and was, I believe, used to say, 'This is part of the reality for women, we know it, we have seen it, we want something done about it but what this magazine is about, is being naughty. If it was not like this, what kinds of fun could we have?' Thus male violence is part of the real world but inside the magazine there is a space to discuss sex without having to keep one eye open for it. *For Women* offers an 'evasive' pleasure, ways of side-stepping some of the codes of femininity and enabling the imagining of behaviour that might well be circumscribed by male sexual violence. But therein lies the editorial dilemma at the heart of *For Women*: is it actually possible to articulate sexual freedom for women in our society?

As a sexually explicit enterprise *For Women* cannot be seen as a space where everything goes. The differences between what is possible for men and for women are obvious within its pages. The magazine is not about wild, frantic couplings between faceless strangers, or sexual conquests running into thousands and this reflects an awareness of the dangers of sexual activity for women. Even fantasy is problematic for the magazine and this is perhaps the reason why there are so few 'true' stories. Sharing fantasy outside of the peeping-in articles is strictly limited. A letter to the Mailshot (Readers' Letter Page) illustrates the imposing of a code not by explicit criticism or condemnation of the letter writer but by a friendly disbelief of her tale. The reader writes of an encounter with a well-hung stranger on a train. The magazine replies:

> Your story may be tall, Mary, but even if you're telling porkies we're impressed with your vivid imagination. If the tale is true, all we want to know is did he have to pay a half fare for his extra leg? (August, 1994, p. 94)

This response would break the rules in a similar kind of magazine for men but it may be the only option for *For Women*: the reality for most women is that it is not safe to indulge in casual sexual encounters with strangers. It is this constant return to the theme of safety in sexual activity that most potently signals the magazine's difference from male pornography and highlights the problems of producing a 'pornography for women'.

Sex in the outside world can be dangerous and/or unpleasant for many women. *For Women* cannot ignore this but it can attempt to construct a space within the magazine to discuss and share a sexual agency often denied women. In *For Women* physical pleasures are both private and communal. Readers share in an individual's pleasure and perhaps experience their own alone. Such pleasure is possibly a refusal of the social control and constraints placed upon women's sexual agency, allowing readers to feel powerful and energetic in the face of those discourses which seek to site women's pleasure in the family or limit their sexual activity to certain approved areas. In seeking to construct a space in which women can experience sexual agency, *For Women* makes use of a number of issues that are central to the feminist agenda. For instance, a woman's right to the control of her body is perhaps the most important to the magazine. This is an absolute in *For Women* and not open to negotiation. Also the ways in which women are able to indulge in non-monogamous sex or have multiple serial partners is an indication of the magazine's acknowledgement of the feminist repudiation of the double standard. However, enjoyment of the magazine is not necessarily limited to this manufactured space. Other pleasures are made available.

'Good' taste, 'bad' taste?

Current debates about sexually explicit material for women rely very heavily upon notions of good taste and what is acceptable behaviour for women. These arguments are naturalized by their reliance upon age-old categorizations of women, the use of the historically grounded dichotomies of good/bad, high/low, madonna/whore and the concomitant linking of the good with the bourgeois non-sexual woman and the bad with her 'low' class sister. Furthermore, they are explicit calls for a return to 'authorized' versions of sex talk. Through their constant reiteration of the need for sex education they place sex talk within the domain of the medical and educational institutions as the only appropriate sites for discussion of sexual activity. I would argue that we are currently witnessing a struggle for the right to talk of sex.

Recent years have seen a significant increase in the amount and variety of sex talk made available to and by women. Many commentators, drawing on libertarian discourse, have viewed this as a good thing: openness creates happiness by allowing the articulation of pleasures. Discussions in the press and elsewhere by those currently designated 'experts' stress the educational function of sexual communication: the acquisition of knowledge. But at the same time as they are applauding the freedom to discuss sensitive matters in such a way that the horrors of the past – unwanted pregnancies, fear of sexual intimacy, vulnerability to disease – are avoided or made less likely, there is still a sense in which embargoes on sex talk as a pleasurable activity in itself are enforced and strengthened. While *For Women* may well offer information about sex under the guise of knowledge as protective device, it also opens up a space for the discussion of sex as an object of pleasurable conversation in and of itself. In other words, the pleasures made available owe as much to titillation as they do to information.

That women are entitled to information about sexual matters is not seriously disputed. Commentators on our changing attitudes to sex appear to be most disturbed by the movement away from sex education to explicit speaking of the body as a sexual presence. It is not so much that discourse has become increasingly sexualized but that the words which are used to describe sexuality have moved away from a vocabulary centred on medicine or morality to words which stress the bodily nature of sexual pleasure. The explicit speaking of bodily pleasures represents a move away from the respectable discourse of 'experts' to a language of unrespectable interactions of the flesh. Moreover it is the presence of women talking sex which is seen as most challenging to the exclusive right of 'experts' to comment on the sexual body.

In her discussion of the systematic conceptualization of a distinct working-class persona through the 'silent organising discourses of sexuality', Lynette Finch shows how the imposition of 'expert' dialogue contributed to the eradication of certain kinds of language in nineteenth-century Australia. Social and juridical campaigns were utilized in order to produce a 'respectable' discourse for the describing of bodily functions and, in particular, sexual activities. At the same time as references to physical phenomena like menstruation and defecation were removed from respectable conversation, the medical profession began to write at great length about the body and its natural functions as a medical entity, moving the body into the authorized sphere of public medicine. Finch writes that

> through the nineteenth century, the creating of a space for the new official discourses to emerge resulted in the reality that, except for doctors and scientists, people did not have a day-to-day language with which to speak about sexuality. Among the middle class ... it became increasingly difficult to make any reference at all to sexual intercourse. (Finch, 1993: 135)

In the silencing of 'ordinary' discussions of sex, official discourses contribute to the delineation of a particular practice of feminine sexuality: the construction of an ideal woman, the female bourgeois, who is unable to talk of sexual activity as a bodily experience and who is, moreover, *naturally* disgusted at any representation of bodies engaged in sex. Her disgust becomes a signifier of her distance from the pollution or taint that is sex and sexual bodies and thus encodes all that which the 'proper' woman must not be in order to preserve a stable and correct sense of self. That such discursive constructions still hold sway is illustrated in Sue Lees' work which shows how the category 'slut' is still used by girls and boys to delineate those girls who have exceeded the norms of 'feminine' behaviour and that this classification acts as much as a signifier of one's own proper behaviour as it is a mark of the 'other'.

Sophie Laws has also shown how menstruation and female sexual desire are still unacceptable topics for public discussion while at the same time retaining their power within the 'illicit economy of ribaldry' (Finch, 1993: 130) and 'dirty' jokes. The recent debate in Parliament and the British press about the sexual content of teenage girls' magazines illustrates the seeming inappropriateness of young women's freedom to discuss sexual matters outside of legitimized public and private spaces. It is argued that the correct place for the discussion of sexuality lies either in the sex education class where the mechanics of sexual function are discussed (often with reference to the 'sex life' of frogs) or in the family home where the 'sacredness' of the sexual union between men and women can be stressed. The disgust expressed by Tory MP Peter Luff at the 'squalid titillation, salaciousness and smut' of young women's magazines points to a continuing construction of women's sexuality as an area of public concern. An area which needs to be policed in order to retain 'the value and importance of sex [as a] God-given gift that, in a loving relationship, is one of the best things about being a human being' (Hansard, 6 February 1996).

In attempting to produce a space for the discussion of sex as a fun and pleasurable activity *For Women* pushes against the boundaries of the acceptable and challenges the normative rejection of women's pleasure and agency in heterosexual sex, a conceptualization shared by bourgeois ideology and, ironically, radical feminist theorization. That the magazine is regarded as less than respectable is surely clear – I have already outlined the ways in which it lies at the intersection between women's magazines and an embryonic 'pornography for women'. What I want to illustrate now are the ways in which *For Women* deliberately sets out to offend 'good taste' by allowing 'excessive' sex talk through the assertion of enjoyment in sexual activity and its focus on the centrality of the body to such pleasure.

As other magazines celebrate women's abilities, *For Women* valorizes female sexuality. Where men are weak-willed and often highly conventional[13] women are shown as strong and unconventional. The magazine recognizes the pull on women's sexuality to clean, pure disembodiment and rejects it as stifling. Women who break the rules (although the boundary of safe sex is not to be transgressed) are shown as liberated, and powerful. Deodorizing sex, playing along with the idea of 'good girls don't' or retreating into good manners are all repressive of women's sexuality. Thus Owens' article is positive about Suzanne's experiences in a Dutch go-go bar where she threw off the mantle of 'good wife' and played the role of 'dirty whore'. What was not permissible was her rejection of the safe sex message.

What seems most striking about *For Women* is its use of first-person testimonies as a means of conveying information about certain sexual practices. These testimonies work in a number of ways. First, they stress the ordinariness of the practice in that some ordinary women experience and participate in, for example, group sex. But most importantly, it is this act of speaking, of breaking silence, which is most transgressive. If the 'ideal' sexual woman is one who remains silent about her experiences and activities, then the open discussion and frequent assertion of pleasure in a particular activity is symbolic of women out of control. The sexual experience itself is related as a pleasurable performance but is doubly significant in its being brought out of the bedroom and into the public sphere that is the women's magazine. That these experiences are related with no sense of shame or disgust makes the assertion of personal fulfilment through sexual experience noteworthy – it is not only what is said but how it is said that offers up a variety of pleasures to readers. Alongside descriptions of pleasure, these testimonies illuminate the emotions and motivations of the women concerned. It is not only physiological pleasure which is represented as important. Feelings also form a significant part of the narrative. Many critiques of pornographic material focus on the dehumanizing effect of repetitious accounts of sexual activity.[14] The emphasis on personal circumstances and feelings in *For Women* in preference to narrations of the pneumatic stuffing of orifices creates a personalization of the individuals featured in the article. In Owens' story, which some readers may find titillating, the testimonies also work to produce compassion for the women. This indicates the magazine's complex relationship to sex. The meaning of pleasure is physical and emotional. The act of speaking the body, of relating specific bodily and emotional reactions, addresses the reader directly and brings into play her own body. The text asks 'How might you feel doing this?', inviting a particular and intensely intimate relationship between text and reader which, if my interviewees are representative,[15] arouses the reader and acts as a spur to fantasy, masturbation and orgasm. As one wrote, '*For Women* plays a big role in a very important part of my sex life, my masturbation, that is the reason I read it.'

Good taste is seen as a repressive tool and is critiqued in articles like 'Miss Manners: or how to put out with dignity', in which vaginal deodorants, faking orgasms, abstaining from sex during a period, etc. are all held up for ridicule (Figure 8.3):

'Should a lady use a vaginal deodorant?'
No, no, no! Let's talk about smegma. . . . Why isn't there a product called Homfresh? Actually, Mrs Shirley Doherty swears by her Femfresh. I pity my father as it must be like going down on an Airball. We may pluck, we may paint, but the beautiful scents which emanate from between our thighs are what makes us WOMAN. Leave it alone. (June 1994, p. 28)

Farting, smells, vaginal wind and urine are all described as natural, part of the sexual experience. Being uptight about odours or bodily fluids is silly and if that means you dare not broach the subject of using a condom with a partner, dangerous. Explicit descriptions of the body are also found in more 'serious' sections of the magazine – letters to the problem page are answered with practical advice for ensuring that risks to health are minimized:

The anal canal is a delicate structure and it's a good idea for anyone considering penetration to take things easy . . . any abrasion of the mucosa anywhere in the body will allow easy access to the HIV virus, and the anal canal is particularly delicate – so it is essential to use a condom. (May 1994, p. 121)

186

Figure 8.3 Miss Manners and body etiquette. (Reproduced by kind permission of *For Women* and Portland Publishing)

The magazine also suggests that fantasy cannot be separated from the body and reality. It is clear that it perceives the body as an important factor in desire, and often fragile. When acting out fantasies women must remember where sexual activity impacts on their emotional, sexual and physical health:

> Then forget it! In a menage a trois, jealousy or being possessive definitely do not fit the bill. It will only cause problems in your relationship and could wreck your friendship, too. I think it is something which is best left as a fantasy. You can get your sexual kicks just by talking about it. (January 1994, p. 121)

The recurring focus on bodily fluids, the article on semen, a story about menstrual blood, and references to vaginal lubrication all point to the magazine's militating against a feminine ideal which denies the siting of sexual pleasure in the body. Physical sensation can be a liberatory experience, and thus throwing off sexual repression, clothing and societal restraint are important to the magazine. Sexual coupling is not sublimated through the language of romance or relationships: interviewees do not talk about 'making love' or end a narrative with 'we went to bed'. They talk of 'fucking', 'sucking', 'licking', 'touching'. Sex is firmly rooted in actual body pleasure for women and men, offering a critique of

187

class-based sexuality for women – the bourgeois notion of women as moral gatekeepers of 'good' sex saving men from immorality and 'bad' sex. Understanding your own desire and listening to the needs of your body and recognizing the solidity of other bodies are all references to a critique of femininity as a disembodied sexuality. That *For Women* sees the discursive construction of the 'proper' woman as damaging to 'real' women is highlighted in its constant assertion of men's inability to deal with women's bodies:

> Of course semen smells funky. That's what makes it sexy. Who wants to make love to a bottle of air freshener? Ignorant men have always used the natural smell of our bodies against us. To say that we're not too fond of theirs either may redress the balance but it also legitimates their feelings about us. (February 1994, p. 48)[16]

This might illustrate a sense of female disenfranchisement within sexual discourse, that women are at a disadvantage in sexual relations, but it is a disadvantage that *For Women* sees as one to be struggled against within heterosexuality, not outside it. Even when promoting the idea of loving heterosexual relationships, *For Women* is often highly critical of men, holding up their attitudes and behaviour to ridicule. *For Women* is all about men as beautiful, sexy and desirable but they constantly fall short of the ideal. The recurring focus on getting a man to do the things which turn women on suggests men are viewed as sexually inadequate. In advocating women's right to sexual pleasure, women's sexuality is represented as having an investment in that which our society usually denies women. Sex does not have to be clean or pure, it can be rude and base.

This may seem to be a reiteration of women's 'natural' alignment with the body and with nature but the critique of good manners and good behaviour actually points to an understanding of the ways in which other discourses intersect with sexuality. I would argue that in order to fully understand *For Women*'s address to its women readers we have to recognize that it does not speak to a 'natural' female sexuality. It has no interest in the radical feminist account of an 'authentic' female sexuality wrested from women under patriarchy. The magazine asserts that our sexual bodies are subject to discourses; desire is not in-born or biologically driven. It talks of women and men as being repressed by social discourses which seek to limit sexuality to romance, relationships or 'good' behaviour.

Contradictions within the magazine militate against any reading which necessarily positions women's sexuality as inherently mutual/responsive or men's sexuality as inherently individualistic or harmful. The magazine seems to reject any idea of women as passive and men as active – in fact, it is difficult to pin down exactly what the magazine means in sexual terms by active and passive. That the magazine is preoccupied with men is undeniable but this focus permits a certain questioning of gender. Shifting notions of masculinity and femininity abound. In the nude photosets, images of men are both hard and soft. Muscles might be pumped up to ridiculous proportions but the manner in which they are photographed detracts from their 'hysterical' manliness. Fashion pages, which act as spurs to both commodity purchase and fantasy, often feature women and men in exotic and fantastical dress or cross-dressing. Certainly fashion pages that dress male models in women's underwear cannot be seen as rigidly adhering to traditional gender stereotypes. Female models and the heroines of the erotic fiction are often portrayed in more dominant roles than their male counterparts. Such images play with the norms of gender and to some extent must be seen as subversive of the codes of masculinity and femininity.

The construction of male sexuality in drag?

The 1990s versions of the 'erotic' magazine for women were greeted with varying degrees of enthusiasm and suspicion but for some feminist theoreticians their arrival appeared to confirm the fear that contemporary discourses of sexuality owed little to women's autonomous desires and everything to an attempt to discipline women's sexuality in the cause of patriarchy and capitalism. One theme of such theorization (Forbes, 1994; Hawkes, 1996) has been the identification of 'domestified pornography' which, it is claimed, attempts to manufacture consent and coercive practices of the self through incitement rather than repression. As Forbes (1994: 5) writes

> A dominant theme in contemporary discourses of sexuality is the construction of female sexual desire as a means of self expression, which is now demanded of women by heterosexuality. It is no longer sufficient for women merely to submit or be the responsive partner to male desire. ... The difference today, compared to the

past, is that women are constructed as eager, desiring subjects and willing participants, who, in order to express themselves, are turning themselves into erotic objects of sexual consumption for men.

The problem with this conceptualization lies of course in its implication that women are non-desiring. As a theoretical tool the discipline critique cannot understand or illuminate the ways in which a magazine like *For Women* attempts to negotiate heterosexual pleasure for women, nor can it cope with comments from readers that they love the magazine without dismissing those women as foolish and blind to their own oppression.

It is important to realize that to focus on the surface elements of the magazine only leads to its dismissal as a male construct. For example, to target its most recognizable element, the inclusion of male nudes, might suggest the application of a male model of sexuality for women. The magazine's discussions around sexuality could also be used as evidence of the construction of women's sexuality along the lines of that defined for and by men. Articles focusing on the size of the clitoris or female ejaculation seem to support the argument that we are offered a view of 'women's sexuality ... premised on a male model of ... size and performance' (Forbes, 1994:9). Although the surface elements of the magazine are important they cannot be seen as indicative of the magazine as a whole. Indeed, Forbes' analysis seems to be premised entirely on surface elements, merely citing the 'cover-lines' of her chosen object of study as if they are capable of conveying in a phrase all that the relevant articles require three pages to cover. In this chapter I have stressed the need to look to the modes of address within *For Women* to understand the kinds of issues which the magazine is trying to negotiate. This may point to the ways in which publications of this type can be seen to offer invitations to 'listen' or 'converse' of a particularly 'female' kind and, in turn, may identify those elements of the magazine which are empowering, liberatory and/or arousing for its women readers.

To focus on the disciplinary nature of magazine publishing, as proposed by Forbes and others, relies, moreover, on a reading of these publications as tools used in particular ways by readers. It is not clear that we can be sure of the ways in which the magazines are used but by highlighting the use of conversation and personal testimony in one magazine, I have attempted to illustrate the ways in which *For Women* allows its readers to partake in discussions of sex in a very direct way. In inviting its women readers into the conversations the magazine directly addresses their sexual emotions. It is this directness which is perhaps most pleasurable for the magazine's readers and most offensive to its critics.

Notes

1. This was not an entirely new phenomenon in that two publishers had previously attempted to create a 'pornography for women' in the 1970s with *Playgirl* and *Viva* but these ventures had been less than successful, in part due to the reluctance of distributors and newsagents to carry the titles (Braithwaite, 1995).

2. Drawing on feminist analysis which suggests that the conventions of photography position women as the passive spectacle of the active male gaze, Richard Dyer (1992: 110) shows how images of men must attempt to 'disavow this element of passivity if they are to be kept in line with dominant notions of masculinity-as-activity'. Images in *For Women* which feature men directly addressing the female reader and doing nothing other than displaying themselves can be seen to contravene the 'active/passive nexus of looking' (109).

3. Criticisms run from labelling women's magazines 'trash' to seeing them as downright dangerous and reactionary. At the risk of generalizing, many feminist accounts focus on what is wrong with women's magazines by applying a notion of bloc ideology to their reading: the reinforcing and creation of an oppressive femininity through the constant examination of romance, the domestic and the 'trivial' concerns of beauty and fashion. However, some writers, such as Janice Winship, suggest that we would do well to recognize that many magazines focus on these 'reactionary' themes in ways which allow for the contestation of traditional femininity.

4. In publishing *For Women*, Northern & Shell clearly hoped to break into the incredibly lucrative market of women's magazine publishing where successful monthlies can expect sales figures of at least 250,000 copies per month. The first issue of *For Women* had to be reprinted three times and achieved a fairly healthy figure of 145,000. This high was not to be sustained and the magazine currently enjoys sales of around 50,000. Obviously such a level of sales suggests a flop in women's magazine terms but as a 'pornographic' magazine this figure is relatively respectable. Northern & Shell's top-selling men's porn magazine *Penthouse* has sales of 120,000 per month.

Playboy achieves around 50,000 sales per month in the UK (Joanna Coles, 1995) and 'niche' magazines such as *Fat & Forty* or *Asian Babes* perhaps fall somewhere between – all short of the kinds of figures consistently achieved by *Cosmo et al.*

5. Both these companies refuse to handle any publication they deem to be 'unacceptable', thereby functioning as informal, yet effective, censors of sexually explicit material.

6. The distinction between hard- and soft-core used here is somewhat different from that used in standard definitions of sexually explicit material. Hard-core in this sense means a move away from those elements which might be characterized as standard features of traditional or mainstream magazines for women towards a more streamlined sexualized content. Ruth Corbett (*For Women* editor during this period) wanted to cut out all such elements – the problem page, fashion, beauty, interviews and discussions of relationships – thereby limiting the magazine to its 'top shelf' elements – the nude photograph, erotic fiction, and readers' letters with an emphasis on fantasy.

7. That the magazine is still undergoing significant changes is witnessed by its recent relaunch (September 1996) with a lower cover price and the injection of more humour.

8. Two 'types' of women appear in *For Women*: the woman who can be seen as extraordinary because of her talents, her sexual bravado or her sexual experience (Madonna would perhaps typify the extraordinary woman) and the ordinary woman, those women who are 'like' the readers, that is not particularly beautiful, famous or spectacularly sexual.

9. The main focus of the magazine is undeniably heterosexual but same-sex relationships are introduced as a variant on (hetero)sexual experience. Women's sexuality is not seen as exclusively heterosexual: lesbianism is not a 'perversion' in *For Women*, but equally it is never suggested as a real alternative to heterosexual relations. In fact homosexuality occupies a rather uncertain place in the magazine. It is seen as something very positive for some women and experimentation is not to be condemned but obviously that is a long way from suggesting that lesbianism could be a life-time practice excluding sexual relationships with men.

10. The male sexpert page stands out as a rather hierarchic textual feature given the construction of intimacy in the rest of the magazine. During an interview with Ruth Corbett it emerged that its inclusion was the result of an outstanding contractual obligation entered into by a sister publication *Women On Top* and was regarded by the editorial team as inappropriate to *For Women*. Dr Stanway's page was the first casualty of budgetary cuts.

11. It is significant that the author's credentials have been explained: by highlighting her role as a columnist for a men's magazine, Tuppy Owens offers readers a privileged insight into these out-of-the-ordinary practices and is also uniquely placed to explain male sexual behaviour to her less knowledgeable readers. She has some knowledge of men's motivation for these activities and she knows that it is not always in accordance with the female partner's best interests.

12. This article by Robin Warshaw was first published as a *Ms* Special Report.

13. For example, the article on breasts in the May 1994 issue makes much of men's stereotypical reactions to large breasts.

14. See, for example, Andrea Dworkin's *Pornography: Men Possessing Women* and the collection of essays in Catherine Itzin's *Pornography: Women, Violence and Civil Liberties*.

15. Since 1994 I have been conducting interviews with readers of *For Women*. The women were self-selecting; they responded to a letter I wrote to the magazine and thus it would be difficult to argue their being representative of all readers of *For Women*. However, all of them (despite their often highly critical commentary on elements of *For Women*) have asserted their right to buy and enjoy the magazine and have made explicit the ways in which they believe the magazine speaks to them as autonomous sexual agents.

16. The male body is often romanticized in the magazine. The use of sepia tints, soft focus and exotic locations in the photosets site female desire in eroticism but there is also a more 'dirty' use of men's bodies. Photosets which stress the sweat and the idea of toil are regular features in *For Women*. Rebellious, working bodies are also used: motorcycle men, mechanics, etc. Here dirtiness, albeit stylized, is seen as attractive, earthy and sexually arousing.

References

Braithwaite, B. (1995) *Women's Magazines: The First 300 Years*. London: Peter Owen.

Coles, J. (1995) Soft flesh, hard cash. *Guardian*, 11 October, pp. 10–11.

Driver, S. and Gillespie, A. (1993) Structural change in the cultural industries: British magazine publishing in the 1980s. *Media Culture and Society*, **15**.

Dworkin, A. (1981) *Pornography: Men Possessing Women*. London: Women's Press.

Dyer, R. (1992) 'Don't look now: the instabilities of the male pin-up. In *Only Entertainment*. London: Routledge.

Finch, L. (1993) *The Classing Gaze*. Allen & Unwin.

For Women. London: Northern and Shell, 1992–. (At its launch the magazine was given a volume and issue number in the style of pornographic magazines. In late 1993 it moved to the month and date system favoured by mainstream women's magazines.)

Forbes, J. (1994) Punishing sex: disciplining women in contemporary discourses of sexuality. Paper presented at the BSA Annual Conference 'Sexualities in Context', 30 March.

Hawkes, G. (1996) *A Sociology of Sex and Sexuality*. Buckingham: Open University Press.

Itzin, C. (1992) *Pornography: Women, Violence and Civil Liberties*. Oxford: Oxford University Press.

Laws, S. (1985) Male power and menstrual etiquette. In H. Homans (ed.), *The Sexual Politics of Reproduction*. Aldershot: Gower.

Lees, S. (1993) *Sugar & Spice: Sexuality and Adolescent Girls*. London: Penguin.

McNair, B. (1996) *Mediated Sex*. London: Arnold.

McRobbie, A. (1996) More!: new sexualities in girls' and women's magazines. In J. Curran *et al.* (eds), *Cultural Studies and Communications*. London: Arnold.

Parliamentary Debates (Hansard) 6 February 1996, col. 146–51. London: HMSO.

Winship, J. (1992) The impossibility of best: enterprise meets domesticity in the practical women's magazines of the 1980s. In D. Strinati and S. Webb, *Come On Down?: Popular Media Culture in Post-war Britain*. London: Routledge.

9

The Bearded Lesbian

Mandy Kidd

In July 1995 the queer lesbian photographer, Della Grace, appeared on the front cover of *Guardian Weekend* sporting a carefully sculpted goatee beard, sideburns and a moustache. The self-portrait, like Grace's previous work in the explicitly sado-masochistic collection *Love Bites* (Grace, 1991) and later in the unpublished collection 'Lesbian Boys', is a self-conscious attempt to transgress the boundaries of acceptability and normative assumptions about sex and sexual identify. In this chapter, I want to consider the way in which Grace uses facial hair to signify lesbianism and to assess the extent to which this queer reconceptualization of the female body challenges the cultural invisibility of lesbians.

The issue of body and facial hair has been an important one for feminists concerned with the political nature of the body and the ways in which women's bodies have been constructed as such through a range of social pressures and patriarchal discourses – scientific and medical, the beauty industry and pornography, for example. In *Beauty Secrets* (1986), Wendy Chapkis describes the ways in which the association of femininity with hairlessness, especially facial hairlessness, serves to reinforce (hetero)sexual difference (the assumed binary difference between male and female) by collapsing the differences between women onto a single standard of acceptable femininity. The possession of facial hair is experienced by women as a personal failure. The moustached woman, according to Chapkis, fails on two counts. Firstly, she fails, as do all women, to be a normal male. She also fails to appear as a normal female. The acute sense of 'private shame' thus engendered is in part conditioned by and in part supports a beauty industry in which

> Hair removal is no doubt one of the fastest growing profit specialities. ... It is estimated that 85 to 95% of all women have unwanted facial or body hair. Many of these people go to great lengths to solve this often embarrassing beauty problem. (Advertisement for 'Epilator 2700'; Chapkis, 1986: 5)

While many women labour to rid themselves of 'unwanted' hair, individual women, according to Chapkis, harbour a secret conviction that all other women possess femininity 'naturally' while theirs is only a 'disguise'. The knowledge that 'the transformation from female to feminine is artificial' (Chapkis, 1986: 5) is constantly undercut by the figure of the 'real woman'.

Della Grace's beard can be read as a refusal of this figure – a deliberate transgression of the natural as it has been imposed on female bodies and, indeed, used to make the concept of a female body socially meaningful. In the self-portrait, Grace asserts the 'capacity' of some female bodies to grow hair and in doing so presents us with a female body which exists outside of the confines of sexual difference or gender binarism, a body not constructed as the feminine other in appeal to a masculine subject. On this reading, then, Grace's beard signifies the lesbian body and makes lesbian existence visible and intelligible as a threat to heteropatriarchal hegemony. However, I think this reading is problematic. While Grace's beard forces us to confront the socially constructed nature of sex/gender, her queer transgressive aim actually undercuts the possibility of a specifically lesbian representation.

Until quite recently, the deliberate wearing of facial hair amongst lesbians was most influenced by feminist and lesbian feminist politics. Discussions about hairiness in lesbian publications have often been framed in terms of the political necessity to resist female sexual objectification by refusing to pluck, wax or shave. Transforming 'unwanted' and 'unsightly' hair into a symbol of feminist resistance and lesbian strength not only challenged heterosexual conceptions of female beauty but also presented gender as inextricably bound up with men's social power and the institution of heterosexuality.

> Men ... have the power to declare us normal or not. So they've hidden from us the truth that it's quite natural to have facial hair

and 'unacceptable' hair on other parts of our bodies. ... By insisting on being ourselves in such a small thing as keeping our own body and facial hair, we're threatening men and their women supporters at their fragile cores. (Jo *et al*, 1990: 274)

According to Deborah Orr, in the article that accompanies the self-portrait, Della Grace maintains that she 'just stopped plucking' and grew her beard to protest the right of women 'to have beards if they want to and if they have the capacity to grow them' (Orr, 1995). She also wanted to protest against 'the thrashing of butches on the streets ... for being the most "visible" '. The argument is, in Orr's words, a 'straightforward feminist' one. It asserts a political allegiance to women and a solidarity with lesbians as women who risk harassment by being openly lesbian in appearance.

The 'simply stopped plucking' line is one that Grace no longer uses. This is not a trivial point and will be returned to later. The question I want to pursue first is the relationship between Grace's feminist rationale and the queer theoretical framework that informs her work.

The queer beard

Taking its inspiration from postmodern cultural theory, queer theory is dedicated to undermining the notion that gender and sexual identity are expressions of an internal and 'natural' self. The normative categories of gender are not 'real' in any essential sense but are rather performances which, through continual repetition in actions and discourse, create the illusion of realness and stability. From this perspective, gender can also be seen as the means by which heterosexuality is naturalized and achieves its hegemony:

> Acts and gestures, articulated and enacted desires create the illusion of an interior and organising gender core, an illusion discursively maintained for the purposes of the regulation of sexuality within the obligatory frame of heterosexuality. (Butler, 1990: 136)

This view of gender as a construction which makes sex a socially meaningful category has, as Sue Wilkinson and Celia Kitzinger have pointed out, a long history predating queer theory. The vision of a world in which sex and, by implication heterosexuality, are no longer organizing principles owes much to the lesbian and women's liberation movements (Wilkinson and Kitzinger, 1996). The Radicalesbians paper 'The Woman Identified Woman' (1970), for example, defines heterosexuality and homosexuality as 'inauthentic categories' which would disappear in a society not organized on the basis of sex. Similarly, Monique Wittig (1981: 446) argues that 'the category "woman" as well as the category "man" are political and economic categories not eternal ones'.

One of the key differences between these earlier approaches and queer theory is the strategy envisioned for getting 'there' from 'here' (Wilkinson and Kitzinger, 1996). For lesbian feminists like Wittig, the strategy of resistance emerges from the perception that sex/gender is the basis of men's tyranny over women through heterosexuality. Such resistance aims at destroying the categories of sex, ending the use of them (Wittig, 1981). Within lesbian theory of recent years, this has been displaced by the queer strategy of transgression, which has grown out of a very different set of political allegiances and theoretical concerns.

In queer theory, performance is not only a means of constructing and regulating gender and desire. Knowingly performing gender, parodying the conventions of dress, style and physicality is also the means of undoing the rigid binary of gender, exposing it as artifice. For Judith Butler (1990: 137), gay male drag is just such a performance, denaturalizing the normative coherence between anatomical sex and gender.

> As much as drag creates a unified picture of 'woman' (what its critics often oppose), it also reveals the distinctness of those aspects of gendered experience which are falsely naturalized as a unity through the regulatory fiction of heterosexual coherence.

Grace's beard is meant to function in much the same way. Grace borrows from the traditional camp performances of gay male culture, 'putting on' masculinity to reveal it as a cultural fabrication. While referencing feminist arguments which take gender as a social construction which can and should be resisted, Grace is much more concerned with confounding binary oppositions by celebrating 'the infinite capacity of gender to mutate and cross all numerical boundaries' (quoted in Orr, 1995).

The 'mutation' and proliferation of gender which much of Grace's later work is about is reflected in the infinite range of sexual and social identities made possible by queer theory and advocated by practitioners of queer. These identities deliberately incorporate contradictory subject positions, ostensibly confounding the essentialist coherence between sex, gender and sexuality. Thus it is possible to have the male lesbian (Jacqueline Zita, 1992), the heterosexual lesbian and the female gay man. Della Grace's beard is part of the 'gender-fucking' strategy which allows her to 'perform as' a 'gay butch boy' (quoted in the *Big Issue*, 1995).

In queer performance masculinity and femininity are not problems to be overcome so much as poles of a rigid binary to be crossed and recrossed, parodied and mimicked. In fact, queer theory makes the idea of escaping gender or replacing gender with a different type of social and cultural organization an impossibility. The argument is that all social meanings are constructed through language or conventions of discourse. Since the Self comes into being only through these meanings and since these meanings are founded on the concept of sexual polarities, there can be no other 'reality' outside of current conventions and power relations. Thus, appealing to a

> 'before', 'outside', or 'beyond' power is a cultural impossibility and a politically impractical dream, one that postpones the concrete and contemporary task of rethinking subversive possibilities for sexuality and identity within the terms of power itself. (Butler, 1990: 30)

In so far as human beings are able to create change and to exercise political agency it is, as Sue Ellen Case (1991) has noted in relation to postmodern theories of the Self, in terms of 'a distance from the dominant' rather than a difference. The significance of this in relation to female facial hair is that Della Grace's queer beard does not signify a break with gender but rather an opposition to the conventions of gender which refuse women the 'right' to grow beards. Within this, however, facial hair remains a signifier of masculinity. In so far as facial hair on a woman represents a refusal of the 'real woman', the lesbian figure which emerges has crossed the gender divide to the masculine side. The fact that Della Grace sees herself (albeit temporarily) as a 'gay butch boy' underlines the intractability of gender within queer.

The lesbian that Della Grace creates is a product of queer's romance with gender as a 'free-floating artifice' which suggests that 'man and masculinity might just as easily signify a female body as a male one' (Butler, 1990: 66). In one interview, she underlies her affiliation with this view:

> I think the stereotype of the lesbian who hates men needs to be addressed. Instead of demonising the masculine, I admire and like men. My fantasy is to be a muscleman ... I don't take hormones, I'm a fully functioning woman and I intend to stay that way. (quoted in the *Big Issue*, 1995)

It can, of course, be objected that Della Grace is a photographer and a performance artist rather than a theorist and that her comments do not reflect the complexity of queer's deconstructive analysis. In this interview, for instance, she conflates 'men' with the 'masculine' and refers to her womanness in the kind of essentialist terms which queer theory has problematized.

I think, however, that Della Grace's comments are significant for what they suggest about how queer is understood and practised in the lesbian community and how queer is shaping the meanings available to lesbians for constructing identities in the 1990s. I would suggest that the value of both queer theory and representation should be judged by the extent to which they address the marginalization and invisibility of lesbians and the extent to which they provide political strategies for overcoming them. As Susan Bordo has argued, the potential of texts to destabilize normative assumptions and values can only be determined in relation to 'actual social practice' (quoted in Jeffreys, 1994: 106). I would suggest that the practices which have been informed by queer theory fail to challenge the invisibility of lesbians.

There are two aspects of some current lesbian practices which are particularly problematic: firstly, the valorization of gay male culture, and secondly, the participation of lesbians in transgenderism. Both of these have been shaped by queer.

Gay male culture

Much queer theorizing on the relationship between gender and sexuality sidesteps the question of who holds or exercises power within the system of sexual difference. One article that has particularly influenced the development of queer thought is Gayle Rubin's 'Thinking sex' (1984), in which she argues that gender and sexuality have separate social existences and should therefore be analysed within different theoretical frameworks. Gender and the oppression of women is the appropriate concern of feminism while sexuality is the province of a theory which is better able to account for the oppression of lesbians 'as queers and perverts' in a system of sexual, rather than gender, stratification. The theoretical disconnection of gender and sexuality is a major theme in queer writing. Cindy Patton (1991), for instance, talks of creating transgressive desires freed from the bonds of gender while Julia Creet argues that 'queer foregrounds same sex desire without designating which sex is desiring' (quoted in de Lauretis, 1991: introduction)

Some feminist theorists have argued that postmodern approaches to identity, of which queer is one, lead to a gender-indifferent view of the world which ignores the larger cultural stage on which the power of men to define and control sexuality is guaranteed (Kintz, 1989; Bernick, 1992). As feminist understandings of sexual oppression drop from the analysis of sexuality, so too does the idea that lesbians are oppressed as women whose existence challenges the gender binary on which male power rests. Within queer, lesbianism becomes a marginal sexuality, positioned alongside male 'queers and perverts' as a dissident sexual identity. Several lesbian feminist theorists have noted the centrality of gay male culture in queer theory and the appropriation of gay male imagery and sexual behaviour by lesbians (Wilkinson and Kitzinger, 1996; Jeffreys, 1994). Julia Creet, for instance, refers to gay male sexuality as 'the very possibility of lesbian radical sex' (quoted in de Lauretis, 1991: introduction). Cindy Patton (1991: 239) exhorts lesbians to 'conquer heterosexuality' by appropriating gay male images of 'fuckability in black leather'. This strategy, she argues, is part of deconstructing 'any female desire that insists that it must be constructed against masculinity'.

The idea that lesbianism should be constructed outside of (hetero)sexual difference, that is not as the other to masculinity, has been put forward by other lesbian writers, most notably Monique Wittig, to whom Patton refers in her article. In this sense, Patton shares with Wittig the belief that 'lesbians are not women' (Wittig, 1981). However, Patton is tied to a queer framework which insists that gender must be 'worked through' before any 'outside' is possible. Wittig, on the other hand, is clear that lesbianism is already outside and need not participate on either side of the polarity.

In keeping with Patton's ideas, Della Grace's lesbian performs on the masculine side, the performance relying on the beard as a masculine signifier and echoing the celebration of exaggerated masculinity in contemporary gay male culture (Jeffreys, 1994). In order to avoid positioning lesbianism against masculinity, Grace's lesbian puts it on. Being a visible lesbian means appropriating the signifiers of sexual subjecthood and performing as a (gay) man. Cherry Smyth (1992: 44) argues that this imitation of gay male roles has grown out of a dissatisfaction with the butch-femme dynamic which is seen as 'borrowing from' the heterosexual model. Instead, 'the butch daddy dyke and lesbian boy ... appropriate masculine codes without denying the femaleness of their protagonists'.

However, the effect of this strategy is to trap lesbianism in a heterosexual dynamic in which maleness defines the terms of sexuality and identity. The appropriation of maleness is justified by Cindy Patton (1991) on the grounds that, since we are inevitably confined within existing discursive spaces of masculine presence and female absence, lesbian sexual subjecthood must rely on disassociating from female desire and claiming masculinity from gay men. Although Patton sees this as a subversion of gay male culture and as a way of making lesbianism visible within hegemonic discourse, lesbian feminist writers have argued that queer strategies lead to the disappearance of a specifically lesbian identity. Sheila Jeffreys, for instance, suggests that the concept of queer disconnects lesbians from women and feminism and subsumes us under a generically male category. Her analysis puts queer theory and practice in an historical context in which the social and economic power of men has allowed them 'to define what culture is and make women invisible'. The transgressive imitation of gay men, which finds its theoretical justification in queer, is seen as a sign of low self-esteem amongst lesbians.

> Taking man, even gay man, as the measure of all things is not a sign of lesbian pride but of the woeful decline of lesbian confidence in the eighties. It is a humiliating retreat from the heady days of lesbian nation in the seventies when the idea that

lesbians were inferior to gay men and should emulate them would have been laughable. (Jeffreys, 1994: 179)

In the view of lesbian feminists, the gender system operates in the interests of men and is a tyranny over women. Queer theory, however, is opposed to gender as it operates to marginalize and oppress all those who deviate from the dominant discourses of gender. This can include SM heterosexuals, transsexuals or 'transgendered' people and bisexuals as well as gay men and lesbians. All of these groups are seen as crossing the boundaries of gender, providing evidence of 'the infinite capacity of gender to mutate and cross all numerical boundaries'. In terms of queer, there is an inescapable pleasure in gender and a desire to thwart the dominant binarism by creating more, rather than fewer, possibilities for its expression:

> Genderfuck ... is the destabilisation of gender as an analytic category, though it is not, necessarily, the signal of the end of gender (whose binarisms I have grown quite fond of in some respects). ... It is a discourse of pleasure, producing desire in a subject who is able to get over herself and have it make a difference. (Reich, 1992: 125)

Lesbian subjects of genderfuck have a relationship to gender which is very different to that of male 'queers and perverts'. In queer theory, gender has been re-invented as a harmless 'put-on' or 'sex toy', something which, as Sheila Jeffreys (1994: 98) has pointed out, is 'difficult to associate with sexual violence, economic inequality, women dying from backstreet abortions'. The idea that masculinity and femininity are simply subject positions which can be taken up at will by anyone obscures the power accorded to the masculine term and to actual embodied men. It is not surprising that 'the return to gender' (Jeffreys, 1994) in the context of the queer alliance of lesbians with gay men and other sexual minorities should produce an admiration of lesbians for gay men which is not reciprocated. As the queer theorist Cherry Smyth (1992: 44) is prepared to admit, this is because 'of the relative lack of sexual and social power to which women have access'.

Queer theory sets itself against the naturalizing discourses of sexology in which sex, gender and sexual object choice proceed from one another and in which the lesbian is the product of a biological or psychological male predisposition, a 'third-sex'.

However, queer also relies on the continued production of the myth of gender. No longer determined by biological essence, the intractability of gender is determined by discourse. The terms of reference have shifted but the practices that result entrench masculinity as an inevitable reference point for lesbianism.

Transgenderism

The story of Della Grace's beard dramatizes both the gender determinism of queer and the way in which lesbian queer practices can lead to the recuperation of lesbianism to a sexological framework.

In one interview, Grace maintains that although she is not a transsexual, she does consider herself to be transgendered. Here, she uses this term to signal her refusal to stay on any one side of the gender divide and to explain the significance of her decision to stop plucking. More recently, however, it has become well known in the lesbian and queer communities that Grace is using the term in a slightly different way. She is now, if not at the time of the *Guardian* article, taking testosterone. In an article in the British lesbian magazine *Diva*, Grace talks about becoming involved in transgendered activism and 'trying to be a bridge between the lesbian/gay and transgendered communities'. She believes that her genetic inheritance predisposes her to 'masculine' characteristics, both physical and behavioural. Before taking the hormone, Grace apparently felt 'the elevated male hormones fighting the others and I had to decide who was supreme'; now, she adds, I feel 'more myself' (quoted in Brosnan, 1996.) The *Diva* article also contains testimonies from several other female-to-male transgendered lesbians who echo Grace's seemingly contradictory involvement in both queer and sexological thinking. On the one hand is the view of gender as endlessly multiple and capable of resisting all attempts to confine it to conventional binary terms. On the other is the belief that all possible variations are biologically based and ultimately refer to 'real' maleness and femaleness. One FTM insists that 's/he' does not 'believe there are two sexes, biologically there are a lot more than that', but she also sees testosterone as a chemical which 'embodies – something spiritual or psychic I feel inside myself. It's the juice or the essence ... of maleness' (Brosnan, 1996).

The appeal to gender as an internal essence replays dominant sexological assumptions. The idea of variations in degrees of masculinity and femininity also echoes the ideas of sexologists from Krafft-Ebing to Freud. But the celebration of diverse gender transgressive identities and the belief that they are on the cutting edge of a new 'post-feminist' sexual politics have been made possible by queer theory.

In this sense, queer has also cleared a space for the potential growth of a 'broad' transgender community in Britain which apparently includes a growing number of women. Stephen Whittle, founder of the British FTM Network, states that: 'Testosterone is a positive way for some women to affirm who they are. ... We are seeing many more who don't actually want to become men, but who find their own expression' (quoted in Brosnan, 1996).

Given the significance and status accorded to masculinity in queer, it is hardly surprising, as Sheila Jeffreys suggests, that transgenderism has emerged in the lesbian community and that some FTMs are defining themselves as 'gay male identified'.

Conclusion

Della Grace's lesbian is a product of a queer framework which, in practice, has fed into and sustained naturalistic perceptions of gender through its deterministic and gender-indifferent approach. Grace's beard is conceptually tied to 'the masculine' and functions to make lesbianism disappear rather than to make it visible. Her performances as a gay butch boy and a female-to-male transgendered self do very little to suggest how lesbians might constitute or represent a lesbian body. My suggestion is that, contrary to Gayle Rubin, lesbian feminism provides the most useful analytical frame in which to speculate about a lesbian body which neither poses itself against masculinity nor appropriates it. Female facial hair, for instance, need not be 'masculine' nor a signifier of 'natural femaleness' but could be understood in terms of the specificity of lesbian experience in a heteropatriarchal world. Growing facial hair does not have to be a celebration of what the female body is capable of doing. This approach also obliges us to celebrate other aspects of our 'biological potential' which would more obviously reinforce the idea of women as a natural group (e.g. menstruation, pregnancy, childbirth). The idea of lesbians as a social category existing outside the social relations of heterosexuality suggests a very different kind of body which might signify a social identity as, in Monique Wittig's terms, escapees from 'the class of women'. (Wittig, 1981) This is not to suggest that in the current world lesbians and women would ever find it easy to opt out of the plucking and waxing rituals which are, for some of us, a daily concern. It suggests, however, that there are alternatives to both biological essentialism and queer determinism and that we need not constitute our bodies within the terms of gender and heterosexuality.

References

Bernick, S. E. (1992) The logic of the development of feminism. *Hypatia*, 7(1).

Big Issue (1995) London edition, August 21–7, 144: 21.

Brosnan, J. (1996) Masculine women. *Diva*, August, 39–41.

Butler, J. (1990) *Gender Trouble: Feminism and the Subversion of Identity*. London: Routledge.

Case, S. E. (1991) Tracking the vampire. *Differences*, 3 (Summer).

Chapkis, W. (1986) *Beauty Secrets: Women and the Politics of Appearance*. Boston: Southend Press.

de Lauretis, Teresa (1991) Introduction. *Differences*, 3 (Summer).

Grace, D. (1991) *Love Bites*. London: Gay Men's Press.

Jeffreys, S. (1994) *The Lesbian Heresy: A Feminist Perspective on the Lesbian Sexual Revolution*. London: Women's Press.

Jo, B., Strega, L. and Ruston (1990) *Dykes Loving Dykes: Dyke Separatist Politics for Lesbians Only*. Oakland CA: Jo, Strega and Ruston.

Kintz, L. (1989) Indifferent criticism: the deconstructive 'parole'. In J. Allen and I. M. Young (eds), *The Thinking Muse*. Bloomington: Indiana University Press.

Orr, D. (1995) Say Grace. *Guardian Weekend*, 22 July.

Patton, C. (1991) Unmediated lust: the improbable space of lesbian desire. In T. Boffin and J. Fraser (eds), *Stolen Glances: Lesbians Take Photographs*. London: Pandora.

Radicalesbians (1970) The woman identified woman. In S. L. Hoagland and J. Penelope (eds), *For Lesbians Only: A Separatist Anthology*. London: Onlywoman Press.

Reich, J. L. (1992) Genderfuck: the law of the dildo. *Discourse*, 15(1).

Rubin, G. (1984) Thinking sex: notes for a radical theory of the politics of sexuality. In C. Vance (ed.), *Pleasure and Danger: Exploring Female Sexuality*. Boston: Routledge Kegan Paul.

Smyth, C. (1992) *Lesbians Talk Queer Notions*. London: Scarlet Press.

Wilkinson, S. and Kitzinger, C. (1996) The queer backlash. In D. Bell and R. Klein (eds), *Radically Speaking: Feminism Reclaimed*. London: Zed Books.

Wittig, M. (1981) One is not born a woman. In S. L. Hoagland and J. Penelope (eds), *For Lesbians Only: A Separatist Anthology*. London: Onlywoman Press.

Zita, J. (1992) Male lesbians and the postmodern body. *Hypatia*, (Summer).

10

The Girls Can't Hack It: The Changing Status of the Female Body in Representations of New Technology

Julia Moszkowicz

Recent developments at cineplexes across the country are casting new light on feminist readings of gender and technology, in particular those which suggest women are situated at the margins of technological developments. For while the statistics support an understanding of the digital age in terms of continued sexual differentiation[1] and justify an overall emphasis on the productive and receptive contexts which seem to make such discrepancies possible, cinematic representations of women and new technology suggest a more complex relationship to the machine. Indeed, the most recent releases incorporating new technology as a theme locate female protagonists not at the margins but at the centre of narrative production. In this article I have chosen to focus on one particular film, *The Net* (Irwin Winkler, US: 1995) starring Sandra Bullock, because it is a good recent example of this cycle.

Making sense of these developments, at least within cinematic accounts of digital culture, requires a reappraisal of the status of the female body within contemporary signifying practice. Psycho-analytic conceptualizations of 'woman', for instance, as the Other of patriarchal discourse who surfaces either as an absence from, or object of desire within a text need re-evaluation. So too do structuralist readings that understand 'woman' simply in terms of a binary logic, as signifying through (sexual) difference from 'man'. Such theorizations around the female body seem inadequate in the face of the emergent cinematic representations I hope to describe. For female protagonists are becoming the signifiers *par excellence* for a particular aspect of the digital age, signifying the disembodiment and fluidity of the subject in cyberspace which cyberpunk writers identify as one of its key features.

Acting out both masculine and feminine characteristics, it would appear that the latest female protagonists are able to speak not only about, but *for* others. Neither marginal nor absent, nor solely object or subject, they are dominating films designed for a wide audience – films that is, that cannot be described as pejoratively gendered. In this most recent of incarnations, the female form is reminiscent of the male protagonist identified within feminist film criticism who is forever taken (and mistaken) for the sole articulator of human qualities. The male body has been found wanting, however, unable to articulate feminine identities (and therefore gender fluidity) without recourse to drag performance. From Dustin Hoffman's *Tootsie* to Robin Williams' *Mrs Doubtfire*, the male lead has failed to articulate a wide range of gender identities while retaining sufficient coherence at the level of the image to be recognizable as 'man'. The female body has been found to retain a greater degree of integrity at the level of the sign – as 'woman' – even when understood diegetically as someone who is not specifically female/feminine but 'person'.

The profile of women in cybernetic texts calls for a second look at those taken-for-granted assumptions about gender and sexual difference. As female protagonists increasingly enact transgressive behaviours, operating in the public world with 'masculine' technologies, it becomes difficult to maintain correlations of sex with gender – that is to say, male with masculine and female with feminine. Likewise, the centrality of the female protagonist within representations of computer networks (such as the Internet) seriously questions common assertions that cyberspace heralds the end of corporeality and an identity rooted in the body. The prominence of the female body suggests it is the discursive contexts, not the inherent characteristics of the machines themselves, that make such meanings possible.

Within cinema it is the thriller genre that largely provides the discursive context for gender and technology. Its conventions, which place female protagonists at centre-stage and in peril from attacks to the body, lend themselves to plots dealing with parallel threats to identity. Indeed, the main thematic thrust of *The Net* is a woman on-the-run from an assassin who wants to cause her physical harm and who uses new technology to bring about her virtual death before an actual one. The thriller genre is one that enables the female body to provide the narrative focus of *The Net*, that is, to emerge as an area of cultural/digital contestation.

In an article entitled 'Feminist theory and information technology', Liesbet van Zoonen (1992: 9–27) has urged feminists to analyse the social and discursive contexts of technology and it is partly in response to her call that this chapter has been written. She is interested in the social and cultural practices which surround evolving technologies, explaining how they constitute our knowledge of the world and, in particular, affect our relationship to machines. She suggests that the project of feminism, within the field of sociology at least, is to accumulate sufficient evidence to demonstrate how the system of meaning around technology works towards a sexual division of labour, that is, towards women's marginal relation to technical practices. Like others in the field she sees technology as gendered, predominantly configured and understood as 'masculine' within contemporary culture. Unlike ecofeminists, however, she believes this identity is a product of the relations of consumption – an identity mapped onto the machine at the point of reception rather than fixed into its structure during the productive process.

Research carried out in the field of gender and technology has shown that representations of femininity and women as, at worst, completely untechnological/absent and, at best, able to achieve heavily circumscribed levels of technical competence/marginal, *do* make a difference in the lives of real women. In a research paper entitled 'Computational reticence: why women fear the intimate machine' Sherry Turkle (1988: 41–58) describes how the ultimate computer user is most frequently configured in terms of masculine characteristics, and is embodied in the image of the male computer hack. The hacker, she argues, is usually portrayed as a young man who is an extreme risk-taker. He sets himself impossible challenges and is prepared to push himself to the limit of physical endurance, even to the point of putting his body on the line in his quest for a more intimate understanding of his machine. Certainly this is how he surfaces within contemporary culture. In a recent radio broadcast for instance, listeners were introduced to the whole concept of cyberspace by a computer enthusiast named Hacker Dan who was interviewed at the

Cyberia Café in London.[2] He was described as someone who spends most of his time 'surfing' the World Wide Web, communicating with fellow computer addicts and speaking a mysterious brand of technical jargon known as 'cyberlanguage'. This choice of cyberwitness is given added interest when one considers that it is a woman, Eva Pascoe, who is a co-founder and director of the Cyberia Café. In women's magazines such as *Women's Art*, it is Ms Pascoe who is more usually called upon to give testimony about cyberspace.

When Turkle carried out her study among twenty-five women taking computer courses at Harvard University, she discovered that it is through their conception of the computer hack as both male and masculine that these women have come to see in computing a cultural symbol of what woman is not. They have come to define themselves in relation to, and as distinct from, the extremities of practice that appear to constitute technological genius. In particular the hacker's total disregard for his body poses a problem for female users and his insistence on taking a machine for an exclusive partner is a further obstacle to their own technological interaction. Jessie, for example, is a woman who self-consciously works against the image of the Hacker when she responds to Turkle's questions.

> It seems to me that the essence of being a hacker is being willing to muck around with things you don't fully understand. ... Women are less willing to take things apart and risk breaking them, to try things when they don't know what they're doing. (Turkle, 1988: 49)

Turkle's respondents feel it is inappropriate for a woman to have the type of relationship with a computer that is valorized within their particular educational establishment. They believe that intimacy with an inanimate object puts their femininity at risk, going against normative conceptions of woman as 'loving' and 'people-centred' and the integrity of the female body. They prefer, instead, to treat the technology as a tool rather than a personal adventure, cherishing an ideal of womanhood (as emotive and bodily-focused), even if this allegiance secures their exclusion from the highest echelons of technological achievement. For this reason she concludes:

> I believe that the issue for the future is not computerphobia, needing to stay away because of fear and panic, but rather

computer reticence, wanting to stay away because the computer becomes a personal and cultural symbol of what woman is not. (Turkle, 1988: 50)

While Turkle has focused on the total exclusion of women from representations of the computer hack, others have examined their marginal but acknowledged status within other discursive contexts of technology. They examine how women appear in the literature around computing, discovering that even in publications with a progressive image, women are largely configured as objects of male cybernetic pleasures, making an appearance predominantly through advertising campaigns and pornographic services directed at male consumers of computer networks.[3] They examine articles on female computer users, pointing out that rather than failing to appear in the media, these women are accorded a specific profile in relation to digital networks, surfacing as peculiarly 'feminine' practitioners of the medium. Systems analyst Karen Coyle (1996: 42) notes that despite the fact that two out of every three on-the-job computer users are women and that 8.3 million households in America name women as primary home computer users, the act of computing is still seen as a 'guy thing'. She suggests that this masculine image is the product not of user practice nor inherent characteristics of the machine but of cultural configurations – images of computing which are circulated around the technology.

> Cultural bias *is* strong enough to give us a view of the world in which what men do is inherently important and the activities of women are only auxiliary ... the bias is strong enough to determine when and where women can go into the world and whether they will be accepted there, long before they have a chance to demonstrate their skills and prove their competences. (Coyle, 1996: 45)

When computing magazines assess women's contribution, it *does* appear that their endeavours are generally articulated as exceptions to the rule. Feature-writing tends to focus on women's difficulties in working in a male-dominated environment. When Jude Milton (aka hacker Saint Jude) is interviewed for *Wired* magazine (Cross, 1995: 118–19), she answers questions about feminism, patriarchy and the possibility of 'virtual rape', something that compares unfavourably to features on men working in this area, who are continually asked to comment upon the future of technology and its implications for the population as a whole. In an article entitled 'All wired up and raring to go' (Cochrane, 1995), the Head of Advanced Applications and Technology at British Telecom is asked for his predictions for (all) future lifestyles. He is not restricted to answering questions about sex differentials within technology and although he is ultimately articulating a gendered discourse of (masculine) digital futures, he does so under the cover of 'universal' experiences. When asked how he sees the world developing in the light of technological research, he replies:

> From a personal and professional point of view, one of the objectives is to do ten times more in a working life. That's what we've been doing ever since we started, I mean going back two million years. (Cochrane, 1995: 32)

Despite recent attempts within feminist accounts of new technologies to focus on women's ability to work through and around the constraints imposed by limited configurations of their technical function or gender identity,[4] what still remains to be challenged is the consensus that women's bodies fail to signify 'active' or 'creative', or even to attain the status of 'subject', in relation to technology. The traditional correlation of male as technological and female as untechnological has been shown to have its roots in culture rather than nature and to constitute a representation which is subject to female agency and social change. But insufficient attention has been given to change in the widest sense – in the actual status of the female body within (engendering) representation. Representations of women and new technology are far from monolithic, in fact, there are certain areas of cybernetic discourse in which the female form predominates in meaning production to the exclusion of men (and vice-versa).

Within cinema, male characters function differently from their female counterparts. In the film *Clear and Present Danger* (Philip Noyce, US: 1994) Harrison Ford plays a character who uses the very latest in information networks to investigate the activities of a South American drugs ring and to undertake surveillance. Once upon a time in movie history, men did battle with guns and the showdown revolved around the speed at which a weapon was retrieved from its holster. In *Clear and Present Danger* men do battle with information networks and the showdown revolves around the ability to retrieve data stored digitally on computer. It is a narrative which is dominated by images of computer networks and one which confines female protagonists to the margins of meaning production. The limited configuration of their function suggests that women both within and beyond the text have no knowledges to bring to technology; that the female body does not make sense in relation to technology; and that ultimately femininity is the antithesis of technology. Indeed *Clear and Present Danger* is a film that treats technology as a pre-given entity, assuming its meaning is determined by the material product. When male protagonists battle within a stream of information, they are understood as simply harnessing the power of the machine and its networks – the power to know about everything and be surprised by nothing. By contrast, women emerge as central characters within techno-narratives to make meanings largely about fluid subjectivity.

It is therefore important to acknowledge how images of men and women are set in differential relation to new technologies within filmic texts and to decipher the specific areas of cyberculture in which they emerge as *chief* signifiers. For rather than being marginal/absent figures within all representations of cyberculture, women have a distinct function to perform. The question, therefore, is no longer simply why is femininity seen as the antithesis of technology, but rather, how are female protagonists overcoming antagonisms established between femininity *and* technology in order to make meanings in and around cyberspace? The emphasis is more on the *process* of signification than the *effects* of prescriptive imaging. For it is a significant feature of the latest digital blockbusters that claims for gender fluidity and boundless identity within cyberspace are being made, and further, that these claims are predominantly played out across female bodies. Actresses are being accorded star billing in films which deal primarily with popular anxieties around the perceived loss of identity at the computer interface.

In *The Net* (Irwin Winkler, US: 1995) the main protagonist (Angela Bennett) suffers the terror of losing her socially recognized and coherent self when her personal documents are stolen on holiday. She is then set up by an adversary from the world of computer networks, who deletes her files from all public records and secures her re-emergence in cyberspace, not as Angela Bennett at all, but as a more dubious character by the name of Ruth Marx. Her dislocation within cyberspace is a focus for anxiety, contributing to the film's success as a thriller by working on popular fears of technology, and proves an interesting contrast to an earlier film featuring women and new technology within a contemporary setting, *Jumpin' Jack Flash* (Penny Marshall, US: 1986). In this film, the dislocated subject is configured as a man – a mysterious British agent who is trapped in Eastern Europe/cyberspace and is trying to get back to base/to a body. However, his loss of coherent subjectivity is not enacted or portrayed by the actor but is a problem established at the beginning of the film which requires narrative resolution by another protagonist. Indeed, the main character in *Jumpin' Jack Flash* is Terri Doolittle (Whoopi Goldberg) – an unconventional computer operator within a financial corporation – who assists the British agent in his re-emergence into the world/narrative as a recognizable person. She facilitates his transition from fluid subject to coherent entity by a gruelling process of investigation, and the outcome is enunciated in terms of the male protagonist's transition from a diegetic, bodiless voice-over to an actual, realized character on the screen.

In *The Net* the audience actually witnesses Angela Bennett's disappearance from all government records. The audience is invited to share in the nightmare of misrecognition as this computer programmer is reconfigured as a prostitute with copious criminal convictions. The film explores the gulf between an individual's personal sense of self and her public/social identity in much more depth than *Jumpin' Jack Flash*, a film that only hints at such sensitive issues. *The Net* lays out the whole process of dislocation as narrative content, rather than confining itself to the joys of plot resolution. The female body is integrated within the whole process of meaning production around this aspect of new technology, signifying in a way that male protagonists find difficult in popular cinema. Whereas Harrison Ford plays a character who assumes control and utilizes the power of technology, Sandra Bullock's character operates in a world of ambiguity, unable to presume or maintain the same distinction between embodied computer user and ephemeral data.

Within the film itself there are other such contrasts to be made, for while Angela Bennett is seen to be struggling to maintain a coherent identity, her adversary, Jack Devlin, is seen to have resolved this particular issue for himself. When he speaks about a 'crisis of self', his fragmented persona is located firmly in the past.

It is not the prime motivator of narrated events, but spoken as an aside, something which he experienced as a little boy.

'You know the film *Breakfast at Tiffany's?*' he asks.
'Very well, it's my favourite film!'
'... Well, when I was about thirteen I had this sort of identity crisis. I used to think I was one of the characters.'
'You thought you were Audrey Hepburn?' Bennett responds.
'No, I used to think I was the cat.'
'The cat?!' she responds incredulously.

Jack Devlin's anecdote hinges around an improbable character that serves to undermine his testimony. It seems unlikely that the confession is valid, establishing the female protagonist's own impending crisis of subjectivity as a discretely sexed experience. The audience is thus left wondering not only if she can be both 'woman' and 'hacker', (and resolve a perennial contradiction), but whether she can, as 'woman', lay claim to a coherent self at all. This ambiguity is drawn out and intensified when Angela Bennett becomes the very embodiment of such popular fears, when she starts to represent the extra-cinematic technophobia of identity loss. When the female protagonist reaches the comparative safety of her hotel room, her/our nightmare begins:

'I need my room key.'
'Name.'
'Angela Bennett.'
'No, I'm sorry. Angela Bennett checked out last Saturday.'
'No. You don't understand. I AM Angela Bennett ... I didn't check out.'
'According to my computer you checked out.'

While Angela negotiates cyberspace under a pseudonym and 'false' identity it might appear that Devlin's allusion to his own crisis of subjectivity only surfaces to draw a momentary parallel between himself and Angela, serving diegetic purposes alone. However, as events proceed, this seemingly innocent diegetic device points to an important and related aspect of this feature which sees a tendency to emphasize parallels between the characters of Devlin and Bennett. Indeed, it is only in relation to continuities such as this that the female protagonist can be understood as, in any sense, universal – as standing in for any man or woman participating in cybernetic culture. At the outset of the film there is an awkward sequence which can only be understood in these terms. Angela Bennett is seen to communicate via the information superhighway with a couple of computer boffins named Iceman and Cyberbob. Bennett deflects their romantic interest, declaring herself for a life of work/social solitude until Mr Right comes along. After revealing the image of her ideal man she is then treated to the following recitation:

'Listen Angel. You are one of us. We accept you. You're one of us. One of us.'
'Yeah, I know,' she replies.

'One of us' being someone who is single, unloved/unlovable and committed to a relationship with a machine.

This example shows how meaning is produced tentatively by the female protagonist who must first and foremost establish herself as a hacker – as a coherent and recognized subject of technology – in order to reach a position from which she can lapse into a bodiless cyberspace, and all this in the face of her being a woman or more widely understood as untechnological. In this example it is the protagonist's sexuality that surfaces as the textual problematic, but time and again it is her female body that disrupts the spectacle of 'a person' capable of navigating cyberspace. When the camera dwells on her bikini-clad form soaking up the sun on an exotic island, her breasts seem to detract from her status as computer hack. The lap-top appears ensconced in flesh, framed as it is by her voluptuous curves and smooth pink skin. There is a tension in the image as the exposed body is foregrounded to the detriment of her relationship to the machine. The swimsuit describes her body so well, it serves as a distraction, highlighting a tension that goes beyond the image and resides in her ambivalent status as hacker-WOMAN. In *Wired* magazine, for instance, images of scantily clad women are used in advertising features to mobilize specifically-targeted (male) desires for commodities. Among the column inches it is not unknown to find pictures of beautiful women set apart from pages of technical information and contextual analysis – such as one comprising a bikini-clad female form (reminiscent of Angela Bennett) emblazoned with the words 'She's a he. Life is harsh. Your tequila shouldn't be.'[5] This places women's bodies on a par with the digital commodities the magazine sets out to describe, undermining women's status as visions of technological savvy by their depiction as comparable aspirational objects. With such representations of women circulating in the media, the Angela Bennett character has difficulty in sustaining her profile as computer genius while she shows more flesh than robe.

This example suggests that some corporeal interludes function as narrative intrusions and need to be reconfigured in order for the female character to make sense as a computer expert within a text dealing in new technology. The overtly sexed body is at odds with popular images of the computer hack, who is after all predominantly configured in the physiognomy of Microsoft giant Bill Gates! Such disruptions to the norm have to be carefully negotiated, and hence the film's overall attempts to play down the body, clothing it in unglamorous attire and re-articulating its disruptions in terms of other forms of difference. Whenever Angela Bennett is seen to indulge in untypical behaviours associated with her sexed body (eroticized or not) the disruption of the sex/gender correlation is reorganized around a non-sexual signified. After she has initiated intimate relations with the smooth-talking Devlin (a transgression of 'femininity' in itself!), it is her quick-wittedness combined with a knowledge of guns which prevents Devlin concluding the evening with the murder he had planned all along. Angela finds a loaded weapon in his jacket pocket and realizes she has 'given' herself to the wrong guy.

'So. What's this for?'
'It's for shark fishing.'
'Shark fishing? With a silencer?'
'You certainly know your weapons.'
'In Colorado you grow up with guns.'

From the previous diegetic content of the film, in particular from conversations about her upbringing in La Junta, Colorado, the audience is encouraged to interpret Angela Bennett's familiarity with the male culture of guns (a disruption of common-sense notions of sexual difference) within a discourse of origins. Angela's upbringing within an outback border town with its nominal connotations of an ethnic community (there is a La Junta in Mexico and a more obvious choice in Denver, Colorado) leads to conclusions that she is clued-up and resourceful. It is her familiarity with the male culture of hunting and killing which has prepared her for such eventualities. Her transgression of culturally coded notions of femininity is effectively displaced and reconstituted within a discourse on race.

This re-coding of the female body in digital discourse has precedents elsewhere, for example, in that prototype film starring Whoopi Goldberg – *Jumpin' Jack Flash* (Marshall, US: 1986). In the latter, transgressive/technological behaviours are once again articulated in terms of racial signifiers when the female computer expert (played by Whoopi Goldberg) is reconfigured as a street smart Afro-Caribbean American. When a colleague's computer breaks down, Terri Doolittle goes to her assistance. She tampers with the machine and her ability to provide the technical solution is greeted with surprise.

> 'The shielding on the isle port is loose. ... How's that?' asks Doolittle.
> 'I don't know how you know how to do that anyway. It's like a gift. An electrical gift,' says a female colleague.

It is Goldberg's capacity to operate within two parallel systems of signification that apparently allows her (female) body to signify 'active user' in relation to new technology. For rather than simply representing 'woman' Goldberg is also black and as such is able to work with circulating notions of urban American ghetto culture, such as that eulogized by mainstream rap artists. In a collection of essays entitled *Postmodernism and Popular Culture* Angela McRobbie (1994) has proposed a reading of *Ghost* (Jerry Zucker, US: 1990) which supports such analysis. Using Derrida's notion of the 'floating signifier' she argues that the same (raced) body can create different meanings within cinema. She describes how Goldberg's body contrasts with that of a 'dark stranger' at the beginning of the film, to create different signifieds. In *Ghost* representations of non-white people link a world of drugs and violence to one of spirituality and sisterhood, mapping out the city as a place of both urban racial conflict and mixed-race female friendships. In *Jumpin' Jack Flash*, however, it is Whoopi Goldberg herself who can be seen as a floating signifier, signifying both active and passive uses of technology and overcoming the aforementioned contradiction between technical genius and femininity by allowing her gender to be reconstituted in racial terms (as well as providing a focus for comedy).

As we have seen, this strategy which sees masculine characteristics (or sexual signifieds) transformed into racial signifieds is utilized within *The Net*. However, there is a significant moment of gender incoherence within the female character which escapes such decisive re-articulation. When Angela Bennett is stalked by Devlin behind the scenes of a conference hall, she soon runs out of places to hide. Finding herself trapped, rather than cowering away she decides to make a stand against her aggressor. Framed within a doorway, her body becomes a shadow, its details erased by severe back-lighting. As Devlin approaches across a gangplank, Angela appears as a dark figure who is cradling a blunt instrument to raise against him. As she takes a swing at him with (what is revealed to be) a fire extinguisher, Devlin is seen to stagger. Then Angela hits him again, only harder, this time forcing him over the precipice. The shots within the sequence are so fragmented and cut about, so determined to hide Bennett/Bullock's features from the gaze of the audience, that she becomes an ambiguously sexed body. This performance of great physical strength against her male adversary proves a memorable and startling climax to the film, a moment of (culturally coded) masculinity which is expressed in more amorphous and universal terms as an intuitive 'survival instinct'.

Within *The Net* the female body therefore shows a tendency to signify transgressive behaviours increasingly as themselves, as disruptions to the feminine coherence of the main character. This ability is partially facilitated by a narrative which carefully constructs continuities between the male and female leads. From the outset Angela Bennett is understood as one of the best computer experts in her field. She is given a particular computer virus to examine because she is 'the best in the business' not simply a competent woman self-consciously working in a man's world. Further, the Jack Devlin character spends much of his time drawing parallels between himself and Angela, and whilst this device is designed primarily to reveal his surveillance of her via the digital networks (and position her as passive object in relation to his active gaze), this function seems to exceed its narrative purpose and spills into an appreciation of the progressive fluidity of the world of computing. When Devlin first meets Angela on holiday, enjoying privileged information about her, he imitates her behaviours. He attracts her attention initially by ordering her favourite drink – a vodka and tonic with an onion – which she is seen to enjoy at the outset of the movie. Devlin draws on knowledges, however, which have nothing to do with such dubious activities as spying, and is able to address Bennett as an equal within the world of computing, basing many exchanges around the shared language of digital culture.

> 'Is that business or pleasure?' he asks, as she works on her lap-top computer.
> 'Is there a difference?'
> 'Not a great deal if you're a hacker.'
> 'That's a nice piece of hardware. I assume you're in the business,' she says, looking at his possessions on the beach.
> 'Isn't everybody?'
> 'Nope.'
> 'God, we're pathetic aren't we?'
> 'Excuse me?'
> 'Well we're here. We're sitting on the most perfect beach in the whole world and all we can think about is ...'
> '... where can I hook up my modem?'
> 'Exactly.'

Feminist readings which have understood films as reflections of the sexed and gendered social relations of technology – as mirrored images of women's subordinate role in digital culture – will experience difficulties accounting for Sandra Bullock's prominence within the text. Equally, those who seek to describe the limiting and prescriptive nature of cinematic images circulated around gender and technology will also have trouble making sense of certain aspects of the film. For while the sequences in question can be interpreted by biological and cultural determinists alike as femininity surfacing problematically in relation to technology, as something that has to be explained away by the text or reconfigured as another form of difference, such a reading fails to take account of the audience. This is not a film specifically designed for men, nor exclusively for women, but one that claims to speak for and about the terrors of technology for *all*. Indeed it is unusual precisely because its claims to universality are articulated by an actress and played out by the figure of a woman. It negotiates multiple experiences of digital technology – of fear and expertise – and ones that, at risk of contradicting itself, are not understood as mutually exclusive. The opposing forces are not assigned to two characters but *one*, who as such plays out the gendered characteristics normally associated with differentially sexed bodies. It is through the attempts to establish continuities between Devlin and Bennett that the latter can be understood as addressing, and speaking on behalf of, an entire audience, for instance, with her monologues about the threat posed by digital culture.

> Just think about it. Our whole world is sitting there on a computer. ... There's a little electronic shadow over each and every one of us just begging for somebody to screw with it. You know what? They've done it to me, and you know what? They're going to do it to you!

Rather than seeing the continuities established between the female lead and her adversary, therefore, as mechanisms either to alleviate anxiety in a specifically male spectator or create a circumscribed area in which femininity and 'woman' can offer points of identification for women in the audience, I am proposing that a space has been opened up for the female protagonist to traverse gendered positions, appeal universally and simultaneously, and yet secure herself as an image of woman. More than mere gender performance by a thoroughly androgynous body, this amounts to the acquisition of multiply gendered characteristics by a discretely sexed one. As spectators watch the female protagonist transgress feminine territory and tread on the proverbial toes of her significant other, rather than being fetishized or seen to occupy an alternate system of meaning (as raced, for instance), she walks a tight-rope of cross-gendered womanhood. This space is largely maintained by the very claims being made within science fiction, the media and cinema about the status of the body and personal identity in cyberculture.

Self-styled cyberpunks have applauded technological developments as a point of liberation, taking the concept of fluid identities in cyberspace to an extreme and claiming that corporeality is redundant in the new post-industrial era. It is a proposition taken up and sustained by a number of texts, including *The Net* itself. In the film *Disclosure* (Barry Lewinson, US: 1994), for instance, the character of Meredith Johnson (Demi Moore) delivers the ultimate speech on behalf of the digital age, a populist rendition of cyberpunk discourse:

> We offer through technology what revolution and religion have promised but never delivered: freedom from the physical body, freedom from race and gender, from nationality and personality, from place and time ... we can relate to each other as pure consciousness.

Similarly, 'Cyberfeminist' work abounds with claims of such

developments, seeing in a post-corporeal future (taken as a technologically-determined given), potentially progressive aspects of a digital society. In *The Cyborg Manifesto* Donna Haraway (1991: 149–74) outlines her ideas about the computer age, describing how the image of the cyborg in contemporary science fiction challenges deep-rooted dualisms, the dualisms established between human and animal, between organism and machine and between the physical and the non-physical. The cyborg – who is half human, half machine – appears at the boundaries that constitute social reality, crossing carefully constructed knowledges of difference which have structured and organized our world. The emergence of the cyborg in contemporary literature, she argues, blurs traditional distinctions and at the risk of creating chaos, offers hope for the formulation of new social identities. 'My cyborg myth is about transgressed boundaries, potent fusions and dangerous possibilities which progressive people might explore as one part of much needed political work' (Haraway, 1991: 152). Haraway's cyborg is a vision spoken in culture and embodied, she argues, by those who operate within increasingly digitized environments. She cites Fritz Lang's woman/machine creation in *Metropolis* (Fritz Lang, Germany: 1926) as one of the earliest examples of cyborg imagery, but she is at pains to point out that the cyborg is more than a creature of fiction – it is also a social reality, '... a cybernetic system, a hybrid of machine and organism' (Haraway, 1991: 154). She alludes to the feminizing effects of digital technology as it traverses cultural categories and social boundaries, such as those perceived and tentatively established between 'home' and 'the workplace'. Haraway believes the stable categories of nature/culture and masculinity/femininity look decidedly fragile as society (in parts of the West at least) moves from an organic industrial community to a polymorphous information society.

> Late twentieth century machines have made thoroughly ambiguous the difference between natural and artificial, mind and body ... and many other distinctions that used to apply to organisms and machines. (Haraway, 1991: 149)

The Cyborg Manifesto is just one of a growing number of texts which offer an alternative view of representation, and it is not without its critics.[6] Of particular relevance here, however, is the way in which Haraway challenges old assumptions about how people use images, breaking affiliations with psychoanalytic theories of identification to propose female subjectivities based not so much on earliest childhood experiences of gendered positions, but on post-developmental experiences of social discourses. It allows for the possibility of subjectivity being construed as an understanding based on conscious experiences of the social, rather than unconscious responses to normative representations. It allows the spectator to contribute knowledges of extra-filmic discourses, for the possibility of women in the audience recognizing masculine behaviours in female bodies (and vice-versa), rather than limiting their role to one of identifying with the restricted feminine characteristics exhibited by these bodies. In the process, the feminist theorist is freed from the work of outlining the limited parameters of femininity 'permitted' by a text and from establishing structures of sexual difference. She is encouraged to look for contradictions within these structures and for continuities across so-called engendering representations, establishing a research agenda which allows for the possibility of change in the status of the female form within imagery, of feminine identities becoming partial (rather than totalizing) points of view for women.

Whilst Haraway's work is useful in describing how images of the cyborg are helping to disperse the resilient dualism of masculinity and femininity which has dogged feminist theory, and its reading of femininity as absent/marginal and masculinity as central and universal, it does not readily admit its own part in bringing about a reconfiguration of dominant stereotypes – its role in assisting the female protagonist to signify (as a presence) in relation to new technology. For it is partly, I would argue, through the writings of cyberfeminists and cyberpunks in contemporary culture (and media representations of them), that we can identify a 'digital age' and make a reading of the same in terms of fluid subjectivity and redundant corporeality. Popular conceptions of cyberpunks are among the knowledges that enable female bodies to take up central positions in microchip-saturated texts. Angela Bennett's female body and unfeminine technological genius are successfully combined because they make reference not simply to technology in and of itself, but to circulating claims around computer networks. *The Net* perpetuates, in the process of utilizing, this very tension between femininity and technology (and femininity and universality) working within the particular

224

receptive context provided by cybernetic discourse.

What is interesting about *The Net*, however, is that claims to cybernetic futures are neither played out within a science fiction genre nor by utilizing the image of the cyborg. They are articulated within a contemporary thriller genre and one that is forced to work with recognizable female bodies rather than futuristic mutations. Indeed generic convention demands that these bodies are constantly under attack. So although Angela Bennett is 'lost' in cyberspace, her body is far from dead and forgotten. Her body is stalked by Devlin throughout the film, for his ultimate goal is to eliminate her physically. So, in the process of signifying the fluid qualities attributed to cyberspace, the female body (as it functions within the thriller genre) serves to contradict the very notion of a 'virtual reality', presenting an actuality that cannot be spirited away. The body, with its insistent materiality, is disruptive of cyberpunk claims to free-play in cybernetic worlds. *The Net* indicates that, like the machines themselves, discourses around new technology cannot overturn social relations overnight. They are forced to work with existing knowledges and experiences of the world, namely, those based on the facticity of being. They can claim that identity is no longer tied to the body, but experiences of the social – of the film itself – suggest the body still provides fundamental clues to meaning and identity.

In this respect Angela Bennett comes to represent not so much the a-gendered cybernetic citizen of Haraway's vision, but the cross-gendered/highly-gendered female body who articulates conflicting assertions within discourse. A fundamental pleasure in the film is derived from the ambivalent status of an actress who is clearly sexed and *in spite* of her female form is seen to transcend the confines of culturally-coded femininity and rigid binarisms to indulge in a variety of uncharacteristic behaviours and signify 'universal' experiences. The narrative unfolds without sacrificing the integrity of Bennett's female form and allows for the possibility of a fluid gender identity within sexed corporeality.

While I have argued that female bodies are emerging as important signifiers within aspects of digital culture, of which *The Net* provides my main example, two further points need clarification. Firstly, only certain types of women/female bodies appear to function as signs in relation to new technology. Sandra Bullock and Whoopi Goldberg have already been mentioned, but there are other actresses to be found in films dealing in new technology and loss of identity, such as Julia Roberts in *The Pelican Brief* (Alan J. Pakula, US: 1993). What is interesting here is that both Julia Roberts and Sandra Bullock have been similarly configured within the media, that parallels have been made between them. Both have been portrayed as young actresses plucked from relative obscurity and propelled into the limelight at the turn of a movie to become highly bankable stars. All this is apparently achieved while retaining an endearing innocence and girl-next-door charm, characteristics which critics believe form the basis of their universal appeal. The dominant image of Angela Bennett circulated in reviews, for instance, is one of a uniquely a-sexual individual – an image that maps nicely onto media portrayals of Sandra Bullock. *Time* magazine writes of Bennett:

> She's shy, lonesome and doesn't do much with her natural prettiness. It's only after you get to know her you realise she's bright and eager to break out of her shell and that crisis is her preferred cosmetic. It is the source of the transfiguring glow that makes Sandra Bullock's screen character into a doofus dream girl, a sex symbol the nerdy nineties can relate to. (Schickel, 1995)

This sexed but incoherently gendered character works with an image of the actress who plays the part, for, like Angela Bennett, Sandra Bullock is portrayed as a woman with broad appeal. *The Face* depicts Bullock as one of the few actresses with the capacity to attract men and women in equal numbers to the cinema, demonstrating an unusual ability among women in Hollywood to 'open a movie'. *The Net* took $10,000,000 in its first weekend despite a lack of supporting names. *The Face* writes, 'She's the girl next door who audiences adore and Hollywood is currently throwing shed loads of money at' (Bernard, 1995: 76). Further, comparisons are often made between Bullock and Julia Roberts, who at different times have been attributed with an unassuming femininity. *Film Review* describes how 'her innocent sex appeal has made comparisons between Sandra and Hollywood Princess Julia Roberts inescapable' (Rynning, 1995: 26). Bullock responds to this comment by saying, 'It's incredibly flattering to be compared to her because Julia's a phenomenon. If it means she's got a wholesome sexuality, or if she's funny, then I don't mind those comparisons, but I think we're very different in our own way' (Rynning, 1995: 26).

Indeed, there is a suggestion that this particular capacity to embody an unassuming brand of femininity and sexuality is the very formulation of characteristics that has enabled Bullock and Roberts to feature in films where 'woman' signifies in ways which transcend the confines of normative representations of untechnological femininity. Numerous reviews comment that only Bullock could have played Angela Bennett, a character who is seen as feminine in terms of her vulnerability yet attributed with a harder street-smart edge and attendant cultural connotations of lack of femininity/masculinity. *Film Review* states:

> Sandra Bullock as Angela is aces, alternatively and believably vulnerable, spunky and super-smart in that sort of way that a deer caught in the headlights is. In fact, she is so convincing you tend to forgive the major lapses in logic and the blatant coincidences that turn this story towards its inevitable happy ending. (Rynning, 1995: 64)

Similarly, *Empire* magazine (Dutka, 1991: 84–90) has described how Roberts, in 1988, was 'just another unknown Southern girl trying to make it in the movies' and, only three years later, found herself in the position of highest-paid actress in Hollywood. Like Bullock she is initially configured in terms of contradictions, attributed with an appeal that crosses sex and gender difference. In the early years of her career, and including the release of *The Pelican Brief*, the predominant image of Roberts was that of an actress with Bambi-like qualities. Actress and producer Sally Field describes how 'men think Julia is extraordinarily beautiful, and women think they went to school with her, that they can call her up and be her best friend' (Dutka, 1991: 88–9).

Bullock and Roberts operate in an area of cinematic discourse which appears closed to men and some of the more glamorous actresses in Hollywood. When Demi Moore makes pronouncements for the digital age in *Disclosure*, she does so within a film that focuses largely on her relationship with the male lead (Michael Douglas) and incorporates new technology within the plot only to place events at the cutting edge of social developments. The main thrust of the narrative is directed towards a different problematic, dealing with the issue of male rape and women's entry into management positions within corporate America. When Demi Moore surfaces in relation to the machine she does so as content, appearing as a character within a virtual reality sequence which is operated by the male protagonist. Her body is suggestive of such signification, valorized as it is within media culture for its perfection. Indeed, Demi Moore actively markets her corporeal self as an asset, modelling nude for the cover of *Vanity Fair* (even when pregnant) and appearing as a *Playboy* centrefold. She stars in films which utilize and make meaning in relation to her assets – vital statistics which sit less comfortably with images of the computer hack than those of Bullock *et al.*, although as she grows older we may see a change in emphasis.

By contrast, to invoke more populist images of the computer hack as computer nerd or cybercriminal would require producers to arrange the narrative around a less than adequate specimen of manhood in terms of the Hollywood ideal. Again it is a question of glamour, although on this occasion the worry is of too little (rather than too much!) to sustain a movie at the box office. When more conventional representations of hackers appear, it is they – the bespeckled males with pallid skin – who occupy positions normally associated with untechnological 'woman' – who appear at the margins of technological texts. In *Goldeneye* (Martin Campbell, US: 1995) a young man is seen to adopt a less than healthy relationship with a machine, pushing himself to the limit of physical endurance in order to outwit his rivals on digital networks. Despite his recurrent catch-phrase 'I am invincible!', it is his dedicated relationship to his machine that ultimately secures his untimely demise. It would appear that the street-smart, 'girl-next-door' epitomized by Sandra Bullock is a success born of compromise – satisfying the need to represent topical techno-phobias without losing a strong Hollywood image.

The prominence of (certain kinds of) women in images of new technology is partly explained by yet another development. For while digital networks have infiltrated nearly every aspect of cultural life, aspects of feminist discourse have also been entering the mainstream. Feminism has emerged as a relatively popular body of knowledge, in relation to which many different kinds of audiences make meaning. The idea of women being objects of male desire, for instance, argued so convincingly by the likes of Laura Mulvey since the early 1970s, are so well rehearsed in contemporary life that even without knowledge of specific texts, it is possible to interpret certain kinds of image as detrimental to and objectifying of women. Indeed, it seems the 'feminine' is invoked each time there is an understanding of someone (or something) who is spoken of and spoken for, who lacks personal autonomy and control of social practices.

It would therefore appear that the female protagonist is emerging as an important sign within new technological discourse, embodying the fragmented and incoherent subjectivity which is seen by some to characterize the post-industrial individual. Furthermore, the female protagonist works by contradiction, undermining, in the very process of personifying, visions of a social identity which is no longer rooted in the body. The unusual feminine configurations presented by Sandra Bullock and Julia Roberts (with their capacity for tomboyishness) and Whoopi Goldberg (with her ability to embody racial rather than exclusively sexual signifieds) have the ability to signify fluidity while using a familiar discursive tool – the female body. The male protagonist fails to signify in the same way, lacking (amongst other things) the equivalent body of knowledge which feminism provides for Bullock, Roberts and Goldberg to sustain him in a state of gender ambiguity. Until this knowledge is developed and/ or a greater degree of equilibrium is attained within the lived social relations of technology, images of 'He' will continue to dominate films where computer networks are understood as powerful tools working towards global expansion and control. Until the statistics reveal that women are no longer marginal or exceptional figures in the world of computing, all the philosophical considerations and uncertainty surrounding the status of the sexed and gendered subject in cyberspace will be left to the masters of articulating ambivalent positioning – women.

While science fiction genres are saturated with images of the cyborg and claims to redundant corporeality, within a growing number of social realist texts dealing with equivalent issues, the resilient dualisms between masculine/feminine, man/woman and sex/gender are actually being demolished *through* configurations of the female body. Such conclusions are sympathetic to more recent work on cyborg imagery which sees in the image of the half-human, half-machine strong traces of a gendered being/ body.[7] Cyberpunks propose a fluid future free from the constraints of materiality, yet the preponderance of actresses in narratives around cyberspace suggests, for the present at least, that the body still performs a central function in contemporary cultural practice and the construction of social identity. Also, lest we forget, the state of fluid subjectivity is more generally perceived as undesirable – as a cloud on the digital horizon – and it is possibly due to this fact that the female protagonist has accrued her own area of expertise in cinematic discourse, specializing in the embodiment of popular technophobias.

Notes

1. The most recent figures suggest that almost 70 per cent of World Wide Web users are men, confirming that women are predominant among the 'information have-nots'. Quoted in Stuart Miller, 'Move to bridge gender gap on Internet', *Guardian*, 21 December 1996.
2. Part of a radio broadcast, *Word of Mouth*, BBC Radio 4, 10 October 1995.
3. See Paulina Borsook, The memoirs of a token: an ageing Berkeley feminist examines *Wired*. In Lynn Cherney (ed.), *Wired Women: Gender and New Realities in Cyberspace* (Washington: Seal Press, 1996), 24–41.
4. See Teresa de Lauretis, *Technologies of Gender: Essays on Theory, Film and Fiction* (London: Macmillan, 1987).
5. See good examples in *Wired*, August 1995, 45.
6. See Andreas Huyssen, The vamp and the machine. *New German Critique* 24/5 (Fall/Winter 1981–82), 221–37 for the problematizing of Haraway's notion of the genderless cyborg.
7. See Samantha Holland, Descartes goes to Hollywood: mind, body and gender in contemporary cyborg cinema. In M. Featherstone and R. Burrows (eds), *Cyberspace, Cyberbodies, Cyberpunk* (London: Sage, 1995), pp. 157–74, for an exploration of the gendered cyborg.

References

Bernard, E. J. (1995) Six million dollar girl. *The Face*, October, p. 76.

Cochrane, P. (1995) quoted in All wired up and raring to go. *New Scientist*, 5 August, pp. 30–35.

Coyle, K. (1996) How hard can it be? In L. Cherney (ed.), *Wired Women: Gender and New Realities in Cyberspace*. Washington: Seal Press, pp. 42–55.

Cross, R. (1995) Modem grrrl. *Wired*, February, pp. 118–19.

Dutka, E. (1991) A star is made. *Empire*, August, pp. 84–90.

Haraway, D. (1991) *Simians, Cyborgs and Women: The Reinvention of Nature*. London: Free Association Books.

McRobbie, A. (1994) *Post Modernism and Popular Culture*. London: Routledge.

Rynning, R. (1995) A load of Bullock. *Film Review*, November, pp. 26–9.

Schickel, R. (1995) Sandra Bullock discovers the downside of the Internet. *Time Magazine* 31 July, and at time-webmaster@pathfinder.com.

Turkle, S. (1988) Computational reticence: why women fear the intimate machine. In C. Kramarae (ed.), *Technology and Women's Voices: Keeping in Touch*. London: Routledge Kegan Paul, pp. 41–58.

Zoonen, van L. (1992) Feminist theory and information technology. *Media, Culture and Society*, **14**, 9–27.

Filmography

Clear and Present Danger (Philip Noyce, US: 1994)
Disclosure (Barry Levinson, US: 1994)
Ghost (Jerry Zucker, US: 1990)
Goldeneye (Martin Campbell, US: 1995)
Jumpin' Jack Flash (Penny Marshall, US: 1986)
Metropolis (Fritz Lang, Germany: 1926)
The Net (Irwin Winkler, US: 1995)
The Pelican Brief (Alan J Pakula, US: 1993)

Index

Absolutely Fabulous 14, 137, 144–51, 159, 161
adolescence 130–1
advertisements 17–18, 34–5, 146, 169, 196
aerobics 10, 91–5, 111
  feminist critiques 95–7, 100–1, 112
  male participation 107
aesthetic norms 139
ageing, attitudes to 17–18, 150
aggression 141, 158–9
AIDS 61, 79
Altenloh, Emilie 41
'ambiguous transcendence' 105
androgyny 6, 10, 82
anorexia (nervosa) 95, 97, 124–6, 151
  see also eating disorders
appearance, women's 11, 117, 121
  feminist critiques 117–19, 123, 132
  women looking at each other 129–30
  see also 'doing looks'
Aquinas, Thomas 52
Aragon, Louis 22
'armoured masculinity' 30–2
Aron-Brunetière, Robert 80–1
Arthurs, Jane 12–13
Asendorf, Christoph 32–3
'aura', loss of 31
Avengers, The 146

Baartman, Sarah 71, 86
Bahr, Hermann 32
Baker, Josephine 82, 86
Bakhtin, Michael 140, 142
Bardot, Brigitte 76
Bartky, Sandra 94, 97, 132
Bartmann, Sarah 68
Baudelaire, Charles 30–1, 33
Beard, George Miller 21, 24, 33
beards for women 14, 195–205
beauty, ideas and ideals 67–86, 93
Beauty Secrets 195
beauty therapy 120–1
Beizer, Janet 22
Belotti, Elena 2
Benjamin, Walter 8, 19, 30–1, 33, 40–3
Berger, J. 132
Big Issue, The 200
biological determinism 8

biological essentialism 53, 206
Birks, Jan 172
'black', as colour and as racial term 67, 72–5
black models 82, 84–6
black women, attitudes to 9–10, 68–86, 93
Bloomingdale model 78
bodily movement in human action 103–14
  transcending previous limits 110
  women's inhibitions 105–8, 110, 114
'body' humour 140, 160
body image 94
body schemas 110–12
Body and Soul 1
body-building 56–7
body-shaping 92
Bordo, Susan 75, 92–4, 97–100, 200
Botting, Douglas 76
Bourke, Joanna 24–5
Bourke, Joanna 24–5
Bradstock, L. 79
Brand, Jo 14, 137, 151–60
Breton, André 22
Britt 76–7
Buck-Morss, Susan 26, 40
bulimia 95
  see also eating disorders
Bullock, Sandra 208, 215, 221, 226–9
Burke, Edmund 72–4, 78
Butler, Judith 3, 49, 54, 56, 197–200

Calvinism 128
Campbell, Naomi 85
career, gender as 60
carnival 140–7, 156
Case, Sue Ellen 199
celebration of the body 129
censorship 3–4
Chapkis, Wendy 195–6
Charcot, Jean-Martin 1, 20, 37
Cheddie, Janice 84–6
Chernin, K. 126
cinema-going 41–2
  see also film
class differences 12–14, 38–43, 139–40, 147, 151, 188
Clear and Present Danger 213–14
codes of behaviour 138, 142, 147

colour, psychology of 79
comedy 13–14, 141–61
  see also jokes
computer technology 14–15, 209–30
  women's reticence towards 211–12
condoms 179, 186
Connell, R.W. 107
consciousness as a shield 27–30
conspicuous consumption 147–8
contraception 61
'conversations'
  involving the body 57
  in magazines 190–1
Corbin, Alain 40
corporeality 53–4, 222–4, 229
cosmetic surgery 125, 128
Cosmopolitan 166, 180
Coyle, Karen 212
craniology 69
Creet, Julia 201
cultural norms 118
culture and nature, distinction between 7
Cuvier, George 68–9, 81
Cyberia Café 211
cybernetics, *see* computer technnology
cyborg imagery 223–5, 229
Cyborg Manifesto, The 223

Dabydeen, David 72
Darwinism 52, 55
date rape 180
Davis, Ann 118
Davis, Kathy 125, 128
de Beauvoir, Simone 2, 15, 99, 104–6,
  131–2
decorum 137–49, 152, 155, 158, 160, 166
department stores 38–9
dermographism 22–4
dieting 125–6
Dion, K. 127
Dirie, Waris 85–6
disabled people 100, 114–15
disciplining of the body 1–2, 10, 94,
  99–100
Disclosure 222, 227
'discontinuous unity' 105
distraction 41–3
Diva 204
division of labour, sexual 210
Doherty, Kitty 171, 173, 175, 178
'doing looks' 11–12, 117–34
'doing woman' 126
domestic violence 141
Douglas, Michael 227
drag 56–7, 147–8, 198
drug use 148–9
drunkenness 40–1
Dworkin, Andrea 12
dynamic nominalism 55
dys-ease and *dys-order* 114
dysmorphic disorder 124

eating disorders 92–3, 95, 119, 124–6, 154
effeminacy 26
egalitarianism 154
electricity, phenomenon of 8, 19, 32–8
Elias, Norbet 138–41, 153
Elkins, Richard 61
embodiment 48–9, 115
emotional repression 138–41
Empire 227
eroticism 6, 12, 50–1, 53, 138, 166, 180, 190
Essence 76
eugenics 9, 55, 70, 78
events in time, bodies as 61–2
exceptionalism, female 145–6, 152
exercise 113
exercise programmes, *see* aerobics
exoticism 81, 84–6

Face, The 226
facial hair 195–6, 199, 205
Factor, Max 77, 79
'fat', negative view of 94
Featherstone, Mike 56
femininity 25–6
  norms 143, 184
  passivity 19
  racialization 67–75
feminism 3–4, 133–4, 182
  popularity 228–9
  see also aerobics; appearance; second-
  wave feminism
Ferguson, Harvie 29
fetishization 96, 101, 156
Field, Sally 227
film 2–3, 15, 36, 41–3, 208–9, 213–30
Film Review 226–7
film stars 129–30, 226, 228
Finch, Lynette 183
fitness and health, pursuit of 4–6, 10,
  91–3, 96, 100–1, 112
floating signifiers 219
Fonda, Jane 6, 91, 95
Fonda, Shirlee 95
food 154, 156
  see also eating disorders
For Women 13, 165–91
Forbes, J. 189–90
Ford, Harrison 213, 215
Forum 172
Foucault, Michel 1–2, 10, 50, 55, 94,
  99–100
fragmentation
  of the body 76
  of sense of self 120
Frame, Janet 119
France 30, 40–1
Frank, Arthur 61
Freud, Sigmund 1, 3, 8, 19, 28–31, 130–1,
  138
Frost, Liz 10–12
FTM Network 205

Futurism   31–2

Gates, Bill   218
gay male culture   201–2
Geddes, Patrick   52–3
gender identity   9, 60–1, 126, 131
genderfucking   199, 203
Germany   27, 41–2
Giddens, A.   126–7
Gilman, S.L.   70–2, 78
Gimlin, D.   126
glamour   228
Goethe, J.W. von   26
Goldberg, D.T.   69
Goldberg, Whoopi   215, 219, 226, 229
Goldeneye   228
Goude, Jean-Paul   82–4
Grace, Della   14, 195–200, 202, 204–5
Grant, Hugh   155
Greer, Germaine   122
Grimshaw, Jean   10
grotesques, female   142–6, 149–52
group sex   174–5, 185
Guardian, The   85, 195, 204

habit   102–3, 108, 112
hacking   211–12, 228
Hacking, Ian   55, 57
hairdressers in hospitals   121–2
Hake, Sabine   43
Hamer, Fannie Lou   75
happiness with one's body   99, 115
Haraway, Donna   223–5
Harrison, Dianne   120
health care, *see* fitness and health
hedonism   147
Henning, Michelle   8–9
Hepburn, Audrey   76
hermaphrodites   60
heteropolarity   51, 55, 58–60
Hill Collins, Patricia   80
HIV   178
Hoffman, Dustin   209
Hogarth, William   72–3
Hollywood   2–3, 227
   see also film
homosexuality-as-pathology   54
Hottentots   68–9, 71
Hurley, Liz   155
hysteria   19–25, 28–9, 37, 39
   'seduction theory' of   29

Ian, Marcia   56–7
'ideal' bodies   2, 130
   see also male bodies; white womanhood
identity, sense of   125
   see also gender identity; self
images of womanhood   3–4, 150
Iman   86
Independent, The   160
individualism   31, 43

industrial accidents   20
information technology, *see* computer
   technology
'inhabiting' a body   111
inheritance of traits and memories   29–30
'inhibited intentionality'   105
'intentional arc'   103–4
intoxication   38–42
Italy   31–2

jaw size   76–7
Jeffreys, Sheila   202–3, 205
Jewishness   70–1, 153
jokes   138, 141–2, 155
Jones, Grace   82–3, 86
Jumpin' Jack Flash   215, 219
Jungle Fever   82–3

Kant, Immanuel   26, 28
Kidd, Mandy   14
Kitzinger, Celia   197
Klein, Melanie   123
kleptomania   38–9
Kofman, S.   131
Kracauer, Siegfried   8, 19, 41–3

'ladettes'   157, 159
Lang, Fritz   223
language, sexual   183, 187
Laqueur, Thomas   52–3
Laws, Sophie   184
Lees, Susan   184
Lenin, Vladimir Ilich   33
lesbianism   72, 195–206
   'male' and 'heterosexual'   199
Lessing, Gotthold   68–9, 71
Lewis, M.   78–9
lifestyle   127
Lloyd, Moya   93–4, 97–8
London, J.   79
Love Bites   195
Luff, Peter   184
Lumley, Joanna   145, 150
Lunas, Donyale   85

McGrath, Roberta   61
Mach, Ernst   32
Mackinnon, Catherine   12
McRobbie, Angela   219
Madonna   6, 98
magazines   75–6, 81
   for teenage girls   184
   women's   165–6
   see also For Women
male bodies, idealization   105–7
'manning' and 'womanning'   61
Mapplethorpe, Robert   83–4
Marie Claire   75–8
Marwick, Arthur   69, 74–5, 79–80
masculinity, ideas of   25–7
   see also 'armoured masculinity'

Index

masculinization 143, 145
masquerade 140, 142, 147, 151
masturbation 174, 180 186
materiality 49–50
medical discourse and attitudes 11, 54, 59
Mellor, Philip 61
'melodic flow' 104, 108
memory trace 29–30
Men Only 180
menstruation 184
Mental Health Act Commission (MHAC) 121, 124
mental health and mental illness 11–12, 112–13, 119–21, 124
Mercer, Kobena 84
Merleau-Ponty, M. 11, 101–5, 108–9, 111–13
Metropolis 36, 223
Millett, Kate 120
Milton, Jude 212
mirrors 129–31
misogyny 119, 127, 154
Miss World competition 122
modalities of bodily existence 113–15
Monroe, Marilyn 93, 134
Moore, Demi 222, 227–8
moral superiority and moral guardianship 141–2
Morrisroe, Patricia 83
Moszkowicz, Julia 14–15
movement, see bodily movement
Mrs Doubtfire 209
multiple personality 38
Mulvey, Laura 2, 132, 229
mutation of gender 198, 203
mutism 37

narcissism 118, 127, 130–2, 138
National Geographic 81
'natural' body 99
Nazism 43
negrophilia and negrophobia 84
Net, The 15, 208, 210, 214–15, 220, 222, 225–6
neurasthenia 21–2, 25, 39
neuroses 20–1, 25, 28–9, 124
new technology, see computer technology
New York Times, The 78
'normal' actions 104, 108–10, 115
normalizing processes 98–101, 124
norms of femininity 143, 184
    see also aesthetic norms; cultural norms; social norms

objectification of the body 110
oestrogen 77
oppositional theories of the body 59, 62
Orbach, S. 126
organic memory theory 29–30
Orlan, H. 127
Orr, Deborah 197

Owens, Tuppy 175–6, 178–9, 185–6

Pacteau, Francette 76, 83
Palmer, Jerry 140
Pascoe, Eva 211
passivity, feminine 19
patriarchy 10, 12, 118–19, 122, 127, 133–4, 195
Patton, Cindy 201–2, 205
Pearson's Weekly 19
Pelican Brief, The 226–7
Pembroke, Louise Roxanne 120
penis 51, 106
performance, gender as 3, 197, 199, 202, 205
perfume 39–40
Perkins Gilman, Charlotte 119
Perrett, Dave 76
'personal' and 'political' 133
Perutz, K. 120–1
Petro, Patrice 41–3
Pfeiffer, Michelle 76
phallocentricity 51
phenomenological analysis 101, 109–15
'plastic' bodies 56, 93
Plath, Sylvia 119
Playboy 228
Plummer, Ken 49
Pond's Institute 18
pornography 3, 12–13, 166, 180–1, 185, 189
postmodern theory 133, 197, 199, 201
power, relations of 15, 51
    inversion of 142, 147
    see also patriarchy
promiscuity 142, 154
prostitution 12, 72, 142, 155
psychiatric hospitals 119–21, 124

queer theory and activism 6, 9, 14, 48, 53–4, 62, 197–206
Question Time 160

racialization of femininity and beauty 67–75
Radner, Hilary 95, 98–9
railway travel 20
Rampton Special Hospital 121
Reich, J.L. 203
Reich, Wilhelm 1
reproductive capabilities 71, 76–8
Reservoir Dogs 158
Richards, Jonathan 167
Rimbaud, Arthur 34
Roberts, Julia 226–7, 229
role-playing 151
    see also performance
Roseanne 161
Ross, Kristin 38, 40
Rubin, Gayle 201
Russo, Mary 143, 145
Ryan, Meg 76

235

safe sex 178–9, 181
scent 39–40
Schudt, Johann Jakob 70
science fiction 229
second-wave feminism 2, 91, 118, 121–2, 132–3
self, sense of 57–8, 115, 120–2, 129–31, 199, 215
self-appreciation 128–9, 134
self-depreciation 152–3, 155–6, 159–60
semen 171–2, 179, 188
sensation, concepts of 8
sex categories 50
sex education 182–4
sex and gender, distinction between 7–8
sex symbols 6
sex talk 182, 185–7
sexology 203–5
sexual abuse of children 124
sexual identity, *see* gender identity
sexual politics 6, 205
sexuality, female 12–13
    portrayal in magazines 188–90
sexually explicit publications 166–9, 180–3
shell-shock 20–1, 25, 28, 37, 39
Shilling, Chris 61
shoplifting 38–9
Showalter, E. 37
Simmel, George 8, 19, 27–8, 37
Simpson, O.J. 79
skin conditions and skin care 5, 17–18, 22
sleepwalking 38
Smith, Clarissa 13
Smyth, Cherry 202–3
social class, *see* class differences
social constructionism 15, 50, 55, 57, 119, 195–9
social norms 14
soldiers, bodies of 2
    see also shell-shock
Sontag, Susan 131
space, personal occupation of 107
Spencer, Diana 80
split personality 38
sportswear 4–5
Stacey, J. 129
Stafford, B.M. 70–1
Stanway, Andrew 172–3, 200
stimulus-response theory 29–30
Stone, Sandy 58–9
Stone, Sharon 76
stress 20–2
surrealism 32

taboos 153, 157
technology, damaging effects 18–22, 30
    see also computer technology
television viewing 143
terminal illness 114–15
testosterone 204–5
Thailand 174

Theweleit, Klaus 26–7
Through the Cakehole 137, 151–60
Tootsie 209
Torday, Emil 81
Toukie 82
trance-like states 39
transformations of the body 6–7, 57–8
transgenderism 200, 203–5
transgressive desires and behaviours 13–14, 56–9, 198, 200–5, 209
transsexualism 56, 58–9, 203
trauma 28–9, 39
    see also shell-shock
troilism 173–5
Tulloch, John 144
Tully, Bryan 58–60
Turkle, Sherry 210–12
Turner, Ted 95
Twiggy 79–80, 93

United States 120, 128
Ussher, Jane 119

van Zoonen, Liesbet 210
vanity 117–18, 127–8, 134
Vanity Fair 228
Verni, M. 67, 75
visibility of the body 4
vulnerability of women, supposed 18–19, 24, 38, 43, 227

weight reduction, efforts at 124–6, 151
West, Candace 50
West, Mae 153
Whitaker's Almanack 34
White, Antonia 119
White, Charles 68–9, 78
white womanhood, ideal of 78–81, 86
whiteness, desirability of 79
Whittle, Stephen 205
Wilkinson, Sue 197
Williams, Robin 209
Williams, Simon 114
Wilson, James 81
Wilton, Tamsin 6–8
Winship, Janice 77
Wired 217
Wittig, Monique 198, 201–2, 206
Wolf, Naomi 122, 132
women's liberation movement 198
World War I 20, 24–6, 37, 39

Yealland, Lewis 37
Young, Iris Marion 99, 104–5, 107–11, 113–15
Young, Lola 9–10, 67
youthful bodies, fetishization of 96

Zerstreuung 41
Zimmerman, Don 50
Zola, Emile 38